The Essays

T H Ferraro

Examples of APA style with references.

© 2003 All rights reserved

Essays

Whether expository, narrative or persuasive, essays are a natural progression of the writing process. An essay's chief purpose is to inform or persuade using references from other sources that strive to validate a point of view or the information being presented.

The essays presented here are in APA style and written on various topics broken down into subject matter. Most have to do with the counseling profession. The reader will get a good sense of how to write an essay while presenting references within the text as well as a bibliography at the end. Various styles of writing are presented here based on the instructor's desire of what should conform to strict APA guidelines, or not. The information is informative and is a good read for those considering a career in the counseling fields.

The first two essays, however, were done for other classes and follow MLA writing formats for English classes, while APA is more scientific.

MLA = Modern Language Association

APA = American Psychological Association

The essays were also left in as much of there original form as possible, which means double spaced so the instructor could make the appropriate marks and comments while reviewing the content.

Please note: Phone numbers and emails are no longer valid

Sections

Just for Fun   4

Turn Tale & Pun – The Composition of Satire

Trapped Like Mice; Rats! (The California Freeway System)

Counseling Theories   37

Role and Importance of Theory

Examples

Couples Counseling   123

Substance Abuse Counseling   169

Psychopharmacology   284

Research   397

Till Death Do Us Part   457

Death with Dignity

Commentaries on Universities/Professors   470

Just For Fun

Turn Tale and Pun: The Composition of Satire

Satire, as we will see, is one of the most difficult forms of writing.

Uses in metaphor, simile and alliteration will prove valuable as well as a clear understanding of irony and paradox.

This preface is composed of a brief history of satire, and a look at what satire is, and some of the problems faced by the satirist from the books: The Anatomy of Satire by Gilbert Highet and Introduction to Satire by Leonard Feinberg.

Examples of the styles and types of satire are offered through the writings of Dave Barry, Dennis Miller, Will Rogers and Mark Twain. A further example, in preparing to write satire, is included by way of my own personal experience with satirical writing.

This expose does not attempt to give a step by step account as to how satire should or could be written; for the question: "Can someone be taught to write satire?" is a subjective one. While people may be able to recognize and appreciate satire, the ability to compose may linger in one's own inborn gifts and/or satirical breeding as a child. However, after carefully examining what satire is, where it comes from and citing examples of good satire, the writing process begins; and through the writing itself, a degree of success may be achieved.

After the crucifixion, a Roman centurion turned to his companion and said, "You've got to admit He was a great teacher." "Yes", said the other, "but was He published?" (Author unknown)

Composition as Satire

"It's all been satirized for your protection" (Maher).

Composition—mothers pull frightened children indoors.

Composition—dogs howl, cats hiss and small rodents scamper to safety.

Composition—the very nature of the term is enough to send teenagers into hysteria, especially on a Friday night with a composition paper due first thing Monday morning.

Now add satire to the mix of writing's plethora of mixed metaphors, dangling participles and sentences ending with prepositions. Where will it all end at? Though satire, considered by many to be the most difficult form of writing, may not be the greatest form of literature, it is one of the most energetic and memorable forms.

We had a good laugh at the satirists' view of the President and his interpretation of "staff benefits," but would not touch the 1999 Columbine High incident in Littleton, Colorado.

Satire is not sarcasm, though can come uncomfortably close. For where sarcasm may leave a chasm of scars, emotional, psychological and/or otherwise, satire is a blend of amusement and contempt. The purpose of satire is to the see the truth, or that part of the truth that is generally ignored, or the absurdity of a person, statement, situation or institution. It is used to shock and move people to feelings of protest, the sharing of the author's emotions and to evoke the same in his audience (Highet 19, 20). Satire offers the reader the pleasures of superiority and the safe release of aggressions often through derision (Feinberg 5). Satire is unfair. The satirist is trying to arouse the attention of an audience indifferent to expression of unpleasant truths, and a throng of teachers, officials, and writers who insist that these truths do not exist. Therefore the satirist may need to exaggerate to make the point, seeming unfair to the issue or person being satirized (Feinberg 13, 14). Unfortunately for the satirist, this creates some problems with satire that must be overcome.

The first problem of the satirist is to hold the reader's interest. Most readers assume they will be entertained by a narrative or educated by an informative exposition. Satire rarely satisfies either though it attempts to accomplish both (Fienberg 85). The satiric writer must enter and develop his expose' quickly, make the satirical point and exit, leaving the audience's appetite coveting more of the forbidden fruit. Second, the satirist has the additional problem of being nasty to the victim without antagonizing the reader. Satire has to camouflage the criticism or sugarcoat it to make it more palatable (Feinberg 86). This is usually done through word play, puns and humor.

Leonard Feinberg, Introduction to Satire, defines satire as "a playfully critical distortion of the familiar." Satire achieves its effect less by what it says than by how it says it. Gulliver's Travels entertains the reader wholly apart from its satire, as does The Importance of Being Earnest.

A Modest Proposal gains its startling effect from the unique manner in which it is written (Feinberg 87, 88) — the manner being of serious tone while the topic being (we hope) satirical.

Reading good satire will give us insight on how to write good satire. But that isn't all the ammo we'll need. It's equally important to know satire and practice satire; to know the subject at which one is planning to throw satirical barbs, or at least have a strong opinion based on some facts. The satirist needs to seem credible.

Will Rogers, American humorist and satirist, once said, "I never met a man I didn't like." I feel the same way about food. But Rogers was best known for his political views and expressed them in satirical manner. "Congress is so strange—a man gets up to speak and says nothing, nobody listens and then everybody disagrees." "If we paid congress according to ability instead of a straight salary, we'd save a lot of money." "Congress meets tomorrow morning. Let us all pray: Oh Lord, give us the strength to bear that which is to be inflicted upon us. Be merciful with them Lord, for they know not what they do."

Mark Twain, a popular writer and storyteller in the mid-to late 19th century, expressed many of his views about the world with satirical wit and charm.

In Man's Place in the Animal World, *Descent of Man From the Higher Animals*, he satirically points out, "Man is the only animal that robs his helpless fellow of his country," "Man is the religious animal — the only true religion of which there are several," and "Man is the reasoning animal, though open to dispute." Samuel Clemens' writings remain popular even today.

But satire is not limited to the written word, nor has it ever been. Satirists are everywhere and in every time. Satirical plays and skits used to entertain the Greek and Roman citizenry. Political cartoons date back hundreds of years and today are found in every newspaper. From Gary Larson's Far Side to Bill Watterson's Calvin and Hobbs, satirizing adults' lack of understanding or misunderstanding of a child's world, to the most notorious satirical cartoon of all, G.B. Trudeau's *Doonesbury*, where satire hopes to entertain as well as inform.

In earlier times the late Bob Hope satirized the political landscape, as did Bill Maher in his popular political TV roundtable "Politically Incorrect." "Saturday Night Live" uses monologues and parodies in the form of skits to satirize political and current events and people.

Dennis Miller used profanity, and a very good thesaurus, on his HBO show "Dennis Miller Live" and in his books, Rants and Ranting Again. Aside from the shock value he seeks through profanity, he instills in the potential satirist another tool of the trade, wordsmithing — how to pen a phrase, how to use alternative words to catch the ear and attention of the intended, though unsuspecting, audience. "…Okay, perhaps it's a bit harsh to call all of us liars. Whatever you prefer. Fact reconstructionist… Truth Manager…Reality stylist…Whatever you want… …Another core ingredient of UFO studies is abduction by aliens. Under hypnosis, the abductees' recollection all share the same characteristics: long stretches of time unaccounted for, strange bruises on the body, a suspicion of sexual violation… is it just me, or does alien abduction sound a lot like spring break?

Newspapers carry Dave Barry satirizing any and everything. Dave has also written satirical books on a variety of subjects. One of my favorites is Dave Barry's *Guide to Marriage and/or Sex*. He graciously points out that no matter how hard you try or how well you plan, you're bound to get what you deserve.

Does that explain your last relationship(s)? In Richard Armour's *My Life With Women*, he further explains that no matter how hard you try or how well you plan... Well, it did go on to include that no matter how long you study women or observe them, as a man, you will always be wrong. I felt that comforting. All the satirical artists I've mentioned, and their works, are great sources for an understanding of the sense of satire.

But now the actual awesome task of writing satire awaits. Our tools include: a quick wit—developed since birth, or forget about participating in any family conversations; an acute sense of humor—or forget about participating in any family conversations; a wild and wacky imagination spawned by too much bad TV and being sent to my room too many times as a kid; a sense of the absurd—though not married, I am a teacher; a few basic courses in English, including grammar; a mom—who was an English major, and didn't we know THAT growing up; and a sturdy, thick, well-used thesaurus.

For we are wordsmiths and language is our playground. Ooo, I kinda like that. Now that the tools are firmly in place, or at least somewhat attached, a subject of ridicule must be decided upon. It should be a subject that the writer feels a kinship toward or knows something about. Even if it is merely to offer an opinion, one is more substantial if accompanied by facts or a deep understanding of the subject matter.

Satire embellishes, draws the reader in to certain details, offers opinions and ridicules the situation while exposing truths unseen by the idle or apathetic eye. It's these surprising revelations of truth, the look behind the scenes offered up in a way that tickles our reality bone that makes satire and those who would expound, expose and execute it in an exalted excursion of ecstasy. Okay, alliteration ain't bad either.

Can one be taught to write satire? That is the subjective question. As writers we put all our known skills to the test every time we place pen to paper, or finger to key. And the key to writing satire may just be the attempt to write it. It may not be good at first. In fact, it may not even be recognizable as satire. But one tries.

Glossary

Alliteration-The repetition of the same initial consonant sound in two or more words in a line of speech or writing for poetic or emphatic effect. Example: Simulating smiles sincere in satisfaction.

Anti-climax-A decline in disappointing contrast to a previous rise.

Example: He falls asleep after sex. She falls asleep during sex.

Colloquialism-Of, pertaining to, or suitable to informal speech and writing.

Example: One ain't comin' to me right now.

Exaggeration-To enlarge something disproportionately.

Example: Overdose of Viagra.

Irony-The use of words to convey the opposite of their literal meaning.

Example: The check's in the mail.

Obscenity-Offensive to accepted standards of decency.

Example: Congress.

Paradox-A statement that appears to contradict itself or be contrary to common sense but that may be true.

Example: Anyone can be a parent.

Topicality–Of or relating to current or local events; currently of interest.

Example: Hollywood, Washington, etc.

Violence–Vehemence of feeling or expression; fervor.

Example: The "anti-gay marriage" movement.

Vividness–Active in forming lifelike images.

Example: See example for obscenity.

Works Cited

1. Armour, Richard. My Life With Women. New York: McGraw-Hill Book Company, 1968.

2. Barry, Dave. "Dave Barry's Guide to Marriage and/or Sex", Dave Barry's Guide to Life. New York: Wings Books, 1991.

3. Feinberg, Leonard. Introduction to Satire. Iowa: The Iowa State University Press, 1967.

4. Highet, Gilbert. The Anatomy of Satire. New Jersey: Princeton University Press, 1970.

5. Maher, Bill. "It's all been satirized for your protection." Political Incorrections. New York: Comedy Central and Simon and Schuster Audio, 1996.

6. Miller, Dennis. Rants. New York: Bantam Doubleday Dell Publishing Group, Inc., 1996.

7. Miller, Dennis. Ranting Again. New York: Bantam Doubleday Dell Publishing Group, Inc., 1998.

8. Sterling, Bryan. The Best of Will Rogers. New York: Crown Publishers, Inc., 1979.

9. The Library of America. Mark Twain: Collected Tales, Sketches, Speeches and Essays 1891-1910. New York: Literary Classics of The United States, Inc., 1976.

T H Ferraro

English 101

Warner

May 29, 2002

"Trapped, Like Mice; Rats!"

The alarm goes off, on the other side of the room, forcing you out of your slumber, your bed and a great, though interrupted, dream. You remember it was necessary to put the clock on the other side of the room because the snooze button was just a little too convenient.

You stumble across the floor to turn off the commotion, all the time wishing you had gotten to bed at that reasonable hour you promised yourself. But your mom called and wanted to talk, then there was that damn English paper you had to finish-and rewrite.

The shower helps, as does that little detour to Starbucks. You make your way to the parking lot they've dubbed the 680 and continue your morning routine of shaving or make-up or cell phone or… anything that will get your mind off the two-hour crawl to work, road rage and all this traffic!

So where did all this traffic come from? Why are there so many cars on the road and clearly not enough room? Why is this guy behind me so close to my rear?

According to the 1964, 1985 and 1996 Traffic Census and Volumes on the California State Highway System, we have been growing at an alarming rate for the past 30 years, and it's not just our diet. At the peak traffic hour, where highways 680 and 580 connect, 900 automobiles per hour were counted in 1964. In 1985, that figure jumped to 8,000 automobiles per hour; and in 1996, 15,000 autos per hour.

The 880 did not fare any better. Though there is no data for 1964, by 1985 15,000 autos per hour were passing the 880/238 interchange at the peak hour. However, this figure dropped to 13,000 autos per hour in 1996. So why the big jumps on 680 and the drop off on 880?

The Metropolitan Transportation Commission and the 1990 Census, both figure the cause as more housing, more people and most importantly, more people commuting to work. More people moved to this area as more jobs were created. A lot of these jobs were created by graduates from Bay Area universities who were entrepreneurs and liked the Bay Area. Many high tech and industrial jobs were created in the 60's and 70's by these grads hence creating a population explosion in those decades. The trend has continued. California saw its population grow again in 1995/96 as 312,754 more people entered the golden state, up 13.06 percent (SR1997 416). The 1990 Census puts it in bleak perspective as it defines the population as persons per square mile. In the East Bay, Alameda County came in at 1,734.5 people per square mile, Contra Costa County at 1,115.8. Ouch! As the population grew, so did the need for housing.

As housing became a premium on the peninsula, the prices for housing rose. Folks started migrating eastward. First to the East Bay, then over the hills to Pleasanton and Walnut Creek; then out to Concord, Livermore, Pittsburgh, and even Tracy, all became bedroom communities for the Bay Area (BATMC 3).

Currently the most acreage available for development between 1990 and 2010 is in the East Bay with 31 percent still available for housing (RTP 20). Highways did start to expand, but not at the rate that the demands on housing were being met.

As more automobiles poured onto the highways from the growth of these communities, the commute time was directly affected, increasing 27 percent from Solano County since 1990, with 38.6 percent of it's work force heading south. 40.2 percent of Contra Costa County commuters head out of town to work upping the ante on southbound highways. All this due to the increased work force coming from these and other Bay Area bedroom communities (BATMC 8). While commute times continued to increase, the departure hour from home to work started a backward slide. Only taking commuters 10 to 15 minutes to get to work in 1964, and increasing to only 20 to 30 minutes by 1985; commuters are now faced with an estimated drive time of an hour or more. Those living around the Bay are leaving home between 7 to 8 am, while commuters from Contra Costa County are forced to leave home between 6 to 6:30 am. The drive home is no picnic either (BATMC 14).

Californians love to drive. We are a very independent people. Our philosophy when it comes to our cars is…"you can have it when you pry it from my cold dead fingers" (NRA).

In 1995, Californians drove 276,371,000,000 miles. Ranked number one, that figure put us 11.41 percent of the entire U.S. population. Second was Texas with 7.47 percent. California also had the highest number of licensed drivers with 20,139,586 or 11.40 percent of the U.S. population.

California also comes in first with the most vehicles registered; 22,431,749 or 11.13 percent of the entire United States. The average California driver puts over 12,000 miles on his/her vehicle annually (SR1997 416).

But it's not just the number of cars we own and operate that puts us in such driving turmoil; it's how we drive as well. In 1990, 75 percent of drivers drove alone to work and back. 14.4 percent shared the drive with others while only 10.6 percent used some form of mass transit. It is predicted that by the year 2010, the number of people driving alone to work will have increased to 76.5 percent, while share driving will slip to 14.2 percent and mass transit will plummet to 9.3 percent.

The scenario only gets worse when looking forward to the years ahead. The 2013 predictions have people driving alone increased to 77 percent, while share driving continues to spiral downward to 14 percent and mass transit drops to 9 percent (RTP 23). All this while we're making use of the aforementioned 31 percent of acreage for housing in the East Bay. Double ouch!

Now let's take all the above information and add it to the realities of driving. While you were engrossed in your morning routine in your vehicle, you didn't notice that traffic had, once again, come to a stand still and WHAM! Fender bender, or perhaps worse.

Even after the accident has been pulled over to the side, the phenomenon known as the "Looky Lou" or "Rubber Necker" keeps traffic from achieving its normal flow (or lack of) for hours. The Metropolitan Transportation Commission, based in Oakland, explains the "Anatomy of a Traffic Jam" like this.

Freeways are just the same. A freeway might be able to handle 6,000 cars per hour with little or no congestion.

But beyond that, even a small increase in traffic (as little as 10 percent) can turn a pleasant drive into a nightmare. And an accident, even a minor fender-bender, can have the same effect, even though the cars involved may be long gone by the time you get through the jam.

So with more jobs being created in this booming economy, with more housing being developed and with more folks moving into this area and bringing more vehicles with them; how do we get out of this mess?

Well, people are creative. Some have already discovered alternative routes. But it's not long before more and more people discover that same route, and street congestion ensues. Some believe we should continue to widen our highways, expanding from four lanes to six and adding more expressways and bypasses (RTP 77). Utilizing this strategy, however, would mean that someday we'd all be living, working and playing underneath the freeways. And we were concerned about not seeing the sun this Spring!

In this same vein, others consider doing the same thing to our freeways as we've done with our housing. Build upward. Double deck the highways of California.

Though this idea sounds plausible, we must also consider earthquake hazards as well as promoting more vehicles on the highways, adding to environmental and health concerns.

Driving habits would have to change. Of all the trips that people take during a 24-hour day, almost 30 percent don't have anything to do with work. There are lots of trips like shopping and running errands that could be made at less congested times. Diverting as few as 7 percent of the westbound morning traffic from the San Francisco-Oakland Bay Bridge would result in a 40 percent reduction in delay for travelers in the corridor (CTF 12).

Some solutions are based on Market-based strategies, charging the consumer for peak time usage. These strategies look like the following (edited from CTF 8,9):

- Congestion Pricing: During peak hours on congested routes, drivers could be charged a price equal to the true cost to society of using the facility, including the cost of delay and productivity. Those who wished to pay may experience a faster, easier ride, while those whose schedules were more flexible could avoid these costs. Communication technologies would be employed so vehicles would not have to stop at tollbooths. This technology is also being considered to allow more people to use car pool lanes as single occupant vehicles during peak hours. This strategy ha been nick-named, "The Rich Man's Commute", implying that those with the most money would be more apt, or could afford, to travel during these times.

- Vehicle Miles Traveled Fee: Fees could be collected based on the number of miles a vehicle travels. On average, motorists could be expected to travel less and take other steps to lower the cost of vehicle ownership and use. Fees could be collected as part of the vehicle registration process, which is currently under consideration to be eliminated, or using advanced technology to charge based on odometer readings. Another incentive, for those that would, to turn the odometer back.

- Emission Fees: Fees based on the air pollution emissions produced by the vehicle could be charged to the owner. People could be expected to drive somewhat less, make improvements to emission control systems, and over time, drive more efficient, less polluting vehicles.

- Parking Charges: Free parking is a large but mostly hidden subsidy for auto use. Charges could be collected to offset the costs of providing parking or to roughly cover the costs to society of auto use, such as congestion and air pollution. Some people might switch a portion of their trips to public transit to avoid parking costs, or begin to ride share-to-share costs. Charges would be imposed on all parking, or only on commuter parking, and could be general charges or varied according to time of day.

- Fuel Tax Increases: The existing per-gallon gas tax could be increased to fully pay for system maintenance, operation and improvements. These increases could induce some travelers to combine or reduce trips, take more public transit, or buy more fuel-efficient cars. However, these suggestions are flawed as most Californians feel they are over taxed already. As we've seen from the previous information, rising gas prices don't seem to deter Californians from driving or buying large gas-guzzling vehicles. Many companies already provide adequate parking for their employees and merchants may not appreciate an imposed or additional parking fee, driving consumers away to stores that provide free parking. Taking a hard look at the above proposals really does indicate that only the wealthy be permitted to drive.

Yes, our roads are in a state of disrepair. Yes, some highways could stand to be widened. But these are only band aid solutions for a patient requiring major surgery. I believe the answer lies in mass transit. But mass transit that is well thought out, well developed, well implemented and well used.

Currently the BART (Bay Area Rapid Transit) system covers most of the northern and eastern territories of the bay. It has stretched its tracks to include some of the fastest growing areas in the East Bay. Unfortunately, it stops short when transporting these commuters to the South Bay or down the peninsula. Cal-train does pick up some of the load, but not nearly enough to decongest the 101. And if our focus is indeed the 680 and 880, BART does little to get travelers to their final southbound destination as it stops in Fremont. Voters in Santa Clara County have continually voted down an extension to BART, and this is reflected in the Regional Transportation Plan, as no mention of extending BART is noted through the year 2013 (RTP 72).

> [More information is needed from Santa Clara County, as to why voters back away from a BART extension, or other extenuating factors of why a plan to extend mass transit into the south bay should be examined.]

But there's always the problem of getting from the BART station to the place of employment. I believe employers should provide a company bus to shuttle their employees to and from the station, whether it be BART or Cal-train. A tax break could be given to companies that comply.

Making transportation easier, not more expensive, should be the priority in developing systems that will help in the ever-increasing demand for expediency and productivity. Until that time, we are literally stuck. Stuck with the current system and contemplating it's future while we're stuck in traffic contemplating our own.

And since there is nothing to be done about congestion in the near future, my recommendation to you, is to slow down, take more time, smell the roses, or whatever that is growing on the side of the road, watch where you're going, don't become a statistic, listen and sing along with your favorite music.

Better yet, buy lots of comedy tapes, books on tape or learn a foreign language on tape. Make good use of your time on the road, then you won't think it's wasted time, and you won't develop road rage.

Learn to appreciate life, the ride and the time the drive to work gives you to be by yourself to think, without anyone else making demands on your time. For one day bureaucracy and brains are bound to join forces; and then you won't have any time for yourself.

Works Cited

1964 Annual Traffic Census. State of California. Highway Transportation Agency. Department of Public Works. Division of Highways. Sacramento. 1985 Traffic Volumes on the California State Highway System. State of California. Business, Transportation and Housing Agency. Department of Transportation. Division of Traffic Engineering. Sacramento.

1990 Census of Population and Housing. United States Department of Commerce, Economics and Statistical Administration.

1994 Regional Transportation Plan for the San Francisco Bay Area. Metropolitan Transportation Commission. Oakland.

1996 Traffic Volumes on the California State Highway System. State of California.

Business, Transportation and Housing Agency.

Department of Transportation.

Division of Traffic Operations. Sacramento. Federal Highway Admin. June1997.

California's Transportation Future. Dec. 1995.

Metropolitan Transportation Commission. Oakland.

Citizen's Guide to the Metropolitan Transportation Commission. June 1997.

Metropolitan Transportation Commission, Oakland.

"Demographic and Economic Characteristics". Bay Area Travel and Mobility Characteristics. 1990 Census. Working Paper #2. Planning Section. Metropolitan Transportation Commission. Oakland. Aug. 1992.

State Rankings 1997: A Statistical View of the 50 States. Ed. Kathleen O'Leary Morgan and Scott Morgan. Morgan Quinto Press. Lawrence, KS. "Work Travel Characteristics". Bay Area Travel and Mobility Characteristics.

1990 Census. Working Paper #2. Planning Section. Metropolitan Transportation Commission. Oakland. Aug. 1992.

"Trapped Like Mice; Rats!" Quoted from The Wizard of OZ. Cowardly Lion. 1939.

Counseling Theory

My Take On Theories

Though my theories are eclectic, as I believe a therapist should have an arsenal of theories in practice and to integrate when and where necessary, as one theory may not fit all clients. A true understanding of various theories can only improve a counselor's ability to truly understand the individual dynamics a client brings to the counseling sessions, what a proper diagnosis might look like, and therefore, a plan of therapy based on the correct theory.

However, this does not negate the reality of counselors having a theory that resonates with them as a starting point. As pointed out in Corey (2009), counselors acquire a counseling style that matches their personality based upon a relationship with a major approach to therapy. Mixing approaches without the proper discipline can produce unproductive sessions as the pathway to good therapy may stray with too may theory tributaries polluting the therapeutic river rather than making it run clear. Or, as pointed out by Dr. Seligman (2010), a theory provides a road map that includes a starting point with the opportunity for reevaluation along the journey as new information is revealed. A particular theory also provides a common language between therapists, especially when a client needs to see a different counselor.

This point may be also used to illustrate that as a scholar, the counselor must be aware of the various theoretical approaches of the past, present, and even ones being explored today in order to have a viable working knowledge of all "languages" used in the psychotherapist's world.

Knowledge is power, and with that power comes the opportunity for social change as a practitioner. Counselors advocate for changes and causes they believe in and that will enhance the world in which we all live. Advocacy is mentioned in the ACA Code of Ethics (2005, Standard A.6.b.), as a way of removing barriers that might infringe upon a client's growth or access to those things that would be beneficial. So then advocacy toward social change is a way of improving the quality of life in general; and with the improvement of life may come greater good mental health.

References:

ACA Code of Ethics (2005). American Counseling Association. Retrieved from **http://www.txca.org/Images/tca/Documents/ACA%20Code%20of%20Ethics.pdf**

Corey, G. (2009). *Theory and practice of counseling and psychotherapy* (8th ed.). Belmont, CA: Thomson Brooks/Cole.

Laureate Education, Inc. (Executive Producer). (2010). *Counseling and Psychotherapy Theories,* Baltimore, MD: Author.

Background of Theory

I came from a time and place where conformity was the name of the game. Mine was a middle-class family living in a track home in a nice, middle-class neighborhood, where nobody rocked the boat, said their pleasant hellos and went about their business.

My folks both smoked, as was the fashion of the time, and drank with their friends at parties. My father fought in World War II, and was a proud man. My mother stayed home to raise a family and make sure dinner was served in a timely manner.

My sister and I, on the other hand, grew up in the 60's and 70's, as baby boomers, welcoming the Beatles, longer hair and wilder clothing into our lives. The 60's and 70's gave rise to the non-conformist movements, where being yourself was more important than blending in, though, more and more boomers, hippies and flower children did blend together and conform to the philosophy of non-conformity. Hence, the adage, "The more things change, the more they stay the same (Karr, 1849).

From that era blossomed the central humanist psychologists, Carl Rogers, Rollo May, and Abraham Maslow, who were liberal in outlook. Maslow's ideas on self-actualization were taken over and used by hippies who celebrated free love and drugs. Similarly, Roger's ideas on Encounters became happenings for the radicals. The more radical and utopian energies were institutionalized in the human potential movement exemplified by the Escalon Institute in Big Sur, California (May, Rogers, & Maslow, 1986; Shaffer, 1978 in Schultz & Schultz, 2008).

Though, dress, hair, music and other styles express the times we live, and each generation pays tribute to their individuality through conformity, I believe we are truly different emotionally, cognitively and psychologically. People experience the environment, relationships and their role within each differently.

People also hear, see and experience things according to their own biases, and then interpret that information to conform to their own paradigm.

Therefore, there is no one therapy, theory, or school of thought where one size fits all. Hence my theory of Individualism, the looking at in individual in a holistic manner, then taking bits and pieces from various theories to construct a therapy tailor made for the individual client.

There is no rush to diagnose a client or even begin treatment, but rather establish a rapport and therapeutic alliance which will enhance trust, openness and communication which will enhance the counseling sessions in such a positive way as to encourage the client to move forward and self-actualize their ability to change and grow (Corey, 2009)

References:

Corey, G. (2009). *Theory and practice of counseling and psychotherapy* (8th ed.). Belmont, CA: Thomson Brooks/Cole.

Karr, A. (1849). "plus ça change, plus c'est la même chose" — "the more it changes, the more it's the same thing", usually translated as "the more things change, the more they stay the same," *Les Guêpes*, January.

Schultz, D., Schultz, S. (2008). A HISTORY OF MODERN PSYCHOLOGY (9th ed.). Belmont: CA: Wadsworth, Cengage Learning.

Running head: ROLE AND IMPORTANCE OF THEORY

Role and Importance of Theory to Mental Health Counseling

Tomas Ferraro

COUN 6100

Introduction to Mental Health Counseling

Abstract

This paper will provide an analysis of the role and importance of theory to mental health counseling practice, including an explanation about the role of new and emerging theories and an explanation about why they are important.

The paper will go on to explain what makes a theory a "good" theory, and how a counselor would know if a new and emerging theory was "good," including how one would evaluate a new theory.

According to Levitt and Bray (in Erford, 2010), "Theories ground us as professional counselors. They provide a means to understand what we are doing, how we serve our clients, and how to explain counseling to clients." As the paragraph goes on to say, our clients don't necessarily want the history or detailed description of counseling, but to provide them with enough information so they are comfortable knowing that the counseling they are receiving has merit and based on tried and true applications.

"Counselors use techniques/procedures/modalities that are grounded in theory and/or have an empirical or scientific foundation. Counselors who do not must define the techniques/procedures as 'unproven' or 'developing' and explain the potential risks and ethical considerations of using such techniques/procedures and take steps to protect the client from possible harm" (ACA Code of Ethics, 2005, C.6.e.). Research, not therapy, is the time to be creating empirical data for a new theory.

However, theories are fine as long as they are still relevant to the times. As society changes its own standards, beliefs and priorities, so people change and individually go through a "paradigm shift," or a new way of believing or thinking, and the counseling profession must change in order to reach the new order and thinking of the time. Counseling and psychological theories have come and gone over the years, with always a new concept to be explored. The better mouse trap, as it were. "Theories take time to develop and become empirically validated for use in the profession." Some include: postmodernism, decisional counseling, motivational interviewing, brief and solution-focused counseling, narrative or constructivist approaches, and feminist counseling (Erford, 2010). Many counselors rely on more than just one theory as people differ from each other, their problems differ, expectations differ and outcomes differ as well.

So what makes a theory good? According to Hansen, Stevic and Warner (1986), the following are five components of good counseling theory:

1. The theory is clear and easily understood.
2. The theory is comprehensive.
3. The theory is explicit and heuristic, generating further research.
4. The theory is specifically geared to help clients reach their desired outcomes.
5. The theory is useful to practitioners.

These five components make it easy for counselors, not only to judge the effectiveness of existing theories in their own practice, but to make determinations about new theories being introduced into the profession. "Theories must be sound to be plausible to professional counselors. Literally hundreds of theories exist with more emerging (Ivey & Ivey, 2007). All these theories can be overwhelming to beginning counselors who are trying to do what is in the best interest of their clients (Levitt & Bray, 2010).

Counselors must weigh each theory carefully as to the benefit of his/her practice and the effect that theory will have on the course and outcome of each individual client's therapy. "Theories differ in their perceptions of the roles professional counselors play in the therapeutic process. Whether one is collaborator, expert, equal, or indifferent, the role of the professional counselor differs across theories (Levitt & Bray, 2010).

References:

ACA Code of Ethics (2005). American Counseling Association. Retrieved from http://www.counseling.org/Files/FD.ashx?guid=ab7c1272-71c4-46cf-848c-f98489937dda

Erford, Bradley T. (2010). *Orientation to the Counseling Profession: Advocacy, Ethics, and Essential Professional Foundations*. New Jersey: Pearson Education.

Hansen, J. C.; Stevic, R. R. & Warner, R. W. (1986). *Counseling: Theory and process* (4th ed.). Boston: Allyn & Bacon. (As cited in Levitt & Bray, 2010).

Ivey, A. E. & Ivey, M. B. (2007). *Intentional interviewing and counseling: Facilitating client development in a multicultural society* (6th ed.). Belmont CA: Thomson Brooks/Cole. (As cited in Levitt & Bray, 2010).

Levitt, D. H. & Bray, A. (2010). Ch 4: Theories of counseling. *Orientation to the Counseling Profession: Advocacy, Ethics, and Essential Professional Foundations*. New Jersey: Pearson Education. (As cited in Erford, 2010).

Running head: ELEMENTS OF THEORY- PSYCHOANALYSIS, BEHAVIORISM, HUMANISTIC.

Elements of Theory

Tomas Ferraro

Psy7110

History and Systems of Psychology

3670 Campus Dr.

Oceanside, CA 92056

650-704-0433

Email: **tommytahiti@yahoo.com**

Instructor: Andrew Nocia

Abstract

This paper will review the theories of Psychoanalysis, Behaviorism and Humanistic, explore the theorist attributed to the school of thought and examine these elements as they would apply to my work as a psychologist.

Working within the field of psychology it is important to take stock of the various schools of thought and theories to determine which one, or ones, will be best applicable to the specialization a student pursues.

As students of psychology, some of the names and theories have become familiar to us. Others may need further exploration. Names such as Freud, Jung Skinner, Pavlov, Maslow and more may be familiar, but being familiar with what theory to associate them with may not.

Psychoanalysis and Freud: It has been said that no one person or culture can take clain for any of the ideas or inventions that have come to pass and so it is with Freud and "his" theories. Examples include (Schultz & Schultz, 2008):

Freud's Oedipus theory, whereas in 1897 a Viennese physician, Albert Moll, wrote about childhood sexuality and a child's love for a parent of the opposite sex.

The concept of Catharis (The process of reducing or eliminating a complex by recalling it to conscious awareness and allowing it to be expressed), was popular before Freud published his work.

Dream Symbolism had been anticipated in philosophy and psychology as far back as the 17th century.

Perhaps it took Freud's putting them all together into one school of thought that created and was the basis of psychoanalysis. Yet the field continues to grow and change.

Consider as a case in point the claim that changes in contemporary psychoanalytic theory and practice have yielded a "widening scope" (Stone, 1954, p. 567) of practice that permits effective psychoanalytic treatment for a wider range of patients. The term *widening scope* implies that new techniques and tools are now available that can reach patients who were not treatable by earlier techniques and tools. It is not at all clear whether these presumably new techniques and tools are more effective with more disturbed patients, and whether the "older" techniques and tools were ineffective with certain kinds of patients. (Eagle, 2007)

Behaviorism and Watson: Watson distinguished himself by announcing he was founding a new school, Behaviorism, though his behavior came under fire after love letters to his assistant were discovered resulting in a sensational divorce and ending his career at John Hopkins University. (Schultz & Schultz, 2008) In 1928, he published Psychological Care of the Infant and Child, in which he severely criticized the child-rearing practices of the day. He charged that "parents today are incompetent." (Schultz & Schultz, 2008)

But Watson's name may not be as familiar to those untrained in the history of psychology. Names such as Pavlov and Skinner prevail as potentially more recognizable as their contributions to Behaviorism. A behavioristic model is not just another personality theory whose creator is the subject of such an assessment: It would seem the greatest challenge to those who engage in the process of unveiling the subjectivity of personality theory.

Skinner's model offers no animations of the internal life and focuses purely and squarely on external and observable phenomena, constituting the most direct circumvention, to date, of the very assumption of subjectivity at the basis of this kind of analysis. (Siegel, 1996)

Humanistic Psychology and Maslow: In the early 1960s, less than two decades before the 100th anniversary of the formal founding of psychology, a so called third force developed within American psychology. This humanistic psychology was not intended to be a revision or adaptation of any current school of thought , as was the case with some neo-Freudian positions. Instead, humanistic psychologists expected to supplant both of psychology's two main forces: behaviorism and psychoanalysis. (Schultz & Schultz, 2008)

However, by the time the late 60s were flourishing, Maslow and his hierarchy of needs became the cornerstone for the hippie movement. Maslow's ideas on self-actualization were taken over and used by hippies who celebrated free love and drugs. (Pytell, 2006)

As a practicing psychologist to be, I can glean vital information out of each theory to help my practice be as comprehensive to my clients as possible.

From Psychoanalysis I can explore my clients past and discover what mental impasses block their moving forward. Are there any fears that need to be overcome? I can help them see that from the past we learn so as to develop a brighter future.

From Behaviorism I help my clients look at the present, the stresses and daily trials that may cause one to feel overwhelmed. What external forces are at work that may be both positive and negative. I help my clients develop a "game plan" of how to cope with their daily habits, chores, issues and stresses.

Finally, we would take a look together at Maslow's hierarchy of needs to find out where on the chart they see themselves. Using a Humanistic approach I would help my client evaluate his/her life and lifestyle, how it is affected by others and where they see friends and family in relationship to their needs.

Using and finding ways to combine and compliment the various schools of thought provides the most comprehensive style of therapy for my clients.

References

Eagle, Morris N (2007). **Psychoanalysis and its critics.** Psychoanalytic Psychology, Vol 24(1), Jan, pp. 10-24.

Pytell, Timothy (2006). *Transcending the angel beast: Viktor Frankl and humanistic psychology.* Psychoanalytic **Psychology,** Vol 23(3), Sum, pp. 490-503.

Schultz, D., Schultz, S. (2008). A HISTORY OF MODERN PSYCHOLOGY (9th ed.). Belmont: CA: Wadsworth, Cengage Learning.

Siegel, Paul F (1996). **The meaning of behaviorism for B. F. Skinner.** Psychoanalytic Psychology, Vol 13(3), Sum, pp. 343-365.

Stone, L. (1954). The widening scope of indications for psychoanalysis. *Journal of the American Psychoanalytic Association, 2,* 567–594.

Running head: ELEMENTS OF THEORY- FUNCTIONALISM, STRUCTURALISM, GESTALT

Elements of Theory

Tomas Ferraro

Psy7110

History and Systems of Psychology

3670 Campus Dr.

Oceanside, CA 92056

650-704-0433

Email: **tommytahiti@yahoo.com**

Instructor: Andrew Nocita

Abstract

This paper will examine the theorists and schools of thought as applied to Structuralism, Functionalism and Gestalt and how these theories apply to my work as a psychologist.

As we have seen through other schools of thought, a revolution is sometimes needed within a former theory to create a new school of thought. However, in E.B. Titchener's case he formed a different school of thought while insisting he was being true to Wundt's theories.

Wundt had recognized the elements or contents of consciousness, but his overriding concern was their organization, that is, their synthesis into higher-level cognitive processes through apperception. (Schultz & Schultz, 2008)

Titchener focused on mental elements or contents, and their mechanical linking through the process of association, but he discarded Wundt's doctorine of apperception. (Schultz & Schultz, 2008)

According to Titchener, the subject matter of psychology is conscious experience as that experience is dependent upon the person who is actually experiencing it. (Schultz & Schultz, 2008) This premise works well with my new school of thought, Individualistic psychology as that theory presupposes that based on individual histories, people will react individually and have unique responses to similar experiences.

By the second decade of the twentieth century, the intellectual climate of thought in American and European psychology had changed… many psychologists came to regard (Titchener's) structural psychology as a futile attempt to cling to antequated principles and methods. (Schultz & Schultz, 2008) Despite these criticisms, historians give due credit to Titchener and his structuralists. Their subject matter-conscious experience-was clearly defined. (Schultz & Schultz, 2008)

Charles Darwin, and his notion of evolution, changed the focus of the new psychology from the structure of consciousness to its functions. It was inevitable that a functionalist school of thought would develop. (Schultz & Schultz, 2008)
During this time of structuralism, many intellects were meeting at Cambridge. Calling themselves the Metaphysical Club, the were keen to discuss the scientific and philosophical issues of the day and was led by a brilliant Cambridge sage,

Chauncey Wright. Wright found Darwinism to awaken a new interest in the problems of consciousness. In an audacious extension of the principles of natural selection to the intellectual realm, Wright argued that the stable contents of our intellects are programed from a kind of Darwinian competition among our immediate thoughts. (Green, 2009)

Although Wright remains unknown to most historians of psychology, some philosophers have recognized his importance to the development of Darwin-inspired functionalist psychology in American. (Madden, 1974)

Functionalism and its Darwinian approach to the mind found applications besides mental testing. Whereas mental *variability* was the focus of testing movement, other strains focused on the *adaptation* of the organism to its environment. (Green, 2009)

As we have seen throughout history, the ability to adapt to change is crucial to survival. The ability to accept change is crucial for good mental and emotional health.

Here again I see how Functionalism can play a crucial role in Individualistic psychology as individuals have a variety of thoughts and emotions attached to change, though the only thing certain in life is change.

One of Wright's peers during this time was William James considered to be the greatest American psychologist. Three reasons have been suggested for his overwhelming stature and influence. First, James wrote with clarity rare in science. His writing style has magnetism, spontaneity, and charm. Second, he opposed Wundt's goal for psychology; namely, the analysis of consciousness into elements. Third, James offered an alternative way of looking at the mind, a view congruent with the functional approach to psychology. In brief, the times in American psychology were ready for what James had to say. (Schultz & Schultz, 2008)

To understand the Gestalt protest, let us recall what psychology was like in 1912. Watson's behaviorism was beginning its attack Wundt and Titchener and on functionalism. (Schultz & Schultz, 2008)

The differences between Gestalt psychology and behaviorism were soon evident. Gestalt psychologists accepted the value of consciousness while criticizing the attempt to reduce it to atoms or elements. Behavioral psychologists refused to acknowledge the usefulness of the concept of consciousness for a scientific psychology. (Schultz & Schultz, 2008)

According to Gestalt theory, the brain is a dynamic system in which all elements active at a given time interact. The visual area of the brain does not respond separately to individual elements of visual input, connecting these elements by some mechanical process of association. (Schultz & Schultz, 2008)

The perceptual organization principles are: Proximity, Continuity, Similarity, Closure, Simplicity, and Figure/ground. (See Schultz & Schultz, 2008, p. 379-380)

Simplicity was the idea that we see figures as being as good as possible under the stimulus conditions, known as pragnanz, or good form.

Rudolf Arnheim, a psychologist turned design professor, applied Gestalt psychology to art which allowed him to make contributions to the theory itself.

Using mostly examples from art history and children's drawings, Arnheim noted "relations between art and abstraction presuppose a revision of certain psychological concepts. (From "Perceptual Abstraction and Art, 1966c, p. 28) This phenomenological imperative, of taking the best of art to test the needs of psychological theory, stands diametrically oposed to the trends of contemporary practice. (Verstegen, 2007)

However, using the Gestalt principles of perceptual organization as presented by Wertheimer (Schultz & Schultz, 2008. p. 379) I can use this as a tool when working with my own clients to help qualify their own perceptual organization and therefore, perhaps, organization within the cognitive and affective capacities as well.

Again, these three schools of thought offer other venues from which to glean ideas and develop theories for counseling at the individual level and the construction of Individualistic psychology.

References

Green, Christopher D. (2009). Darwinian Theory, Functionalism, and the First American Psychological Revolution. *American Psychologist*, Vol. 64, No. 2, 75-83.

Madden, E. H. (1974). Chauncey Wright's functionalism. *Journal of the History of the Behavioral Sciences, 10*, 281-290.

Schultz, D., Schultz, S. (2008). A HISTORY OF MODERN PSYCHOLOGY (9th ed.). Belmont: CA: Wadsworth, Cengage Learning.

Versegen, Ian (2007). Rudolf Arnheim's contribution to Gestalt psychology. *Psychology of Aesthectics, Creativity, and the Arts*, Vol. 1, No.

Running head: ELEMENTS OF THEORY- COGNITIVE AND EVOLUTIONARY PSYCHOLOGY

Elements of Theory

Tomas Ferraro

Psy7110

History and Systems of Psychology

3670 Campus Dr.

Oceanside, CA 92056

650-704-0433

Email: **tommytahiti@yahoo.com**

Instructor: Andrew Nocita

Abstract

This paper will explore the schools of thought of cognitive and evolutionary psychology, their beginnings and the theorists responsible for their development. Discussion will also cover how these schools may be applied to my work as a psychologist.

Much like a renaissance, an awakening after the dark ages, so has psychology had it's own rebirth of consciousness with the introduction of Cognitive psychology. Like all revolutionary movements in psychology, cognitive psychology did not spring up overnight. Many of its features had been anticipated. Interest in the consciousness was evident in the earliest days of psychology before it became a formal science. The writing of the Greek philosophers Plato and Aristotle deal with the thought processes, as do the theories of the British empiricists and associationists. (Schultz & Schultz, 2008)

Gestalt psychology influenced the cognitive movement with its focus on "organization, structure, relationships, the active role of the subject, and the important part played by perception in learning and memory" (Hearst, 1979, p. 32). The Gestalt school of thought helped keep alive at least a token interest in consciousness during the years that behaviorism dominated American psychology. (Schulz & Schultz, 2008)

The founding of cognitive psychology did not occur overnight, not could it be attributed to the charisma of one individual who, like Watson, changed the field almost single-handedly.

Like functional psychology, the cognitive movement claims no solitary founder, perhaps because none of the psychologists working in the area had the personal ambition to lead the new movement. Their interest was pragmatic: simply getting on with the work of redefining psychology. (Schultz & Schultz, 2008)

Though Cognitive psychology deals with conscious thought, stimuli, the environment and how the individual creatively arranges it within, the study of conscious mental process sparked a renewed interest in unconscious cognitive activities, (Schultz & Schultz, 2008) and at the molecular level.

As more information piles up about neural transmission, we may hope for the time when it is possible to assess the results of analytic work at cellular levels. (Zabarenko, 2004)

According to Beckman (2003), a new nontoxic fluorescent marker has been perfected that permits "researchers to follow multiple groups of cells or molecules . . . [So it's possible] 'to image the cells while they're doing their normal behaviors' " (Fraser, quoted inBeckman, 2003, p. 76).

"Two-photon microscopy, which uses low-energy lasers to light up tissue bearing fluorescent markers only where the two lasers intersect, allows …
researchers to zoom in three-dimensionally on the junctions without damaging tissue" (Beckman, 2003, p. 77). This means that the study of "how neurons establish long-term relationships [can be conducted using] nerves that have not been stunned by an anesthetic" (Beckman, 2003, p. 77). The new technique enables research on "individual neurons in the cerebral cortex of mice over a period of weeks or even months . . . and the lower energy photons cause far less damage to living tissue" (Miller, 2003, p. 78). Beckman (2003) quotes Cohen-Cory echoing a common scientific realization: "It's interesting how [ideas] change once you have more tools" (p. 77).

And since a miniaturized two-photon microscope that can be mounted on the head of an unanesthetized rat is being developed at the Planck Institute in Heidelberg, may we not look forward to the day when we can "see into the working brain" during free association? (Zabarenko, 2004)

With the cognitive movement in experimental psychology and the emphasis on consciousness within humanistic psychology and post-Freudian psychoanalysis, we can see that consciousness has reclaimed the central position it held when the field formally began. (Schultz & Schultz, 2008)

The most recent approach to psychology, evolutionary psychology, argues that people are biological creatures that have been wired or programmed by evolution to behave, think, feel, and learn in ways that have fostered survival over many past generations. This approach is based on the assumption that people with certain behavioral, cognitive, and affective tendencies were more likely to survive and bear and raise children. (Schultz & Schultz, 2008)

Charles Darwin may be considered the first evolutionary psychologist. At the end of *On the Origin of Species*, Darwin predicted, "In the distant future . . . psychology will be based on a new foundation, that of the necessary acquirement of each mental power and capacity by gradation. Much light will be thrown on the origin of man and his history" (Darwin, 1859, p. 488). (Buss, 2009)

Evolutionary psychology is a broad field that makes use of research findings from other disciplines, including animal behavior, biology, genetics, neuropsychology, and evolutionary theory. It applies these findings to all areas of psychology. (Schultz & Schultz, 2008)

Evolutionary psychology has advanced beyond Darwin's vision in several ways. The first stems from theoretical developments in evolutionary theory that occurred after Darwin's day — the discovery of particulate inheritance, the modern synthesis, the theory of inclusive fitness, and the understanding of the logical implications of genic selection. The second was fashioned by the cognitive revolution — the view that psychological adaptations can be conceptualized as information-processing devices instantiated in the brain (Tooby & Cosmides, 2005). The third followed from exploring new domains, such as sexual conflict and within-family conflict, that are being illuminated by modern evolutionary theory. (Buss, 2009)

Both cognitive and evolutionary schools of thought will play a crucial role in my work as a psychologist and in Individual psychology.

Cognitive recognizes the effect of experiences and the environment of the individual and how each person arranges that stimuli, whereas the evolutionary theory recognizes individual abilities, traits, behaviors and feelings to learn how to survive in an ever changing environment. This will be an important factor in dealing with clients suffering from PTSD or the day to day situations that can become overwhelming if not dealt with through adequate coping skills.

References

Beckman, M. (2003). Play-by-play imaging rewrites cells' rules. *Science, 300,* 76–77.

Buss, David M. (2009). **The great struggles of life: Darwin and the emergence of evolutionary psychology.** American Psychologist, Vol 64(2), Feb-Mar, Special issue: Charles Darwin and **Psychology**, 1809-2009. pp. 140-148.

Hearst, E. (Ed). (1979). *The first century of experimental psychology*. Hillsdale, NJ: Erlbaum.

Miller, G. (2003). Spying on the brain, one neuron at a time. *Science, 300,* 78–79.

Schultz, D., Schultz, S. (2008). A HISTORY OF MODERN PSYCHOLOGY (9th ed.). Belmont: CA: Wadsworth, Cengage Learning.

Tooby, J., & Cosmides, L. (2005). Conceptual foundations of evolutionary psychology. In D. M. Buss (Ed.), *The handbook of evolutionary psychology* (pp. 5–67). New York: Wiley.

Zabarenko, Lucy M. (2004). **Psychoanalysis, Neuroscience, and Cognitive Psychology: Some Samples From Recent Research.** Psychoanalytic *Psychology*, Vol 21(3), Sum, pp. 488-492.

An Adlerian Approach to Abby

Adlerian theory and approach seems to be the best fit with Abby. Abby (Client Profile 1), is concerned that she has not made enough of her life. Though she possesses a Bachelor of Arts degree, she is concerned that by marrying, she gave up the opportunity to achieve her Master's degree. Hence, she may have feelings of inferiority. Adler (Corey, 2009), suggests that it is in dealing with our feelings of inferiority that we overcome our limitations and achieve superiority. The Adlerian approach also takes into consideration cultural issues within the assessment and treatment processes. In Abby's case, her culture may have dictated that when married, the wife attend to the needs of the husband and home. She may also have feelings that at 57, time has passed her by and it is too late to achieve those things she may still wish to do.

Individual Psychology hypothesizes that thoughts, feelings and actions are the responsibility of the individual.

This may not be applicable in Abby's case, as sometimes circumstances arise that one has no control over.

In Abby's case, her husband contracting cancer, which has over whelmed her; and as Abby may feel her time for therapy is limited, an Adlerian approach is another fit as it offers a quick assessment and application to treatment as well as the use of a variety of cognitive, behavioral and experimental techniques (Corey, 2009).

As with any client, the beginning process would involve the sharing of the client's rights to confidentiality, informed consent and working up a counseling plan that would be viable to Abby's time and needs, but also meet the goals of therapy (APA Code of Ethics, Standards A.1.a, A.1.c., and A.2.a.). The following standards would also be applicable; A.2.c., A.4.b., B.1.a-d., and B.2.a. as in Dr. Ford's analysis (Laureate, 2010), he proposes the potential of Abby being suicidal. Standard B.2.a. is not only an ethical responsibility but a legal obligation as well.

After the initial intake and the beginnings of the therapeutic alliance, I would use some of the strategies put forth by Haynes and Corey (2005), as he applied them to Ruth; most notably the cognitive approach involving role-playing, giving the client the opportunity to step outside of herself and view her problems or concerns in another light, and possibly taking a more objective look at herself, and the problem.

As counseling continues, we would need to take a look at her past relationships and how those have influenced how she feels about herself in the present and in dealing with her husband's cancer, her feelings of inadequacy and how that is influencing her physical well-being. Journaling is another therapeutic strategy, whereby the client documents her feelings throughout the week easily going back to read and reflect on those feelings and how and why they manifested (Haynes and Corey, 2005).

The initial therapeutic goals for Abby, within the Adlerian approach (Corey, 2009), are to make her see herself in a more positive light. She needs to see herself as an accomplished woman. In exploring her past, I would touch upon if she were the first in her family to achieve the level of education she has. We would explore the weight loss as a potential positive and ways to reenergize herself.

As mentioned in my discussion post, education would be used as a therapeutic tool to dispel the notion that she was responsible for her husband's cancer through his diet. This relief of guilt will go along way to achieving a state of satisfaction and may reduce any suicidal thoughts Abby may possess. Along with the diminished thoughts of suicide, she may enter into a new longing for life and the energy that comes with it.

We are at the beginning stages of therapy with Abby, and more information and exploration is needed to adhere to a therapeutic solution and final goals. As we learn more about Abby, her past, and emotions connected with it, we may choose to invoke a psychoanalytical approach during some sessions. But for now, I feel an Adlerian approach is warranted, if nothing else than to relieve Abby of her guilt and suicidal thoughts.

References:

ACA Code of Ethics (2005). American Counseling Association. Retrieved from http://www.txca.org/Images/tca/Documents/ACA%20Code%20of%20Ethics.pdf

Client Profile 1: Abby (2010) Transcript.

Corey, G. (2009). *Case approach to counseling and psychotherapy* (7th ed.). Belmont, CA: Brooks/Cole, Cengage Learning.

Corey, G. (2009). *Theory and practice of counseling and psychotherapy* (8th ed.). Belmont, CA: Thomson Brooks/Cole.

Corey, G. & Haynes, R. (2005). Integrative counseling: CD-ROM. Belmont, CA: Brooks/Cole.

Laureate Education, Inc. (Executive Producer). (2010). *Counseling and Psychotherapy Theories,* Baltimore, MD: Author.

An Existential Approach to Patrick

What is Existentialism?

Existentialism is a philosophical approach to therapy rather than a style of practice. It presumes we are free and therefore responsible for our choices and actions (Corey, 2009). A basic existentialist premise is that since we chose our path we are not victims of the circumstances surrounding those choices. It also seeks a balance between human limitations and the tragedy it brings, and the opportunities and possibilities of being human. Existentialism seeks to overcome isolation while creating meaning in a person's life and establishing meaningful relationships.

Strengths & Weaknesses

It is in this way that existentialism can help Patrick (Client Profile #3) overcome his anxieties, break free of his isolation, gain new meaning in his life for self and work, and develop other close friendships outside of work. However, though existentialism makes the client responsible for choices, it fails to acknowledge the fact that sometimes we do not have choices in life. As a firefighter, Patrick may have had a choice whether to enter a burning building or not, but to decline an assignment would be to deny the very essence of who he was. Hence the question is posed, did he really have a choice in his actions with the 9/11 tragedy? If, indeed, this lead to post traumatic stress disorder, as a possibility addressed by Dr. White (Laureate, 2010) was that also Patrick's choice?

Culture, Gender & Age

Dr. White also points out that as a therapist, Patrick's culture, how and where he was raised; his subculture as a firefighter; his definition of what it means to be a man; and his age, what it means to be a 33 year old man, need to be explored. She pointed out within the initial intake that there is no reference to his sexual identity, how he feels about his scarring, and his level of depression, which might trigger suicidal thoughts. Though these things may prove to be useful in future sessions, and as Patrick feels comfortable in talking about them, based solely on Patrick's initial video and transcript, it seems a lot of assumptions are being made.

Ethics & Laws

As Patrick has certain rights within the framework of therapy, he would be privy to and made aware of his rights to confidentiality, informed consent and working up a counseling plan that would be viable to his time and needs, but also meet the goals of therapy (APA Code of Ethics, Standards A.1.a, A.1.c., and A.2.a.). The following standards would also be applicable; A.2.c., A.4.b., B.1.a-d., and B.2.a. as in Dr. White's analysis (Laureate, 2010), she proposes the potential of Patrick being suicidal. Standard B.2.a. is not only an ethical responsibility but a legal obligation as well.

The Therapeutic Goal

The overall therapeutic goal with Patrick, in using the existentialist approach (Corey, 2009), would be a self-awareness that he has the freedom to be the author of his own life; that he has choices. At 33, he is still young enough to go into the military; and with his firefighting expertise, could qualify for entrance into Officer Candidate School, then become a fire fighter instructor, as the existentialist emphasizes a client's current experience. With a renewed outlook that he, indeed, has options, may come a renewed confidence, self-assurance, and increased self-esteem. Therapeutic goals in existentialism (Corey, 2009), do not entail that the counselor, or client, find a solution, but rather to help the client become aware of where and who they are now and encourage them to make life-changing decisions. Hence, the therapeutic goal with Patrick would be just that.

Counseling Strategies

One of the strategies I would use (Corey & Haynes, 2005) would be to ask Patrick what he wants. What are his therapeutic goals? What would he be doing if he weren't a fire fighter? The exploration of those answers might give Patrick a new awareness of the opportunities and possibilities he may have not considered. Also, the existentialist is concerned with feelings, so asking Patrick how he would feel about change, and having him place words with those feeling, would be part of the therapeutic process (Corey & Haynes, 2005).

Summation

The role of the existentialist is to open the door of possibilities for the client, but the client, and in this case, Patrick, must choose to walk through or not. The counselor can encourage and support, but the final decision must come from the client, who is now aware of the freedom and strength he possesses, to make it himself.

References

ACA Code of Ethics (2005). American Counseling Association. Retrieved from

http://www.txca.org/Images/tca/Documents/ACA%20Code%20of%20Ethics.pdf

Client Profile 3: Patrick (2010) Transcript.

Corey, G. (2009). *Case approach to counseling and psychotherapy* (7th ed.). Belmont, CA: Brooks/Cole, Cengage Learning.

Corey, G. (2009). *Theory and practice of counseling and psychotherapy* (8th ed.). Belmont, CA: Thomson Brooks/Cole.

Corey, G. & Haynes, R. (2005). Integrative counseling: CD-ROM. Belmont, CA: Brooks/Cole.

Laureate Education, Inc. (Executive Producer). (2010). *Counseling and Psychotherapy Theories,* Baltimore, MD: Author.

Cognitive or RET Approach

Aaron B

Aaron is a 17 year old Syrian-American male, who is single. He attends high school where he is a star athlete on the track team. He is 5'10" and weighs 120 pounds. He has osteopenia and is an only child of divorced parents. He does not smoke, drink or use illegal substances. However, he does take Vicodin, as prescribed by his doctor for knee and shin pain. Aaron thinks that losing another 10 pounds will enable him to run faster and he keeps lists of the foods he's eaten, people he's talked with and every possession he owns (Client Profile, 2010).

Cognitive Approach

Cognitive therapy may be the best for Aaron right away. As Aaron enjoys writing things down, and as an element of cognitive therapy there is some homework involved, this may be a way for Aaron to keep a record of how he is doing in therapy (Corey & Haynes, 2005). Aaron falls into this type of therapy in the following ways (Corey, 2009): *Arbitrary inferences and selective abstraction*: Aaron believes that he'll run faster if he loses another 10 pounds. He is ignoring important information about the thinning of his bones which may lead to breakage, and masking the pain with Vicodin. *Magnification and minimization*: Aaron is giving everyday events in his life greater value and importance by writing everything down, from people he's talked with, to what they've said. I cannot fault Aaron for writing down his possessions as many insurance companies recommend such should there be a catastrophe. Many people keep track of what they eat and the fat content as well; however, Aaron does seem to be taking things to the extreme making him a candidate for cognitive therapy, for if a therapist can change how one thinks, then behavior can be changed as well.

The one thing that the cognitive approach does not account for is how emotions determine behavior. Yes, the cognitive therapist will say that a change in cognition will produce a change in emotions; but what about theories that suggest emotions help create thought patterns?

RET Therapy

One of the things we have not heard, is how Aaron feels about his parent's divorce, or how he feels about his mom's high standards and expectations and how this might be influencing him to do even better on the track team. Though we know he's on Vicodin (Client Profile, 2010), we still don't know the extent to which he's taking the pills and if there's an addiction problem looming in the near future.

One of the benefits of RET therapy is that it can be a brief therapy. This may suit Aaron better, for as a high school senior, he may be going away to college soon.

However, this type of therapy also invokes a change to emotions as a way of changing behavior (Corey, 2007), and there may be no emotions attached to Aaron's actions.

Integration

Many of the theories lend themselves to integration, and this is true of both behavioral and cognitive therapies (Corey & Haynes, 2005). And though I believe that cognitive therapy may be the best starting place for Aaron, I would not hesitate to bring in a therapy, such as RET, should I discover that what drives Aaron into making his decisions is his emotions.

Code of Ethics

With Aaron we need to be cognizant that he is still a minor, so any therapy we may want to implement needs to be approved by his mother (Code of Ethics, Standard A.2.d.). We need to take into consideration his cultural heritage to see if anything there relates to his cognition and therefore his behavior (Standards A.2.c., A.4.b. & B.1.a.). We need to investigate how much Vicodin he's taking and if there might be an addiction (Standard B.2.a.), then implement the DSM-IV to find out if there are other potential concerns.

Summary

The overall therapeutic goal with Aaron is his health and educating him on the benefits of proper nutrition and health. Through the use of the cognitive approach, the goal would be to make him re-examine why he's writing so many things down and to what benefit. Is he afraid that a conversation he had with someone will come back with the person denying what was said?

These are things worth examining to get a bigger and more detailed picture of Aaron and try to modify the behaviors before he may leave for college.

References

ACA Code of Ethics (2005). American Counseling Association. Retrieved from

http://www.txca.org/Images/tca/Documents/ACA%20Code%20of%20Ethics.pdf

Client Profile 2: Aaron B (2010) Transcript.

Corey, G. (2009). *Theory and practice of counseling and psychotherapy* (8th ed.). Belmont, CA: Thomson Brooks/Cole.

Corey, G. & Haynes, R. (2005). Integrative counseling: CD-ROM. Belmont, CA: Brooks/Cole.

Lois and Family Systems Approach

Strengths and Limitations

The strengths of using the Family Systems Approach (FSA) with Lois is due to the multi lens therapy model. The systematic approach (Corey, 2009), explores the family process and rules. It invites the whole family in right away to seek validation and consensus as to the concerns being presented. It is also concerned with cultural implications and larger systems affecting the family. It will intervene to change the way Lois views herself. Within the lenses that might help Lois, are the multicultural lens (p. 425), the gender lens (p. 426), and the process lens (p. 427). These lenses will help Lois see her role within the family in regards to her culture, her gender and the process of communication between two people, something she may be lacking with her husband, hence the fear of abuse (Client Profile #4).

A potential limitation for this model are practitioners "who assume Western models of family are universal" (Corey, 2009). Therapists need to expand their views of the individual, gender roles within cultures, and extended families. Counselors focusing on nuclear family models will come up short with clients in expended families. In Lois' case, this means the care of her mother.

Culture, Gender and Age Issues

Though Lois is a 41 year old, Hispanic woman, there is too much information missing concerning her culture and the culture of the man she married. If we are to assume that Lois is a "traditional Hispanic woman," what does that mean? Is she Mexican? The term Hispanic is used to cover all Spanish speaking countries in Latin America and Spain. So where is Lois from? Mexico? Spain? Venezuela? The information in her file is unclear and would definitely change the dynamics of the case study and how to proceed if we had more information. Also, there is no mention of her husband's race or culture. So the issues surrounding this area are unclear at this point.

Ethical or Legal Issues

The main ethical issue at stake here is non-maleficence, to do no harm. Lois will be duly informed of her right to confidentiality (ACA Code of Ethics, 2005, B.1.b-d.), but will also be informed of Standard B.2.a., the duty to report any danger that may befall the client. In Lois' case, this is the fear of abuse by her husband.

Using the FSA, input from Lois' husband would be welcome as we look at ways they can bond and communicate to avoid confusion, misunderstandings and any threat of hostilities. Lois wants to change to appease and please her husband, but she, individually, must not get lost in the process.

Therapeutic Goal

The goal for Lois and the success of her family unit is based on the multicultural lens, which uses ten areas of assessment. These assessments produce meaning to the areas of direct experience. Finding the areas that "fit" among family members and those that are different is key in helping families understand the dynamics of individuality and acceptance of the family as a whole (Corey, 2009).

The gender lens will help Lois and her husband better understand the stereotypical roles being played out in the family unit. Once again, this is based on culture. Some cultures embrace what Americans call stereotypical, which is why a clear definition of culture is important.

The process lens helps couples and families to function in ways that meet demands, needs and goals of everyday life. The process of therapy is directly related to the process of change, which in Lois' case, something she wishes to do.

How to Proceed

The first thing would be to gather much more information that what was not given in the Case Study. Once some of the pieces have been filled in , then I would know better how to proceed with therapy and the techniques and strategies I would employ.

References

ACA Code of Ethics (2005). American Counseling Association. Retrieved from

    http://www.txca.org/Images/tca/Documents/ACA%20Code%20of%20Ethics.pdf

Client Profile 4: Lois (2010) Transcript.

Corey, G. (2009). *Theory and practice of counseling and psychotherapy* (8th ed.). Belmont, CA: Thomson Brooks/Cole.

Individualistic Theory

Individualistic theory is what I call my own approach to therapy. It takes a look at the client as a holistic individual; different from others in the unique way he/she relates to and interprets their environment spiritually, cognitively, emotionally, physically and psychologically.

According to Dr. Seligman, "We cannot be all things to all people," therefore an integrated approach to therapy allows the therapist greater room and access to what the client may be in need of (Laureate, 2010).

Arnold Lazarus, the father of clinical behavior therapy (Corey and Haynes, 2005), coined the term "technical eclecticism," meaning that the therapist draws upon many techniques without necessarily adhering to the theory that spawned the technique, but rather taking the technique of various approaches and tailor making them to a clients individual struggle.

This approach could be called the cornerstone of individualistic theory.

View of Human Nature

Individualistic theory integrates approaches from existential, person-centered, cognitive behavior and reality therapies. As with existentialism, individualism does not readily identify therapy with a set of techniques (Corey, 2009, p. 139), but rather trusts the client's ability and desire to move forward (p. 169) to fulfill his/her potential, realizing that he/she will make mistakes along the way (p. 277). The brain acts as a monitor, recording those things in life that are pleasant and make us feel good (p. 318); however, as we strive to repeat those feelings, their may be consequences along the way that we must take responsibility for our actions (pp. 141, 319). One key element shared by these approaches and incorporated within individualistic theory, is the ability to achieve self-awareness and self-actualizing. Hence, we come full circle in incorporating these four approaches to therapy.

Key Factors in Changing Behavior

"Those who cannot remember the past are doomed to repeat it," George Santayana (1933). With that in mind, individualistic theory recognizes that we are all products of our past and present experiences, our environment, and how we interpret them to give them meaning in the now. One of the dawning awarenesses in existential therapy (Corey, 2009, p. 140) is, "They learn that in many ways they are keeping themselves prisoner by some of their past decisions, and they realize they can make new decisions."

Therefore, individualism does look to the past to remember and learn from it as a tool to emphasize the changes that can be made in the present to avoid irrational thinking (p. 276) in the future. Clients are encouraged to take responsibility and stop blaming others, or even themselves (p. 277), as this only inhibits grow, change and self-actualization. Individualism incorporates the ABC framework (p. 278), and choice theory (p. 318) to help clients make better choices and change the behaviors that promote destructive choices.

Therapist-Client Relationship

As with the aforementioned therapies, individualism's therapeutic alliance is based on mutual trust and respect. Therapy is a journey taken together with the therapist modeling such values as compassion and genuineness, and the client using that modeling as an agent for change. The therapist accepts the client unconditionally, but there is no need for an intense relationship. The emphasis is on an understanding and supportive relationship.

Therapist's Function and Role

The therapist acts as a mentor and teacher, informing the client of rights and responsibilities, some of which are outlined in the APA Code of Ethics (2005). The therapist also teaches the client about self-evaluation (Corey, 2009, p. 321), and moving beyond irrational thoughts (p. 280). The therapist accomplishes this by being congruent, accepting and empathetic (p. 171), and helping the client to gain a new understanding of themselves and recovering ownership of their lives (p. 149).

Key Goals of Therapy

The saying, "Half of solving a problem is the recognition of one," is appropriate to therapy. If the client is in therapy at his or her own initiation, then there is a chance that therapy will be successful. Otherwise, one of the first key goals in therapy is to allow the client to take responsibility, as many play the "blame game" or are in denial.

Once acceptance of one's responsibilities has been attained, then true therapy can begin. We can begin by teaching the client that change is possible. That we can learn from the past in order so as not to repeat it, and begin on a journey of self-discovery that allows for self-awareness and actualization. This can be achieved by unconditional acceptance and obtaining mutual respect for one another.

Techniques and Procedures

Though the theories and therapies that influence individualism are not partial to a particular technique in order to quantify a client, I believe that any tool that allows a therapist a deeper perspective into the client's personality is beneficial. I also believe that the client should be involved in his or her own therapy away from the counseling sessions. Therefore, homework may be in order. One of the first homework pieces I would charge my client with would be either the Meyers/Briggs Personality Test, or the Keirsey/Bates Temperament Sorter. I have found over the years what insightful tools these are in helping to understand the unique perspective of individuals.

However, there are other procedures that need application before homework is assigned. This is the beginning of a therapeutic alliance and the building of trust. This can begin with the reviewing of the APA Code of Ethics (2005), and the rights a client has in regards to privacy and confidentiality, and the times those might need to be breached. In individual therapy, the counselor would take some time to introduce him/herself, qualifications, experience, and theories and approached usually used in "diagnosis" and "treatment," though a philosophy of the therapy is not to clinically label the client.

From here, the therapist acts as guide, mentor and facilitator in helping the client through the therapeutic journey, with the client setting goals along the way, some short term, some long term.

Populations Served

The population being served would be dependent upon the specialty the counselor may have chosen. As indicated by the name, individualistic therapy takes into account the individual as a unique entity. Group therapy, therefore, may not be a good fit for this approach. This does not mean, however, that a group would not be beneficial within the therapeutic approach of another theory. This may not be ideal for family therapy as well, as most family therapists want the family unit to engage in the therapy as a whole.

Who this type of therapy would work for, is the man or woman who finds him/herself single again after a long term committed relationship, or who is having a hard time finding one in the first place. Or the high school student who is in need of a counselor to really listen to his/her needs and desires but is locked in peer relationships that are proving to be unhealthy, or whose parents have grown distant. This type of therapy would also be successful for those who seem trapped, lost, unmotivated, in a rut, or who can't seem to generate the will or desire to move forward and become self-actualized.

References

ACA Code of Ethics (2005). American Counseling Association. Retrieved from

    http://www.txca.org/Images/tca/Documents/ACA%20Code%20of%20Ethics.pdf

Corey, G. (2009). *Theory and practice of counseling and psychotherapy* (8th ed.). Belmont, CA: Thomson Brooks/Cole.

Corey, G. & Haynes, R. (2005). Integrative counseling: CD-ROM. Belmont, CA:

    Brooks/Cole.

Laureate Education, Inc. (Executive Producer). (2010). *Counseling and Psychotherapy*

    Theories, Baltimore, MD: Author.

Santayana, G. (1933). Retrieved from http://en.wikipedia.org/wiki/George_Santayana

Compatible theories for integration... and, not.

Compatible

   Existential and Person-Centered Therapies

Both these therapies deal with human nature as the ability to become self-aware. The existentialist (Corey, 2009, p. 139) does so my questioning ourselves, others, and the world. Likewise, with person-centered, examines how a client acts in their world with others over-coming obstacles within and outside of themselves (p. 170).

Therapeutic goals for the existentialist include helping clients redefine themselves in ways that promote greater genuineness. Increased awareness is the central goal of existential therapy (p. 148). Person-centered therapy clients ask, "How can I discover my real self?" Clients recognize that they have lost contact with themselves by using facades. Hence, a therapeutic goal in person-centered therapy is to become self-aware.

Both the existential and person-centered therapists are not looking to define their clients in terms of diagnoses, but rather assist them in rediscovering and recovering ownership of their lives (p. 149). Within person-centered therapy, this is done by the attitude of the therapist and by modeling change for the client (p. 171). Both client and therapist are on the journey of discovery together, working together to attain the therapeutic goal of self-awareness.

Least Compatible

Adlerian and Reality Therapies

The Adlerian view of human nature is how a person's perception of the past and early events has a continuing influence (p. 98), while Reality therapy, Choice theory, focuses on the needs and choices the client is making today (p. 318).

While the therapeutic goals of Adlerian therapists center around the adoption of behaviors in community and social interest (p. 104), and Corey (2010) mentions in the video how the Adlerian therapists believe that it is important or the client to involve themselves in community in order to help feel satisfied, the Reality therapist helps his clients by having them learn better ways of fulfilling their personal needs (p. 321). These include: power or achievement, freedom or independence, and fun.

The therapist's function and role are different as well. Adlerian counselors make comprehensive assessments by gathering information by means of a questionnaire on a client's family constellation.

Once interpreted, the questionnaire gives a picture of the client's early world (p. 105). The Reality counselor acts as a mentor and teacher in how clients can engage in self-evaluation. The role of the reality therapist is to challenge the client to examine and evaluate their own behavior, then to make plans for change (p. 321).

Most of the relationships between therapist and client seem similar in respect to openness, understanding, cooperation and mutual trust. These qualities seem to be a continuous theme throughout most therapies.

As I was trying to deliberate which theories work better together and which do not, I had to agree with Corey (2009) and his evaluation of how each point of view (p. 454) offers a perspective for helping clients in their search for self.

I believe the exercise above helps us to better understand what therapies work well together and which do not. It also helps us to better understand what theories work better with what types of practices we are interested in pursuing. Personally, I am sure I will be selecting a few to integrate as I explore the major theories in depth.

Though Carl Jung is placed in psychoanalytic theories, which may differ from the Roger's person-centered philosophies, Jung's work helped produced the Meyers/Briggs personality test, which lead to the Kiersey/Bates temperament sorter which can prove very useful in counseling sessions.

As Dr. Seligman states (Laureate, 2010), "We cannot be all things to all people," hence integrating theoretical approaches is beneficial as it tens to make us well rounded counselors able to better deal with the various concerns we are faced with as clients enter our offices.

Reference:

Corey, G. (2009). *Theory and practice of counseling and psychotherapy* (8th ed.). Belmont, CA: Thomson Brooks/Cole.

Corey, G. & Haynes, R. (2005). Integrative counseling: CD-ROM. Belmont, CA: Brooks/Cole.

Laureate Education, Inc. (Executive Producer). (2010). *Counseling and Psychotherapy Theories,* Baltimore, MD: Author.

Behavioral and Cognitive Theories

Behavioral theories began in the 1950s and 60s and began to thrive despite harsh criticism from psychoanalytic therapists. By the 1970s contemporary behavioral theory was a major force in psychology. The 80s brought more research and the emergence of cognitive behavior therapy, and by the 90s the ABCT (Association for Behavioral and Cognitive Therapies claimed a membership of 4,500 members. Now, in the 2000s, a "third wave' is emerging, bring with it an enlarged scope of research and practice (Corey, 2009).

Behavioral therapy's key concepts rest on the scientific views of human behavior. The current trend being to give more control to the clients to increase their freedoms thus overcoming debilitating behaviors that restrict choices. The more freedom one has, the more choices one can make, including overcoming their sociocultural conditioning.

Behavioral therapists give their clients a functional assessment, or behavioral analysis, to identify the condition. This is the ABC model, antecedents, behaviors and consequences. Antecedent events promote certain behaviors, while consequences maintain certain behaviors. If the consequence is positive, the behavior will be maintained.

Behavior therapy has been criticized for changing behaviors, but not feelings. However, its strength is the emphasis it places on ethical accountability (Corey, 2009, p. 264). Clients have a great deal of freedom in deciding what the goals of therapy should be.

Developed by Albert Ellis in 1955 (Corey, 2009), Rational Emotive Behavior Theory (REBT) was one of the first cognitive behavior therapies. REBT's basic reasoning is that our emotions come from our beliefs, reactions and evaluations of life's situations. The focus, then, is working on thinking and acting rather than feelings.

REBT looks at humans who possess the potential for rational and irrational thinking. The goal is growth and self-actualization as brought about by the disposition for happiness, loving and communication. REBT realizes humans are fallible and helps clients to accept that they will make mistakes in the future, learn to live with them and make peace with them.

The therapist here is directly involved within the therapeutic process. Education is the key as to illuminate the mystery surrounding the therapy while going through the various steps of the treatment plan. The therapist engages in telling the client what they are doing irrationally to create negativity in their lives, then challenge the client to develop a rational philosophy to overcome it (Corey, 2009, p. 280).

Although REBT allows the therapist to be eclectic in their therapeutic approach, concern is how well the counselor is trained in the cognitive behavioral approaches.

Reference:

Corey, G. (2009). *Theory and practice of counseling and psychotherapy* (8th ed.). Belmont, CA: Thomson Brooks/Cole.

Couples and Family Counseling

Personal Filters

Definition of Family

As the baby boom generation came to be (1944-1964), traditional definitions of family remained as they had been for generations before (Laureate, 2008). A man, a woman, 2.5 children, usually one boy and one girl, living a middle class, worker bee lifestyle. The baby boom generation brought with it social change, women's rights, civil rights, sexual promiscuity, and an exploration of gender roles and gender identification. Though these were not new, they were brought to the forefront and more to the public forum and consciousness than in previous generations. Hence, the traditional family changed as well, and now there is no single definition of family. According to Thomlison (2010), we recognize a vast number of family structures.

The three groups of family, recognized by Health Services Technology (2005), are: Traditional, as described above; Extended, referring to blood relatives or related members of a family living together; and Elected, those coming together out of need or desire to create a family unit. These may include the following family structures: Single parent, stepfamilies, same-sex partners, grandparent-headed, foster or adopted, and non-related households.

Similarities between traditional, extended and elected do exist, as there are still roles of what is considered masculine and feminine to assume. Who is going to work? Who is caring for the children, if any? What household chores are being assumed and by which partner or family members? These roles determine traditions in the daily living of any family.

Personal Filters

Perhaps it was the times I grew up in. Maybe it was due to the open-mindedness of my own family or the fact that it presented me with concepts of diversity that may have eluded another. At any rate, my filters do not include how a family is made up, or if a couple is mixed race or same gender. My aunt is Lesbian, my nephew is gay, and I am privileged to have friends that are diverse in age, race, color and ethnicity. Within the dynamics of a relationship, happiness and fulfillment are the cornerstones for success.

With this being said, my filters center around what makes couples or families dysfunctional. An abusive spouse, teens who are running the household, parents who lost that credibility with their teens by becoming their friend; in other words, those things that may have been avoided by those involved, but they fell into the abyss of dysfunction by their own choosing. I will admit, that I have a low tolerance for blatant stupidity. However, what may appear "stupid" to the casual observer may be naivety or ignorance.

This must be taken into consideration when counseling couples and families. Common sense, as we have found out, is not so common as we once thought; and with more people expecting instant gratification living in a fast food, one hour photo world, this may transfer over to unrealistic expectations within relationships as individuals race into Las Vegas marriages without knowing each other, or families that are formed out of obligation rather than desire.

Therefore, with the recognition of these filters, and a propensity for patience, I am certain I can overcome my own biases while placing myself in the shoes of my clients and emphasizing with their concerns. For I, too, am a victim of ignorance and naivety and must remember that lessons are learned differently by different people.

References

Health Services Technology (2005). In Thomlison, B. (2010). *Family assessment handbook: An introduction and practical guide to family assessment.* (3rd ed.). Belmont, CA: Brooks/Cole, Cengage Learning.

Laureate Education, Inc. (Producer). (2008). Couples and family counseling [DVD]. In Introduction to Couples and Family Counseling. Baltimore, MD: Author.

Thomlison, B. (2010). *Family assessment handbook: An introduction and practical guide to family assessment.* (3rd ed.). Belmont, CA: Brooks/Cole, Cengage Learning.

Diversity in Counseling

Impact of Diversity

Many of us enjoy living in a culturally diverse area. The wide variety of restaurants, shopping, music and dance all testify to that; but living the culture day to day may be a different story, as we can leave the restaurant, go home from the festivals and take a cultural item bought at a store back to our own home. Living within a culture through marriage and family is a different matter.

According to Hecker and Wetchler (2003), Falicov (1995) provides the best definition of culture.

"shared world views, meanings and adaptive behaviors derived from simultaneous membership and participation in a multiplicity of contexts, such as rural, urban, or suburban setting; language age, gender, cohort, family configuration, race, ethnicity, religion, nationality, socioeconomic status, employment, education, occupation, sexual orientation, political ideology; migration and stage of acculturation."

With this definition in mind, we can begin to uncover a plethora of potential diverse issues that might challenge couples, marriages and families alike. The term I would like to focus on is "adaptive behaviors." Many people are aware that adaptation is the key to survival, however some are more adaptable than others and marrying into a culture one is unfamiliar with can cause stress, leading to levels of misunderstanding and miscommunication.

Ideally, it would help if a multicultural family therapist had traveled outside of the U.S. (Odell, Shelling, Young, Hewitt & L'Abate, 1994) and mastered at least one language of another culture. In my case, living in the Southwest, Spanish would be the ideal. Odell, et al. (1994) go on to suggest that culturally immersing oneself can help in learning another's culture as well. However, many would interpret this as those coming to the United States immerse themselves in the "American" culture, as diverse and multicultural as it would seem. Developing friendships that are culturally diverse would be another way to develop a knowledge base in working with multicultural couples and families (Odell, et al., 1994).

Two issues that may arise within a diverse couple is a traditional sense of the man/woman relationship, and how to raise the children in a multiculturally diverse family in regards to religion, education and discipline.

If an independent American, or Americanized woman marries a man of a culture where the man takes charge of most, if not all aspects of a relationship, she may find that her independent nature and his controlling nature provide hostility and friction within the relationship. If this occurred while dating or at the beginning of the marriage, something might have been done; however, in my experience, these men wait until there are children in the mix making it harder for the woman to leave. If the woman exhibits a desire to leave and take the children, then the man, perhaps middle eastern, who may have ties in his home country, may take and hold the children hostage forcing the woman to live in his home country where he can exhibit greater control over her. In cases such as these premarital counseling may prove beneficial. Unfortunately, many people don't feel the need for premarital counseling which may explain the divorce rate in this country.

This scenario also plays out in the second issue of childrearing where most premarital counseling focuses on values as they pertain to gender, roles, finances, family (including whether to have children, how many and how to discipline them), conflict resolution and communication (Jolley, 2008).

Communication is the key to help alleviate the impact of diversity in the first place. Even if it means eventually communicating with a therapist before it is too late.

References

Falicov, C. J. (1995). Training to think culturally: A multidimensional comparative framework. In Hecker, L. L. & Wetchler, J. L. (2003). Contextual issues in marital and family therapy: Gender, culture, and spirituality. *An Introduction to Marriage and Family Therapy.* Hawthorne Press, New York.

Hecker, L. L. & Wetchler, J. L. (2003). Contextual issues in marital and family therapy: Gender, culture, and spirituality. *An Introduction to Marriage and Family Therapy.* Hawthorne Press, New York.

Jolley, D. (2008). Premarital counseling helps couples avoid relationship problems. Retrieved from **http://www.fcconline.org/ExpertHelp/Advice/tabid/93/articleType/ArticleView/articl** eId/50/Premarital-Counseling-Helps-Couples-Avoid-Relationship-Problems.aspx

Odell, M., Shelling, G., Young, K. S., Hewitt, D. H., & L'Abate, L. (1994). The skills of the marriage and family therapist in straddling multicultural issues. *The American Journal of Family Therapy, 22*(2), 145-155.

Resolving Ethical Dilemmas

Case Study Summary

    A family unit consisting of a husband, Tom; wife, Lisa; and two sons, is in discord. Tom and Lisa argue continuously as to whom is at fault. Lisa blames Tom for being unavailable and at work all the time, while Tom states that he might be home more often if Lisa was not a "cold fish." Currently Tom is considering an affair with a co-worker and has secretly divulged this to Jan, the family counselor, while Lisa has also spoken to Jan about an unplanned pregnancy and the potential of an abortion of the baby girl as a way to get back at Tom, as he has always wanted a girl. Jan feels she is over her head with the secrets and the discord within the family. She is unsure if she should keep these clients or refer them to another counselor.

Ethical Dilemma One: Dual Relationships

The first ethical dilemma that was evident is the potential for a dual relationship as presented in Tom wanting to speak with Jan alone and confiding in her the prospect of an affair. The dual relationship is presented in IAMFC Ethical Code, Section I, Letter H. Should a dual relationship become necessary as a way to help curb the conflict, then "family counselors are obligated to discuss and provide informed consent of the ramifications of the counseling relationship."

Ethical Dilemma Two: Termination of the Relationship

According to IAMFC Ethical Code, Section I, Letter M, a counselor can terminate a therapeutic relationship if it is no longer in the best interest of the client. In this case, Jan is considering the possibility of termination due to her own personal reasons or that the presenting case may be more challenging than she desires to take on. Her decision to terminate could also come into conflict with Section I, Letter A (IAMFC Ethical Codes), as her decision might have a negative impact on what is already happening win the family. Further blame could be placed on each spouse by the other for Jan deciding to terminate.

Ethical Decision-making and Potential Solutions

Jan must weigh each of the problems within the family and the ethical dilemmas she is facing (Hecker & Wetchler, 2003). Though both Tom and Lisa are looking at the problem in terms of each other, Jan needs to consider the welfare of the children, including the unborn one, and the welfare of the entire family. In fact, at this point, she may be the only one doing so.

Since it is obvious that Tom and Lisa are looking for counseling separately, Jan must explain the ethical codes and ramifications of entering into a dual relationship as now the client has gone from one, the family unit, to three, Tom, Lisa and the family unit.

This is a common ethical dilemma faced by Marriage and Family Counselors (Hecker & Wetchler, 2003, p. 505).

After explaining the ethical codes surrounding dual relationships and confidentiality, Jan should meet with Tom and Lisa separately to first determine if there is a desire to save the marriage. If so, then she counsels both to open the doors of communication and truly talk and listen to each other. She should meet with Tom and Lisa together to begin to educate them on how to communicate effectively.

As she is working with Tom and Lisa, Jan should also meet with their two sons, Steven and Daniel to get a clear understanding of how the boys are feeling and what their expectations are of counseling and what their hopes are for a positive outcome.

In doing so, Jan may overcome her concerns of termination and therefore overcome that particular ethical dilemma. Since, it would seem that a dual relationship may be initially therapeutic, she can circumvent that ethical dilemma, as long as all parties are aware of the new relationship entered into with the therapist, and all agree that it is for the good of the family unit as a whole (IAMFC Ethical Code, Section I, Letter H).

References

Hecker, L. L. & Wetchler, J. L. (2003). Contextual issues in marital and family therapy: Gender, culture, and spirituality. *An Introduction to Marriage and Family Therapy.* Hawthorne Press, New York.

International Association of Marriage and Family Counselors (IAMFC) Ethical Code (2001). Retrieved from http://iamfconline.com/PDFs/Ethical%20Codes.pdf

The Family Genogram

Ferraro Genogram

I started my genogram with my parents Vince and Nancy, and my mother's sister Suu, who is a lesbian, which was always a source of tension between my father and Suu. This, however, was not indicated in the genogram as my father is deceased and I would imagine the tension died with him.

Below is the Ferraro Genogram. As you can see, I spent more time examining my sister's family, as, not only did I not have one, but as you will see, hers is much more interesting.

Table 1 Ferraro Genogram

Ferraro Family

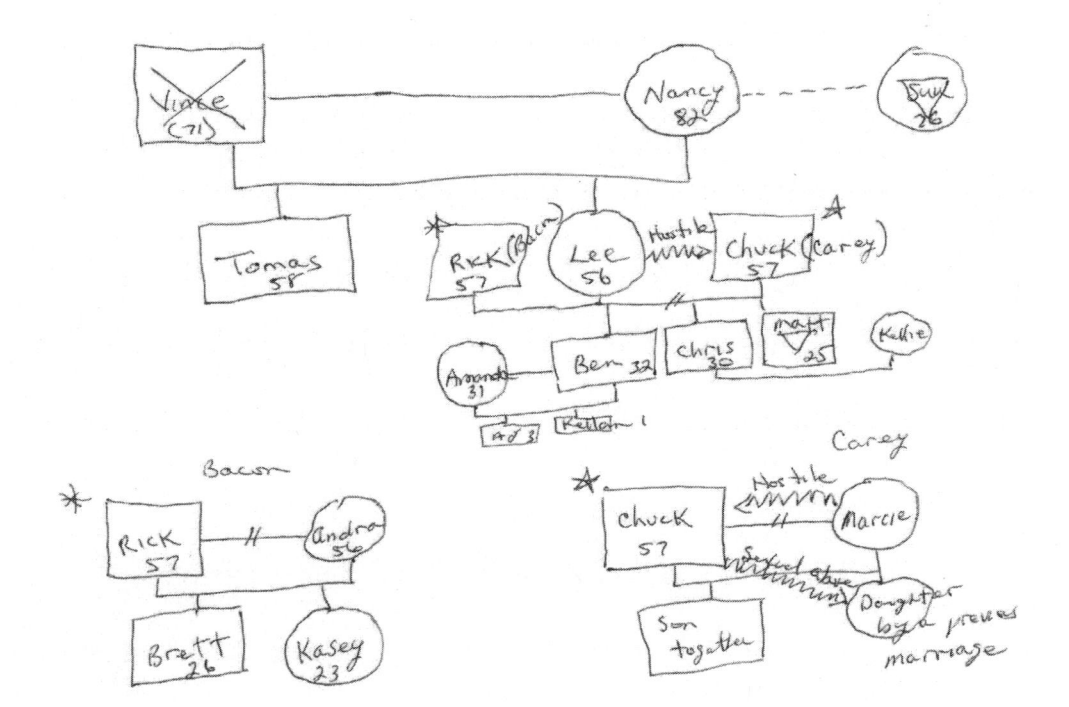

Vince (71) — Nancy 82 ---- Sue 76

Children of Vince & Nancy:
- Tomas 58
- Rick (Bacon) 57 — Lee 56 (Hostile) — Chuck (Carey) 57

Lee's children: Amanda 31 — Ben 32, Chris 30, Matt 25, Kellie

Ben & Amanda's children: Ad 3, Kellan 1

Bacon
Rick 57 —//— Andra 56
- Brett 26
- Kasey 23

Carey
Chuck 57 — Marcie (Hostile) (Sexual abuse)
- Son together
- Daughter by previous marriage

Ferraro Family Genogram: An Explanation

My younger sister, Lee, married Chuck in 1977. She was a party girl and wanted to get out of the house, while he was a tall, dark and handsome, lonely Marine from a Mormon background. After the marriage, Chuck's mom convinced Lee that the Mormon lifestyle was the best in terms of child-rearing and family unity. Unfortunately, Chuck was a "Jack" Mormon (a term used to indicate those Mormons who do not fully comply with the no caffeine or alcohol doctrines of the church) and though the marriage thrived during the birth of the first two boys (Ben and Chris), after the third (Matt), it began to wane. Lee gained weight, and with her newly found religion, Chuck had lost his party girl. Hence the adage: "Women marry men hoping they will change, and they don't; while men marry women hoping they won't change, and they do."

Chuck and Lee's marriage ended in divorce with Chuck leaving Lee for another woman. It was soon discovered that Chuck was a serial monogamous, marrying, having a child, then divorcing another woman before marrying Marcie, with whom he had a child. Marcie brought a little girl into their relationship.

Lee eventually married Rick, and old friend, who had been divorced and has two grown children (Brett and Kasey). Rick, who used to be in construction, has not worked for almost 10 years due to the economy. Lee, who is a nurse, is the sole breadwinner. Rick has taken to drinking and is a self-admitted drunk who does not intend to seek help as he "enjoys" being drunk. This, sometimes, is a source of embarrassment to Lee.

Meantime, Chuck, Lee's ex-husband and the father of her three boys, was "outed" having a sexual relationship with Marcie's daughter (12). He is currently serving a 12-year jail term and will have to register as a sex offender once released. His sons (Ben, Chris and Matt) have written him off, and he is rarely discussed if at all.

Matt, Lee's youngest, recently came out as gay. This has not been a source of tension between the brothers, or with any family member.

Ben, Lee's oldest, has two sons with Amanda, who has gained a great deal of weight. This has made Ben a philanderer as he seeks out affairs with other women. This, however, has not been what has put a strain on the relationship as Amanda may not know, or care, about Ben's activities.

They recently moved, for Ben's job, away from Amanda's parents who helped care for the young boys AJ and Kellan. Now Amanda must become a fulltime parent, which she is not enjoying and the move has become a source of tension between this young couple.

As you can see, there is a great deal of family dynamics happening here and a family genogram can help a therapist get a visual overview of those dynamics and help begin a treatment plan for the family's overall success.

Family Systems

Supra systems: For the Ferraro-Carey-Bacon family, what people see is more important than "fixing" the problems that may eventually tear this family apart. Lee ignores her husband's overdrinking unless it is a source of embarrassment for her. At this time in her life, she would rather be with someone than alone, regardless of consequences. The various family units within this structure are interdependent of each other, where the whole is greater than the sum of its parts (Hecker & Wetchler, 2003).

Subsystems: Within the family units there are many subsystems. Though they all depend on the support and approval of the greater family unit, they function independently of each other as separate units with their own lives and goals. However, the supra system dictates that the larger family unit approves of their choices.

Family Rules: Like the Buckman family (Universal, 1989), there are many "dirty, little, secrets" that are not to be addressed or brought to the surface during family functions for serious consideration. If they are, the discussion quickly becomes one of jokes and sarcasm designed to displace the importance of the topic and eventually deviate from it to lighter subjects. As explained by Hecker and Wetchler (2003), this would be an example of a covert rule. Never verbally stated, but understood by all.

Boundaries: Within these family units and the larger as well, boundaries shift from rigid to diffused based on the needs, desires and whims of the family members. Parents befriend their children until they become an annoyance, then parental roles are implemented. Parental advice is given by Lee, the family matriarch, whether asked for or not, but quickly slips into the friend role so as not be have offended anyone with her remarks. The boundary which is missing is permeability, where all information flows freely resulting in an open system. Once this is achieved, then true communication can exist and the family unit may be able to help itself (Hecker & Wetchler, 2003).

Therapy

The main problem within the family unit is the fear of embarrassment. If problems are not admitted, then there are no problems. There may also be a fear of reprisal and a disconnect from the larger family unit if certain secrets are unveiled. This is based on trust, or the lack of it. A disjunction (Hecker & Wetchler, 2003) that family members will be critical versus supportive if the secrets were revealed.

Though the genogram is a good mapping and graphic tool (Thomlison, 2010), other tools include: the family interview, self-reporting, and teaching, observation and role-playing tools. The more resources that are used, the more information the therapist can gather to help in making a therapeutic determination of how best to help the family. The goal, of course, being to get the family into a healthy family function, as described in Barnhill's "The Health Family," (2001). According to Barnhill, the dimensions of a healthy family include: Individuation-having independent thoughts and feeling; Mutuality-a closeness between individuals with clearly defined identities; Flexibility-a paradigm shift, changing our ways of thinking and accepting as the family unit changes;

Stability- making sure the family unit feels secure despite the changes that occur; Clear perception-seeing things as they really are, not how we wish them to be; and , Clear communication-the successful exchange of information between the family members. Once these have been successfully implemented, a healthy family is destined to emerge.

My Genogram

   Since I do not have an extended personal genogram, per say, I would have to rely on my extended family of friends, and perhaps look upon them as my siblings and how their various roles impact me. As many people are displaced from immediate family members due to geography, the economy, or emotional ties, sometimes friends do become family members that are more important than blood relations.

   Being able to relate to this myself, would give me a greater understanding of the dynamics friends play in one's own personal genogram.

References

Barnhill, L. R. (1979). Healthy family systems. *The Family Coordinator, 28*(1), 94-100.

Hecker, L. L. & Wetchler, J. L. (2003). General systems theory, cybernetics, and family therapy. *An Introduction to Marriage and Family Therapy.* Hawthorne Press, New York.

Imagine Entertainment & Universal Pictures (Producers). Howard, R. (Director). (1989). Parenthood [Motion Picture]. USA: Universal

Thomlinson, B. (2010). Family assessment. *Family Assessment Handbook: An Introduction and Practical Guide to Family Assessment.* (3rd Ed.). Brooks/Cole, Belmont, CA.

A Therapy Model in Study

Strategic Family Therapy

Strategic Family Therapy (Hecker and Wetchler, 2003) subscribes to the interactive view of problems, that is, what is happening between people rather than within them. This is the case of the Lowndes family.

A review of the discord shows a family unit consisting of a husband, Tom; wife, Lisa; and two sons. Tom and Lisa argue continuously as to whom is at fault. Lisa blames Tom for being unavailable and at work all the time, while Tom states that he might be home more often if Lisa was not a "cold fish." Currently Tom is considering an affair with a co-worker, while Lisa who has an unplanned pregnancy is considering the potential of an abortion of the baby girl as a way to get back at Tom, as he has always wanted a girl (Week 3 Case Study).

Though this is affecting the family unit as a whole, sons Steven and Daniel agree that the fighting is continuous, the main concerns center around the dispute and discord between Tom and Lisa.

Washington School's Map

The description of problems is known as PUSH (Protection, Unit, Sequences of interaction, and Hierarchy) is a way therapists can present problems because it emphasizes solutions rather than problems.

Protection is looked at as a way for a loved one to behave in a manner that will improve the situation, as in rising to the occasion for success to occur. Hecker and Wetchler (2003) suggest that the therapist look at the behavior as positively motivated. In Lisa's case, she wants her husband home with her to interact with the children.

Unit is the focus of a triangle, that is, although the problem may seem to be between the two, there is a third party that may help to provide a solution to the problem. In the Lowndes household, the boys represent the third party. Within therapy, it may be the therapist.

Sequence of Interaction not only conceptualizes the problem but points the way to a solution as well. Hostile sequences of interaction are replaced with friendlier ones as solving one problem may cause a domino effect and begin to solve others (Hecker & Wetchler, 2003). In this case, if Tom were home more often to help with the boys, Lisa may have more energy and not be the "cold fish" Tom claims her to be.

This might lead to Tom's decision not to have an affair and Lisa's news of a baby girl. And as Tom has always wanted a baby girl, this might bring them closer.

Hierarchy is the establishment of the power base within relationships. These days, most couples juggle that with the structure of role assumption. Dysfunction occurs when there is an incongruent hierarchy; that is, when people are not behaving in age or role appropriate ways toward each other.

Within therapy there needs to be a strategy for change, and it begins with whom to invite to the therapeutic sessions. In Tom and Lisa's case, the therapist should meet with each separately to determine how string the bond is to save the marriage. Meeting separately will squelch the fighting that happened in the first session (Case Study 3). From there, the therapist can best determine the course of interaction and eventually bring both Tom and Lisa together to work cohesively and productively in saving their marriage, and their family.

References

Hecker, L. L. & Wetchler, J. L. (2003). Contextual issues in marital and family therapy: Gender, culture, and spirituality. *An Introduction to Marriage and Family Therapy.* Hawthorne Press, New York.

Week 3 Case Study: The Lowndes Family

Sexual Issues Affecting a Couple

Infidelity

According to Whisman, Gordon and Chatav (2007), infidelity is one of the most damaging events in a relationship and the hardest to treat in couples therapy. Relationships are built on trust, and when that trust is violated, it is hard to trust again. People look at trust in one of two ways; I will trust you until you prove to me you can't be trusted, or, you have to prove to me you can be trusted. A person of trust who commits an act of infidelity has violated that trust.

There are many factors that may lead to infidelity, the most frequent being marital dissatisfaction. A partner who may be predisposed to having an affair may have a higher neuroticism factor than their partner (Whisman, et al., 2007). On the other hand, compatibility in personality and religion can be a constraining factor on sexual infidelity.

Other factors contributing to the predictability of infidelity was a lower self-esteem by a partner who was suspicious of their partner engaging in an affair.

However, according to Atkins, Marin, Lo, Klann and Hahlweg (2010), treatment specifically designed for infidelity has a high success rate. In recent studies the outcomes of 145 couples revealed solid improvements in both relationship satisfaction and depressive symptoms.

Impotence

Stress, marital dissatisfaction and age all play a part in male impotency. It has been noted that men reach their sexual peak in their late teens and early twenties, while women reach it in mid-life, just as their partner may be experiencing a wane in desire and capability.

Erectile dysfunction (ED) is most commonly noted in accompanying mood disorders and depressive states along with a diminished quality of life (Rosen, Seidman, Menza, Shabsigh, Roose, Tseng, Orazem and Siegel (2004). With a diminished capacity for sex, women may feel the need to seek sexual gratification elsewhere. Hence Impotence may lead to infidelity. This may also help to explain the cougar effect, whereby, older women seek the company of younger men.

However, there is hope here as well. Studies, surveys and tests show that men taking prescription medication to relieve ED, improve their moods and well-being, bringing a new vitality into their relationships (Paige, Hays, Litwin, Rajfer and Shapiro (2005). In fact, 88% of Sildenafil (Viagra, Cialis, etc.) users had an increase in erectile function of 60%. 38% indicated an improved quality of life, while 29% indicated an improved relationship with their sexual partner.

In conclusion, though there are many factors that may tear a relationship apart, it would seem that if the partners are willing, there is a way to overcome what dissolves a relationship in favor of preserving it.

References

Atkins, D. C., Marin, R. A., Lo, T. T. Y., Klann, N. & Hahlweg, K. (2010). Outcomes of couples with infidelity in community-based sample of couple therapy. *Journal of Family Psychology*. Vol. 24, No. 2. 212-216.

Paige, N. M., Hays, R. D., Litwin, M. S., Rajfer, J. & Shapiro, M. F. (2005). Improvement in emotional well-being and relationships of users of sildenafil. *The Journal of Urology*. Vol. 166, Issue 5.

Rosen, R. C., Seidman, S. N., Menza, M. A., Shabsigh, R., Roose, S. P., Tseng, L. J., Orazem, J. & Siegel, R. L. (2005). Quality of life, mood and sexual function: A path analytic model of treatment effects in men with erectile dysfunction and depressive symptoms. *International Journal of Impotence Research*. Vol. 16, 334-340.

Whisman, M. A., Gordon, K. C., Chatav, Y. (2007). Predicting sexual infidelity in a population-based sample of married individuals. *Journal of Family Psychology*. Vol. 21, No. 2, 320-324.

Serial Monogamy

Serial Monogamy is defined as a man, or woman, who leaves one spouse for another. He or she may have gotten tired of the arguing or other factors that made home life unlivable in his view, but the prospect of living without a spouse is intolerable. Hence, he has been courting a potential spouse to marry as soon as the divorce with the current spouse is finalized.

I had never heard of this before until it happened to my sister. It was her first marriage, she a party girl cheerleader type, he a tall, dark and handsome Marine. He came from a Mormon family, which my sister was indoctrinated into. She liked the family oriented values, but he was a "jack-Mormon" who liked his coffee in the morning and his wine at night. My sister had gained some pounds after her third child and the cute, little party girl whom he had married, disappeared along with their sex life.

"Men marry women hoping they won't change, and they do; while women marry men hoping they'll change, and they don't." (Einstein).

Finding out that her husband was already cheating on her, she divorced him. He went on to be a serial-monogamists two more times before settling down, fathering two more children, one with each of his wives.

The impact of the divorce was staggering for my sister's family of three boys, and her oldest, always getting high marks, faltered and began acting out in class. As he grew, however, he regained his talents and became a star pitcher on the high school baseball team.

The actions taken by him left the current family with half-brothers and sisters, all whom live near each other and participate in family gatherings during the holidays. Including all the ex-wives! He is currently in jail due to sexual relations with his last wife's teenage daughter, not his. Which brings me to the second reason for divorce, the first being infidelity, and that is the potential of abuse.

As mentioned in my discussion paper, abuse that is being perpetuated from one spouse to another, and/or to the children is, in my opinion, of a legitimate concern as to divorce the perpetrator.

According to Hecker and Wetchler (2007), 8.7 million couples were involved in spousal abuse in 1985. One can only imagine in these stressful times that that figure may have risen.

Three important findings contribute to an understanding of broader ramifications of family violence. Child and partner abuse co-occur at alarming rated, around 40%, the impact of children seeing spousal abuse may affect them as they were being abused themselves, and children who grow up exposed to violence may become victims and/or perpetrators.

Whether the abuse is physical. sexual, mental, psychological, or emotional, divorcing the one who is acting out may be the only way to save the other and the children. Sometimes divorce saves a family rather than tear it apart.

Between the two, I would have to defend the leaving of a spouse for the safety of myself and of my children. The serial monogamist will do the leaving, though I would questions the motives under which he's leaving and if counseling could have saved that marriage.

References:

Ferraro, T.H. (2008). Personal experience with a serial monogamist.

Ferraro, T. (2011). Divorce and alcoholism. *Discussion Week 8.* Couples and Family Counseling. Walden University.

Hecker, L. L. & Wetchler, J. L. (2003). Contextual issues in marital and family therapy: Gender, culture, and spirituality. An Introduction to Marriage and Family Therapy. Hawthorne Press, New York.

Assessment Techniques and Intervention Goal Plan

The Family Interview

Since Jason has been in and out of his biological parent's home on more than one occasion, and since it is the goal to eventually place him there again, I believe it is important, especially because his step-father seems reluctant to have him back, that a family interview be conducted before Jason be allowed to return home (Thomlison, 2010, pp. 147-150).

Within the interview, the therapist needs to be aware of the surroundings. Do they welcome Jason back? Has room been made for his return? The therapist needs to listen to the concerns and expectations of Jason, Jeff and Carol, as well as watch the body language of all three (Thomlison, 2010, pp. 72-75).

Teaching and Role-Play Tools

Teaching and role-playing also bring the observational component from the family interview into play. However, if Jason is going to successfully matriculate back into the family home, both parents and son, must learn to adjust to the new conditions, dynamics and challenges each are faced with (Thomlinson, 2010, p. 86).

Rehearsing the new behaviors while being observed by the therapist, who offers praise and constructive suggestions, is paramount to the success of families like the Yellowbird's. However, the family interview is the most effective way to establish if all parties are ready for the return of Jason into the home in the first place.

Changing Behavioral Factors

"Behavior is regulated through both cognitive and behavioral processes," (Thomlinson, 2010, p. 96). With that in mind, the Yellowbird family needs to begin the process of changing how they think of one another and the behaviors that come from that cognition. Jason, of course, has a lot of behaviors to change and Jeff his thoughts of Jason. If Jeff can begin to change his thoughts, it may inspire Jason to begin changing his behaviors. However, there is a catch 22, as Jeff may want to see behavioral change before his thoughts about Jason change. From changing behavioral factors, the family, working with the therapist can begin to…

Create Opportunities

Since family systems are influenced by outside sources, and in this case the Yellowbirds have been influenced by many, it is important that interventions be established to create opportunities for the family to take responsibility and begin to build the skills and knowledge that will help be become independent of the therapist (Thomlinson, 2010, pp. 97-98).

Changing Boundaries

As Jason has matured from a child into an adolescent, and now entering high school, he can no longer be treated as a child. With his "street smarts" he would not tolerate that. Hence boundaries must be established to ensure that all members know their roles and responsibilities within the household.

Jeff must recognize that Jason is not a boy anymore subject to his rules and possibly his fatherly advice, but another man living in the house and the son of his wife. Jason must also come to terms that successful living in a family unit means assuming responsibilities that make living in a family unit pleasant and secure (Thomlinson, 2010, p. 100).

Reference

Thomlinson, B. (2010). Family assessment handbook: An introduction and practical guide to family assessment. (3rd Ed.). Brooks/Cole Cengage Learning. Belmont, CA.

Interventions for Sexual Issues and Dysfunctions

Intervention Strategy

Vaginismus

Vaginismus is the painful spastic contraction of the outer third of the vagina, usually due to shame, fear or embarrassment, which in Sandra Wilson's case is brought on by her sexual abuse as a child (Hecker & Wetchler, 2003). According to Masters and Johnson (1970), the physical dilemma can be overcome through a series of vaginal dilators slowly increasing in size. However, while the physical remedy is a temporary solution, behavioral and cognitive therapy needs to begin to reduce, if not eliminate the guilt, or shame, Sandra feels about her sexual abuse. This is where individual counseling would be beneficial, bringing in John only after Sandra has overcome the initial stages of guilt and is beginning to positively process her abuse; which is to say, beginning to deal with it and making positive progress in overcoming it. Only then would it be prudent for John to join the therapy sessions in a supportive role.

Systemic Issues

According to Zimmer (1987), the problem for marital distress may come from outside the relationship and not an actual physical part of the couple themselves. Using the psychoanalytic perspective (Hecker & Wetchler, 2007), a greater scope can be placed on the marriage and causal effects of outside factors. In the Wilson's case, it is the fighting over money issues and John's desire for Sandra to get a better paying job.

Sandra, being dedicated to the children fights it, and therapy can help to see if her sexual dysfunction is not only being triggered by her sexual abuse and subsequent Vaginismus, and/or, psychosomatic response to "punish" John for his badgering her to get a different job.

Challenges

Ignorance can breed fear. It can also breed discontent and anger. The challenges a therapist might meet here is John's interpretation of an actual physical ailment his wife possesses and interpret it as Sandra's pulling away from him physically due to his insistence of another job. If Sandra is just realizing more details about her own sexual abuse, then how much has she divulged to John? This might be new information for him. What will be his reaction to it?

Education is the key element here. John needs to be educated as to his wife's condition and the psychological trauma that has brought it on. In doing so, it is possible he may curb his enthusiasm of Sandra seeking a different job at this time. As Sandra sees she is getting support from John, this may help her in overcoming stressors that may be contributing to her Vaginismus, if indeed it is in part psychosomatically based on her arguments with John.

All in all, open communication, education, and support are going to be key in helping to resolve the issues faced by the Wilsons at this time.

References

Hecker, L. L. & Wetchler, J. L. (2003). Contextual issues in marital and family therapy: Gender, culture, and spirituality. An Introduction to Marriage and Family Therapy. Hawthorne Press, New York.

Masters, W. H. & Johnson, V. E. (1970). Human sexual inadequacy. In Hecker, L. L. & Wetchler, J. L. (2003). Contextual issues in marital and family therapy: Gender, culture, and spirituality. An Introduction to Marriage and Family Therapy. Hawthorne Press, New York.

Zimmer, D. (1987). Does marital therapy enhance the effectiveness of treatment for sexual dysfunction? *Journal for Sex and Marital Therapy*. In Hecker, L. L. & Wetchler, J. L. (2003). Contextual issues in marital and family therapy: Gender, culture, and spirituality. An Introduction to Marriage and Family Therapy. Hawthorne Press, New York.

Substance Abuse Counseling

Assessment Instruments: Interview (CAGE), SMAST & SASSI-3/2

One of the most important aspects of any assessment of substance abuse is the diagnostic interview (Stevens & Smith, 2009). A carefully planned and conducted interview is the corner stone of the diagnostic process, and given the prevalence of denial from substances abusers, it is important during the first interview to gain permission to interview family members, friends and co-workers. Though in itself, the interview may not be considered an actual assessment, it will give validity to the assessments chosen by the clinician and a scope of how honest the client is being with the therapist and especially with him/herself.

Based on the conditions a therapist finds a perspective client would predetermine what techniques and instruments to use. For example, if the substance abuse therapy was court ordered and the client truly believed there was no abuse or addiction, then a CAGE interview followed by SMAST might be more effective (Stevens & Smith, 2009). On the other hand, if the client was seeking therapy due to their own concerns about abuse and addiction, a CAGE interview followed by the self-reflective assessment, the Substance Abuse Subtle Screening Inventory (SASSI-3 or SASSI-2) might be preferred; the 3 indicated for adults and the 2 for adolescents.

The CAGE questionnaire is easily incorporated into the diagnostic interview. A four item questionnaire, it encompasses (C) an attempt to "cut down" on alcohol intake; (A) annoyance to criticism about abusive behaviors; (G) guilt about addictive behaviors; and (E) the "eye-opener," drinking in the morning to relieve withdrawal anxiety. This interview followed by another assessment can help the therapist determine, one, if there is a chemical abuse issue, and two, if there is, what level the addiction has attained. The SMAST is a Short Michigan Alcoholism Screening Test which can be administered verbally. It contains 13 of the 25 questions from the MAST and is easy to score allowing the therapist a quick determination of the extent, if any, of alcohol abuse within the client.

The SASSI-3 is single page paper and pencil questionnaire. On one side are 52 true/false questions while on the other side are 26 items that allow clients to self-report the negative effects of any alcohol or drug use (Stevens & Smith, 2009).

Depending on the client's state of denial and reluctance to therapy, as mentioned above, due to court order, or an insistence by family and/or friends and the desire by the client to "prove them wrong," the SASSI-3 is effective in uncovering abuse patterns that are hidden. Still, it is a longer test by comparison to the SMAST and the therapist would have to predetermine the client's patience level in deciding what test to give. Though the SASSI-3 does not seem like a long test to those seeking treatment as they are there by their own volition, it may be viewed differently by those at an initial interview at the behest of others. Hence, the SMAST may initially be more effective.

Whichever one is used, an initial diagnostic interview seems to be the key to begin the most effective type of assessment used.

Reference:

Stevens, P. & Smith, R. L. (2009). *Substance abuse counseling: Theory and practice* (4th Ed.) Pearson. Upper Saddle River, New Jersey

Prohibition/Off Label Prescriptions

Prohibition

According to Dr. Tom Carguilo (2011), it was prohibition where organized crime first entered the picture to supply people with the alcohol they demanded. The 18th amendment, which began prohibition, was ratified by congress in 1919 and implemented a year later. In the 1920s bootleggers such as Al Capone, highlight the darker side of prohibition. However, prohibition began much earlier.

In 1831 temperance movements begin advocating for abstinence. In 1851 the first prohibition law is passed by Maine (repealed in 1856) and by 1855 thirteen states had enacted prohibition legislation. In 1881, Kansas became the first state to have prohibition in its state constitution. It was in 1917 that the Senate passed the Volstead Act which lead to the War Time Prohibition Act saving grain for the WWl effort (Web).

It was the national ban in 1920 that brought organized crime to the forefront in helping people to illegally obtain alcohol. In 1933, the Volstead Act was repealed. However, the damage had been done, and organized crime was here to stay.

Today gangs battle for territory in which to sell illegal drugs, and there is the speculation that if drugs were legalized, gangs and organized crime would cease to exist.

Off Label Prescriptions

The use of Selective Serotonin Reuptake Inhibitors (SSRI) were found to be clinically effective in treating depression in adults. As such, doctors prescribed SSRIs for children and adolescents as well. However, SSRIs were not clinically tested for use in children and adolescents and hence not approved for their use (Wilton, 2011).

Testing during the first part of the 21st century showed that children and adolescents developed increased suicidal behavior (Wilton, 2011), though suicide attempts using SSRIs tend to be unsuccessful (Paradise & Kirby, 2005). Despite the risks, physicians continue using SSRIs through the guise of Off Label Prescriptions.

Off Label Prescriptions are used frequently in Canada. The troublesome issue with Off Label Prescriptions is that there is little to no information about the content of the bottle, dosages prescribed or warnings or side effects. Doctors use their own experience with the drug via adults, plus turn an ear to the U. S. Food and Drug Administration who has approved certain types of SSRIs for use with children and adolescents.

References

Laureate Education, Inc. (2011). "History and Context of Substance Abuse Counseling," Baltimore, MD. Author.

Paradise. L. V., & Kirby, P. C. (2005). The treatment and prevention of depression: Implications for counseling and counselor training. Journal of Counseling and Development, 83, 116 – 119.

Wikipedia (2011). Prohibition in the United States. Retrieved from **http://en.wikipedia.org/wiki/Prohibition_in_the_United_States**

Wilton, Kim (2011). Dalhousie Journal of Legal Studies, Vol. 20, p89-105, 17p

Alcohol and Caffeine

The two most commonly used drugs are alcohol and caffeine, mostly due to the fact that they are legal and can be purchased easily. Though there are no gangs or cartels associated with these two substances, they can be just as addictive as any of their psychotropic counter parts, and alcohol, just as deadly.

Alcohol (Depressant)

A glass of wine with dinner, a few beers while watching the game, a night cap; from wine tasting to tequila tasting, we find excuses to induce alcohol into the very fabric of our society, our lives and our culture.

Ethyl alcohol (ethanol) is a clear bitter liquid that can be used as an anesthetic, a poison, a foodstuff, or an antiseptic. In a 2005 survey (Stevens and Smith, 2009), over half Americans (51.8%) 12 or older, reported being regular drinkers of alcohol. This translates to 126 million people.

As a depressant, alcohol has a relaxing disinhibiting effect where most people mistakenly assume it to be an aphrodisiac and sexual stimulant. This reaction is due to the influence on the frontal lobes of the brain where neurochemical mechanisms for exercising judgment are located (Stevens & Smith, 2009).

Physiologically, alcohol affects the cardiovascular system by dilation of the peripheral blood vessels, irritates the gastrointestinal tract by increasing the secretion of stomach acid and pepsin, and damages the liver potentially creating a cancerous pathway to many other organs.

Caffeine (Stimulant)

Classified as a "minor" stimulant, caffeine is the most widely consumed psychoactive agent in the world (Stevens & Smith, 2009). It can be found in coffee, tea, chocolate and many soft drinks. The chronic overuse of caffeine is called caffeinism. Data shows that "its overuse induces an intoxication of the CNS (Central Nervous System) that includes habituation, tolerance and withdrawal syndrome" (Greden & Walters, 1997).

Caffeine is rapidly absorbed into the gastrointestinal tract and its effects are felt in 30 to 45 minutes. Two hundred milligrams of caffeine (2 cups of coffee) will activate the cortex of the brain, showing an arousal pattern on an EEG. It also reacts on vascular muscles, causing dilation of the blood vessels.

At higher levels autonomic centers of the brain are stimulated causing increased heart rate, respiration and constriction of the blood vessels in the brain and also increases gastric acidity.

Caffeine is not considered a toxic drug. I'll drink to that!

References:

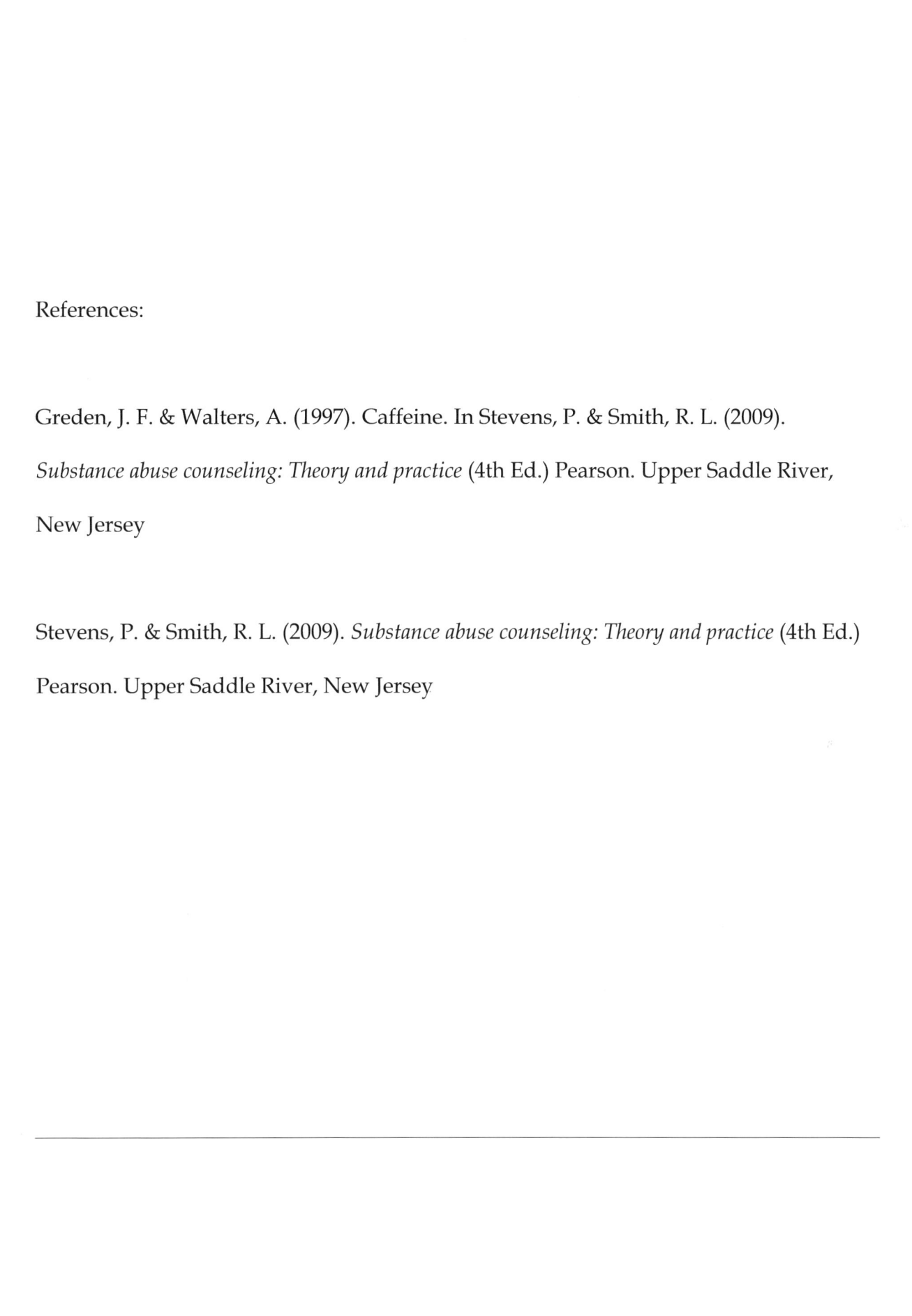

Greden, J. F. & Walters, A. (1997). Caffeine. In Stevens, P. & Smith, R. L. (2009). *Substance abuse counseling: Theory and practice* (4th Ed.) Pearson. Upper Saddle River, New Jersey

Stevens, P. & Smith, R. L. (2009). *Substance abuse counseling: Theory and practice* (4th Ed.) Pearson. Upper Saddle River, New Jersey

History and Context

Tomas Ferraro

Walden University

History and Context

Strengths

The two strengths I bring to substance abuse counseling are the capabilities to be nonjudgmental and impartial. As counselors one never knows who will be referred or will enter the counseling arena either by choice, referral or order. Though the history and the nature of the abuse is important, counselors need to develop a "shock" threshold so as not to disrupt the therapeutic alliance by having the clients feel they are being judged.

Things that shock one person may not shock another; that does not mean that one is more sensitive than the other. Events affect people differently and there is also a trauma threshold that is different for everyone. One does not know that threshold until presented with it. Therefore, the ability to be nonjudgmental when dealing with clients who are involved with drug abuse is imperative.

Also, during the initial intake, and especially when dealing with couples or families, it is important to remain impartial and not take sides, if though the family may want the counselor to do so. This may alienate the client or the support group, which will be needed during treatment and subsequent visits. Impartiality indicates to the client that the therapist is willing to listen and consider all factors of the addiction.

Challenges

My two challenges would have to do with women taking drugs while pregnant, and those who have thrown away wonderful opportunities that others would give their right arm for, all in the name of drugs and alcohol and then are absorbed in self-pity.

As an educator for 30 years, there was a saying I'd share with my students, that if they didn't want to learn they didn't have to listen to the lesson, but they didn't have the right to make that decision for anyone else by talking or disturbing the class in any way.

I feel the same concept can be applied to the girl or woman who is ingesting drugs or alcohol while pregnant. Yes, there may be extenuating circumstances. She may have already been an addict, prostituting herself for her habit and "accidentally" became pregnant. Whatever the circumstance, it is important that she receive treatment quickly, and in a way that will do no further harm to the fetus.

More than this, however, would be my challenge to counsel one who had a blessed life and threw it all away due to alcohol and drug abuse. I would be hard-pressed to see this individual as anything more than selfish, self-centered and self-absorbed. Yes, the prosperous get addicted as well, and I would need to go into depth to find out way and if there were any sincerity in wanting to overcome the addiction. Perhaps a support group might better meet this individual's needs.

NIDA

For all potential clients, I do believe I possess the qualities outlined in Counselor Characteristics and Training, Standards 4.4, 4.5 and 4.6 (NIDA). These standards outline characteristics that center around empathy, flexibility and the desire to overcome one's own prejudices to focus on the presenting problem with an open mind and heart.

For though we may not like the situation our client presents or how they got there, it is not for us to judge, but to develop a therapeutic alliance and the best course of treatment. They may have fallen, but are here now, asking for help, and possibly forgiveness.

References:

Ferraro, T. H. (2011). A personal evaluation of strengths and challenges in counseling clients who have addictions with alcohol and drugs.

National Institute on Drug Abuse (NIDA). Counselor characteristics and training. Retrieved from http://archives.drugabuse.gov/ADAC/ADAC13.html

Biology, Genetics, and Substance Abuse and Addiction

Tomas Ferraro

Walden University

Biology, Genetics, and Substance Abuse and Addiction

Biology

Biological and chemical factors greatly affect how the drug interacts with the body (pharmacodynamics) and how the body interacts with the drug (pharmacokinetics). Since each person is chemically different, it is hard to project how a drug will interact with the body or the brain (Stevens and Smith, 2009).

Metabolism plays a vital role in addiction through biology. Should the body metabolize the drug quickly, the patient may not feel any effect and begin ingesting a larger amount. On the other hand, if the body metabolizes the substance slowly, the individual may feel ill with a desire to discontinue use or appreciate the positive affects received.

Genetics

Heredity has always been speculated as a cause for substance abuse, a generational passing down of genes that have a predisposition for addiction. With alcohol abuse, studies have lent credence to the theory of generational addiction (Stevens and Smith, 2009). Adoption studies have determined that offspring from alcoholics with exhibit signs of addiction though they have been raised in home and by parents who are not predisposed to addictive behaviors.

Genetic epidemiology (Saxon, Oreskovich and Brkanac, 2005) refers to the role in which genetics exerts control over the trait of heritability in addictive behaviors. Tests using family studies, adoptive studies and twin studies have reach similar conclusions in heredity addiction.

The Relationship of Addiction

There is an argument for biological factors being more prevalent in addiction and overdosing than genetic factors. If there has been no history of abuse, then there is no record of pharmacokinetics and therefore an ingestion of a drug is an unknown in how it will react pharmacodynamically. The drug may not be effective in some and create an instant overdose in others.

However, with genetics and heredity, there may be a history of abuse, a history that can be examined by the offspring giving them an opportunity to choose another path, or examine the potential of the urge of addiction and do something other than succumb to it.

This, of course, would be hard pressed in adoption, therefore, examining the birthparents' medical records, including any history of mental health would be ideal during the adoption process.

References

Saxon, A. J., Oreskovich, M. R. & Brkanac, Z. (2005). Genetic determinants of addiction to opioids and cocaine. *Harvard Review Psychiatry*. Volume 13, Number 4

Stevens, P. & Smith, R. L. (2009). *Substance abuse counseling: Theory and practice* (4th Ed.) Pearson. Upper Saddle River, New Jersey

Hallucinogens and Inhalants

Cannabis

Mention the word cannabis or hemp in our society and the first thought people possess is that of marijuana. That would be true when talking about Cannabis Indica, which has higher levels of the chemical THC, which can be addictive. The other hemp plant, Cannabis Sativa, is the industrial hemp with which rope was once made, as this species has more fiber. Paper was made using hemp, in fact the declaration of Independence and Constitution were written on paper made from cannabis sativa (Robinson, 1997).

Dr. Carguilo (2011) initially states that cannabis is difficult to categorize, but would classify it as a psychedelic due to its hallucinogenic nature. Stevens and Smith (2009) do classify Cannabis as a separate substance from Hallucinogens.

The smoking of marijuana can cause euphoria, impaired memory, concentration and knowledge retention, but a more vivid sense of the senses. Stevens and Smith (2009) also mention a loss of appetite, but aren't the "munchies," a distinct rise in appetite, part of the marijuana experience?

Physiologically, the research findings on marijuana are mixed (Stevens & Smith, 2009), whereby some research shows that chemicals found in marijuana can interfere with a cell's ability to manufacture pivotal molecules which affects substances needs for cell division and may cause aging in various organs. However, observations of human marijuana users from several studies do not confirm these findings as little disease or organic pathology has been found in cannabis-using populations.

It is also difficult to distinguish between marijuana as a cause of problems or as the consequence of problems. Many people may become dependent on marijuana and as such develop a dependency because of anxiety or depression (Steven & Smith, 2009). There does seem to be a moderate level of psychological and physiological dependency. An overdose of marijuana can cause fatigue, lack of coordination, paranoia and psychosis, whereas withdrawal can cause insomnia irritability, and anxiety.

Inhalants

This group contains anything that can be sniffed, snorted, huffed, bagged or inhaled. This includes spray paints, hairspray, glues, deodorants, and a variety of household and medical items. There are many more and many more to come. About 17% of teens say they've inhaled a foreign substance for the direct purpose of getting high (Stevens & Smith, 2009). Though tragic, they are our best source in the discovery of the next volatile substance.

A high school friend's younger brother sprayed the cooking spray, Pam, into a plastic bag, then inhaled it for a high. Unfortunately, as Pam is used to coat a pan for non-stick cooking, so it coated his lungs and prevented oxygen from entering the blood stream. He suffocated.

More and more inhalants are being discovered in this same tragic way as inhalants are readily available, easy to obtain, and legal. The toxic fumes make users forget their problems, but can create disruptive and antisocial behavior. However, it is not clear if it is a cause-and-effect relationship, that is, if inhalants produce antisocial and disruptive behaviors, or if those with the capacity for disruptive and antisocial behavior tend to use inhalants (Stevens & Smith, 2009).

Physiological symptoms associated with inhalants include drowsiness, lightheadedness, and agitation. Increasing use can cause dizziness and disorientation. Extreme intoxication can create sleeplessness, muscle weakness and hallucinations. Chronic users can experience weight loss, disorientation, inattentiveness, and lack of coordination. Severe damage to the brain and nervous system may occur over time and cause death as the body is starved for oxygen (Stevens & Smith, 2009).

References:

Robinson, R. (1997). *The hemp manifesto: 101 ways that hemp can save our world*. Park Street Press. Rochester, Vermont

Stevens, P. & Smith, R. L. (2009). *Substance abuse counseling: Theory and practice* (4th Ed.) Pearson. Upper Saddle River, New Jersey

Poly-Substance Abuse and Cross-Tolerance

Some people who drink don't necessarily smoke, but according to Funk, Martinelli and Le (2006) most who smoke also drink. In fact, smoking is three times higher in alcoholics than in the general population (Substance Abuse and Mental Health Services Administration, 2005). This relationship between alcohol and smoking is interesting in the fact that the two are dissimilar in their effects physiologically and psychologically. Then there is the legal combination of nicotine and caffeine to consider.

A few studies examining the role of the mesolimbic dopamine system have found that if the nicotine receptors are suppressed the desire for alcohol is decreased. The role of the mesolimbic dopamine system in mediating alcohol-nicotine interactions is supported by the observation that blocking nicotine receptors in the VTA abolishes the alcohol-induced increase in dopamine release (Funk, et al., 2006).

Tolerance is defined as a reduction in the response to a drug after repeated exposure to the drug. The tolerance resulting from chronic exposure to one drug can create a cross-tolerance to one or more other drugs. It is difficult to evaluate the cross-tolerance between alcohol and nicotine because both are so commonly used and abused together (Funk, et al., 2006).

However, this is not the case when harder drugs are used and abused. Known as a "speedball," the combination of cocaine and heroine is "simultaneous use," which is drug combining, whereas alcohol and nicotine might be considered co-use, the ingesting of two different substances through two different paths (Lankenau & Clatts, 2005).

Heroin is an opiate and can cause feelings of euphoria, while cocaine, a stimulant, can cause feelings of exhilaration, relief of limitless power and decreased inhibitions (Stevens & Smith, 2009). Together in simultaneous use, they can create quite a high.

Poly-substance abuse is found at drug clubs were combinations of ketamine, marijuana, alcohol, heroin, speed, ecstasy, or hallucinogens such as LSD and mushrooms are prevalent. Most users do not have the experience to predetermine the pharmacodynamics or pharmacokinetics of simultaneous use on poly-substance abuse.

References:

Funk, D., Marinelli, P. W., & Lí, A. D. (2006). Biological processes underlying co-use of alcohol and nicotine: Neuronal mechanisms, cross-tolerance, and genetic factors. *Alcohol Research & Health, 29*(3), 186-192.

Lankenau, S. E., & Clatts, M. C. (2005). Patterns of polydrug use among ketamine injectors in New York City. *Substance Use & Misuse, 40*(9-10), 1381-1397.

Stevens, P. & Smith, R. L. (2009). *Substance abuse counseling: Theory and practice* (4th Ed.) Pearson. Upper Saddle River, New Jersey

Family Roles and Dynamics

Tomas Ferraro

Walden University

Family Roles and Dynamics

Interaction With Substance Abuse and Addiction

Based on the research, as indicated in Stevens and Smith (2009), family structure plays an important role in determining and predetermining substance abuse issues. Subsequently, the substance abuse then increases other dysfunctional patterns within the family, such as domestic violence. Substance abuse in families leads to the impairment of children in terms of social, physical and psychological development, which may lead to mental and/or substance abuse issues as an adult.

For example, in families where drug abuse is apparent, children may decide to "leave" the family physically, emotionally or mentally, but knowing that they never belonged makes them question if they can ever really leave (Stevens & Smith, 2009). However, should they "stay," children may take on various roles in order to help them cope. Within the roles children take on in ATOD families, unless they themselves are the abusers, include:

Hero- Usually assumed by the oldest child who knows the family dynamics and may feel responsible for the families pain. Learning to anticipate the needs and wants of others, recognition from the family and the outside world, is a form of achievement. Unfortunately, hero children feel inadequate for they cannot "fix" the problem.

Scapegoat- This is the problem child who minutely reflect the stress in the family. Their disruptive behavior removes the attention from the family dysfunction and demands immediate attention.

The Lost Child- Though acutely aware of the time and energy spent on the abusive person, these children do not strive for attention and withdrawal, whereby communication with others becomes a problem.

The Mascot- Usually the youngest child, the mascot demands attention through humor and fun. They quickly understand that doing something humorous will help break up a heated argument. In adulthood, however, mascots remain immature and unable to express honest feelings.

Characteristics and Complications Within Families of Substance Abusers

Families with ATOD (Alcohol, Tobacco and Other Drugs) communicate through the use of anger, guilt, judgment, blame and criticism, while inconsistencies abound in parenting and boundaries often change and are unclear.

Many addictive families share the same characteristics (Stevens & Smith, 2009), which include:

- Secrecy- Otherwise known as disengagement, this is extremely important. Family members will change their roles in the household to still make it function as normally as possible. Rules will change in order to better keep the secret.
- Denial- Another form of disengagement, the problem does not exist. As children develop they adjust, or adapt, to their surroundings. If the adaptation is that of dysfunction, this will foster the dysfunction within the children.

- Hypervigilance- This characteristic is measured by the unknowing of when the abuser will act out, creating uncertainty and fear within the household. Lack of trust is a by-product of this characteristic.
- Inability to express feelings- The user/abuser is the only one allowed to express feelings. All others must be suppressed, creating dysfunctions in children that will carry over into adulthood.

Many children within these households expressed a desire to network with other children as to not feel so isolated within their dysfunctional family (Stevens & Smith, 2009).

Ethical and Legal Concerns in Counseling Families of Substance Abusers

The first thing a counselor must take into consideration is the client and who the client is. Is it the abuser, or the entire family? Standard B.1.b. and c. (ACA Code of Ethics, 2005) specifically deals with respecting a client's privacy and confidentiality. Hence the need for determining whom the client is, or clients are.

If the client is the abuser, then multiple considerations must be taken into account. First, if other members of the family wish to enter into counseling with the abuser, permission must be granted and a new contract written (Standard B.4.a. and b.). Second, if the abuser shows signs of, or has mentioned intent to hurt himself or others, then Standard B.2.a. must be applied (ACA Code of Ethics, 2005). Thirdly, if the abuser is a minor, Standards B.5.b. and c. apply, and finally, there needs to be a determination if the abuser has the capacity to give informed consent (Standard B.5.).

Should the counseling be entered into by a court order, then therapists may be required to submit their notes for court review. Though this may be in direct violation of patient-therapist confidentiality, Standards B.2.c. and d. are taken into consideration.

By in large, a therapist position should always center on doing no harm when it comes to the counseling relationship.

Reference

American Counseling Association (2005) *ACA Code of Ethics.* Retrieved from

http://www.counseling.org/Resources/CodeOfEthics/TP/Home/CT2.aspx

Stevens, P. & Smith, R. L. (2009). *Substance abuse counseling: Theory and practice* (4th Ed.) Pearson. Upper Saddle River, New Jersey

The Person of the Counselor

STUDENT

Walden University

The Person of the Counselor

According to NIDA (2011), "The counselor's role is to motivate, engage, guide, educate, and retain clients during all phases of the program" (p. 1). As a substance abuse counselor, I will need to be trained to fill these roles when counseling individuals with substance abuse issues. The first stage is to evaluate my current strengths and weaknesses along with personal bias. This application contains a reflection of my strengths, weaknesses, and biases that I bring to counseling substance abusers.

Strengths

My best strength is my ability to create a strong therapeutic alliance. According to the NIDA (2011), "the first and foremost goal of treatment is to engage the client in a friendly, cooperative, positive interaction that increases the client's willingness to examine and change his or her drug-using behavior" (p. 1).

Creating a strong therapeutic alliance will be the key to engaging the client and then leading him or her on a journey to recovery.

The family and support system of the client are critical to the outcome of counseling and preventing relapse (Stevens & Smith, 2009). The ability to create a strong therapeutic alliance with the client and his or her family and social support system will be an asset to my work as a substance abuse counselor.

The NIDA (2011) described the ideal personal characteristics of a counselor as empathetic, nonjudgmental, and tolerant. I believe that I embody these characteristics. I can see the good in individuals, and focus on his or her strengths. I am very good at observing body language as part of the therapeutic alliance process, and use the body language to keep the client engaged. The NIDA (2011) suggested that this skill will also be useful with countertransference and control problems that come up with resistant clients.

Challenges

I have never had a substance abuse problem so I do not have firsthand experience. My personal reframe for this challenge is that I am an excellent example of drinking alcohol in moderation. I have never even tried marijuana or any non-prescription drug. I have no street credibility and it could hamper my efforts at creating rapport. NIDA (2011) suggests that it does not matter if the counselor has been through treatment or is in recovery.

I am not experienced in working with resistant clients. This would be by far the most challenging aspect of substance abuse counseling for me. NIDA (2011) recommends that joining with the client during resistance is helpful, but I do not yet understand how to do this. Through this course I hope to learn how to first engage the client then lead them gently past resistance into a life of recovery and the client's personal goals.

Conclusion

This Application contained a reflection of the personal strengths that I could potentially bring to counseling substance abusers. This application also examined the challenges that I could face due to my personal bias, and suggests ways I could address those challenges. As a substance abuse counselor, I will need to be able to be familiar with assessment instruments to create a custom treatment plan to best need my client's needs (Stevens & Smith, 2009). Becoming fully trained and continuing education to stay on top of the latest empirically effective research will be the best and most ethical way to become an effective substance abuse counselor (ACA, 2005).

References

American Counseling Association "ACA Code of Ethics 2005" Retrieved from http://www.counseling.org/files/fd.ashx?guid=ab7c1272-71c4-46cf-848c-f98489937dda

National Institute on Drug Abuse (NIDA) Retrieved December 10, 2011 from: **http://archives.drugabuse.gov/ADAC/ADAC13.html**

Stevens, P., & Smith, R. L. (2009). Substance abuse counseling: Theory and practice (4th ed.). Upper Saddle River, NJ: Pearson Education, Inc.

Culture and Substance Abuse

Tomas Ferraro

Walden University

Culture and Substance Abuse

Family History

The Browns are an African American family whose lives have been disrupted by the economy, injury, drug abuse and violence. However, it wasn't always that way.

Stan Brown- Father- Suffered a football injury in college preventing him from his dream of a career with the NFL. Dropped out of college and became a warehouse manager until the economy cut his position. Was incarcerated for drug trafficking "for a friend" in an effort to keep his family out of debt.

Mitsy Brown- Mother- Stay at home mother until Stan was incarcerated. High school graduate, married Stan after becoming pregnant. Only skills are household oriented, but was hired by a maid service working days and washes dishes at a diner evenings. Had to give up the house in a better neighborhood and moved to a neighborhood known for drugs, gangs and violence, but was the only thing affordable.

Stanley Brown Jr. –17, oldest son- was doing well in high school until the incarceration of his father and the family's move to a poorer neighborhood. Though he was not gang affiliated, he was shot and killed in a drive-by.

James Brown- 16, 2nd oldest son- was doing well in high school and currently on the football team. Being pressured by the local gang to join and threats of violence has affected his schoolwork.

Letisha Brown- 15, oldest daughter- has always run with a fast crowd in high school and has joined the neighborhood gang. Recently became pregnant. Acts as a drug courier and has started using herself.

Meisha Brown- 13, second oldest daughter- Honor student at local middle school. Outgoing at school, but hides in her room when she's not trying to take care of the family and doing domestic chores around the house.

Steven Brown-10- youngest son- Diagnosed with ADHD at primary elementary school and was getting services. However, with the move to the new neighborhood and a new school, services have been slow in coming, if at all. Has started to act out, though still remains close to Meisha helping around the house. Grades are low and suffering.

Concerns About Substance Abuse

According to Stevens and Smith (2009), African American families are at a disadvantage economically, educationally and socially with the majority of prison inmates coming from that culture, though only making up approximately 12% of the total population. African Americans have the highest illicit drug use at 7.5%. One out of every 14 Black men is behind bars for crimes involving drugs or alcohol.

African Americans are particularly vulnerable to the negative social and health consequences of substance abuse. The number of crack cocaine users among Blacks has risen significantly in the past decade. Hence, the prognosis for the Brown family is not without concern.

The family has undergone tragic and unfortunate events that have placed the children at risk to become gang members and become involved with gang activities, including drug use, trafficking and other illegal activities. For Letisha the possibility of prostitution becomes a reality, while Steven, who is already at risk with ADHD, may become courier for and early indoctrination into the gang. James is being threatened so may join the gang to try to keep them away from his younger siblings. Since the culture of gangs is illicit activities including drug use, the possibility of drug use and addiction exist for the Brown family. Unless the children can begin receiving social services, including counseling, they may turn to the gang as a way to protect the family and earn much need money. However, this will bring a culture of drug use and violence and may destroy the family in the long run.

African Americans and Counseling

African Americans usually have a negative view of mental health services as the perceive therapists as being insensitive to their needs and believe counselors fail to provide enough energy and time working with culturally disadvantage groups. They also feel that counselors do not accept, understand, or respect cultural differences (Stevens & Smith, 2009).

Mitsy Brown may not want outside agencies involved for fear of CPS intrusion and the risk of having her family broken up and taken away. Blacks rarely utilize outside agencies for these reasons, but do look to church and extended families for guidance and help (Stevens & Smith, 2009). Unfortunately with the move, the family has been displaced from their home church and immediate support system, making the potential of succumbing to the new outside pressures the children are experiencing.

The only avenue for help may come from the school and an introduction to social services, including counseling for the children. The keys to prevention are practical strategies where counselors can analyze adaptive behavior patterns and the specific sociopolitical influences of substance abuse (Stevens & Smith, 2009).

Reference

Stevens, P. & Smith, R. L. (2009). *Substance abuse counseling: Theory and practice* (4th Ed.) Pearson. Upper Saddle River, New Jersey

Models and Theories Discussion: Addiction vs. Disease

To predetermine if addiction is a disease, we must first examine the words themselves. Dis-ease, according to many dictionaries, is the disorder of structure or function in a human, that produces specific signs or symptoms or that affects a specific location. This definition in itself would include the brain and the various illnesses that intrude upon it.

Addiction, according to Schaler (2002), on the other hand is defined as a choice.

"The person we call an addict always monitors their rate of consumption in relation to relevant circumstances. For example, even in the most desperate, chronic cases, alcoholics never drink all the alcohol they can. They plan ahead, carefully nursing themselves back from the last drinking binge while deliberately preparing for the next one. This is not to say that their conduct is wise, simply that they are in control of what they are doing."

In Kurtz (n.d.) Bill Wilson did not refer to alcoholism as a disease and AA did not originate the disease concept of alcoholism. It is the members who attribute alcoholism as a disease. Should we look at all forms of addiction as diseases then? Is sexual addiction a disease or a choice? Scientifically, the contention that addiction is a disease is empirically unsupported. Addiction is a behavior and clearly intended by the individual person (Schaler, 2002).

Examining 12-step programs, no cure is being offered for the addiction, but rather coping skills and support to change the decision making cycle and the habitual behavior as found in many theories of counseling (Miller, 2005). Counseling is recommended for addiction, but rarely for disease. Medications are recommended for diseases, but rarely for addictive behavior. Hence therapy has within its resources addictive counseling, but not disease counseling. Though counseling exists for clients who have contracted a life altering disease, e.g., HIV, counseling will not cure the disease, but rather help the client find ways to manage and cope with it. The disease itself is not being helped or cured through counseling (Otten, Zaidi, Wroten, Witte & Peterman, 1993).

Schaler (2002) indicates that there is no dispute that various substances cause physiological changes in the bodies of people who ingest them. There is also no dispute, in principle, that these physiological changes may themselves change with repeated doses, nor that these changes may be correlated with subjective mental states like reward or enjoyment. However, does an addiction lead to disease? Alcoholism has been attributed to liver disease.

According to Larkin, Wood and Griffins (2005), addicts are responsible to themselves and are to blame, by society, of their inability to practice self-control. Whereas, having a disease clearly places the blame elsewhere with the addict assuming little, if any, responsibility for his/her choices. Addiction has also acquired a pathological connotation which can also be referred to as a disease.

However, in conclusion, I must look at the distinction between addiction and disease, and though addiction may lead to disease, addiction in itself is clearly an initial choice that leads to addiction rather than a disease that was inflicted upon a person without a choice being offered.

References

Kurtz, E. (n.d.) *Alcoholics Anonymous and the disease concept of alcoholism.* Retrieved January 11, 2012 from http://www.bhrm.org/papers/AAand%20DiseaseConcept.pdf

Miller, G. (2005). *Learning the language of addiction counseling* (2nd ed., chap. 2, pp. 16-31). Hoboken, NJ: John Wiley & Sons, Inc

Larkin, M., Wood, R. T. A., & Griffiths, M. D. (2006). Towards addiction as relationship. *Addiction Research & Theory, 14*(3), 207-215.

Otten Jr, M. W., Zaidi, A. A., Wroten, J. E., Witte, J. J. & Peterman, T. A. (1993). Changes in sexually transmitted disease rates after HIV testing and posttest counseling, Miami, 1988 to 1989. *American Journal of Public Health.* Vol. 83, No. 4, 529-533.

Schaler, J. A. (2002). Addiction is a choice. *Psychiatric Times.* Vol. 14, Issue 10.

Counseling Models and Theories

Tomas Ferraro

Walden University

Counseling Models and Theories

Theoretic Models

Person-centered Therapy

This theory provides a safe climate for self-exploration for the client to explore blocks to their growth and can experience aspects of themselves that were denied or distorted. Person-centered therapy also enables the client to move toward openness, greater trust in themselves and a willingness to be a process. This model also uses few techniques but stresses the attitude of the therapist to include active listening, reflection of feeling, clarification and "being there" for the client (Miller, 2005).

Behavior Therapy

This theory helps the client to eliminate maladaptive behaviors and learn more effective ones. The therapy focuses on factors influencing behavior and what can be done about behaviors that are problematic. Clients can set treatment goals and evaluate how well these goals are being met. Techniques include: relaxation methods, eye movement, desensitization reprocessing, reinforcement techniques, modeling, social skills training, self-management programs and coaching (Miller, 2005).

Reasons For and Application Of Chosen Theories

In person-centered therapy, Jack will feel that he is listened to and given the opportunity to explore the real reasons for his drinking, reflect on his time in Vietnam and what it meant for him to lose his legs. Behavior therapy will focus on the actual factors that influence his drinking, and through Jack's own realization of his problems, as they relate to his health and relationships, will be able to set goals for himself to begin to eliminate his current drinking habits.

Strengths and Weaknesses

These two models compliment each other in bringing to the other elements that it lacks in order to make it more of a complete therapeutic model designed for substance abuse. Person-centered therapy does not provide for diagnostic testing, taking a case history or provide for questioning for information., however, it does provide for a positive perception of the counselor by the client, an important factor in the therapeutic alliance Jack needs to help build with his therapist (Sevens & Smith, 2009). The behavior model, on the other hand, is more therapist oriented in having the client involved in a series of exercises based on the diagnosis. Hence a combination of the two brings in the needed strengths to assure successful therapy.

References

Case Study (n.d.) Jack. Substance Abuse Counseling. COUN 8728.

Miller, G. (2005). *Learning the language of addiction counseling* (2nd ed., chap. 2, pp. 16ñ31). Hoboken, NJ: John Wiley & Sons, Inc

Stevens, P. & Smith, R. L. (2009). *Substance abuse counseling: Theory and practice* (4th Ed.) Pearson. Upper Saddle River, New Jersey

Dual Diagnosis

Tomas Ferraro

Walden University

Dual Diagnosis

Description of Problem

Jerome is a 48-year-old gay African American who has a crack cocaine addiction. He states that he has not used crack for three days. However, according to the DSM-IV (APA, 2000), individuals with cocaine dependence usually find it necessary to suspend use for a few days to rest or obtain more funds for the purchase of crack. Therefore, Jerome's nonusage for three days does not reflect a willingness to discontinue crack, nor does it indicate a potential road to recovery. As he is also prone to mentally wander and speaks in erratic sentences, it may be questionable about the three day time period.

Jerome may also be suffering from Substance Intoxication Delirium. The DSM-IV (APA, 2000) speaks of this condition as indicated by rambling speech, transient ideas of reference, paranoid ideation, auditory hallucinations in clear sensorium and disturbances in attention. Jerome's rambling statements, unfocused attention, hearing voices and having the Devil coming after him when he tries to stop using crack, are all indicators of Substance Intoxication Delirium.

Though Jerome expresses a desire to stop using, it also needs to be taken into consideration that he is on the run from a gang member and is seeking refuge for safety. It could be determined in a day or two of counseling and treatment how devoted he really is to his own recovery and rehabilitation.

Dual Diagnosis

Since substance abuse almost always occurs within the context of other problems, the therapist must also diagnose the contributing factors that may have lead to the abuse, or recognition that the substance may be exacerbating a current behavioral problem (Stevens & Smith, 2010). As a general rule, a drug or alcohol problem exists if the substance abuse continues after and despite significant interference in one of the six major areas of a person's life:

- Job or school
- Relationships with family
- Social relationships
- Legal problems
- Financial problems
- Medical problems

Jerome falls into three of these areas as his homelessness, and arrests would indicate.

The difficulty in dual diagnoses with substance abuse is how much of the delirium is cause by the drug and how much is attributed by other factors (Stevens & Smith, 2010). Many symptoms of substance intoxication or withdrawal improve or are alleviated within days or weeks.

It is not uncommon for substance abusers to appear more disturbed when initially assessed than they will after a period of abstinence. Other diagnosis categories such as personality disorders, PTSD, mood disorders and thought disorders are common differential or coexisting diagnoses. What may appear to be a substance abuse problem may also be attributed to MS or diabetes, such as focusing attention or garbled speech patterns. Differentiating between bipolar or manic depressive order and the highs and lows of substance abusers is often a complicated diagnosis process (Stevens & Smith, 2010).

Treatment

Historically, major mental illness and substance abuse have been treated in separate service systems with differing and sometimes contradictory philosophical orientations. Typically, a patient is stabilized in an inpatient or outpatient psychiatric unit and then transferred to a separate chemical dependency unit. In the parallel approach, psychiatric and addiction treatments are provided concurrently, but in different settings and by different staff members. While the parallel model improves upon the serial model by providing concurrent treatment, it also shares the limitation of relying upon separate service systems and treatment philosophies that are often in conflict (Bride, MacMaster, Webb-Robins, 2006).

In response to these limitations, a number of experts have promoted an integrated treatment (IT) model. This model combines methods and skills derived from both psychiatric and addiction treatment practices to treat dually diagnosed individuals

in a single setting with a single staff. The IT model has been touted as a more effective approach to treating people with co-occurring disorders than the serial and parallel treatment models. However, according to Bride et al. (2006), after reviewing 36 research studies on the effectiveness of IT models it was concluded that the addition of dual-disorders groups to traditional services, short-term IT in controlled settings and demonstration projects with high-risk groups failed to demonstrate positive outcomes.

Thus, the few available studies that compare integrated and nonintegrated treatment of co-occurring substance use and mental health disorders suggest that IT may improve substance use outcomes, but is no more effective in mental health or community stability outcomes than nonintegrated treatment (Bride et al., 2006).

References

APA (2000). *Diagnostic and statistical manual of mental disorders.* (4th Ed.). American Psychiatric Association, Washington, D.C.

Bride, B. E., MacMaster, S. A., & Webb-Robins, L. (2006). Is integrated treatment of co- occurring disorders more effective than nonintegrated treatment? *Best Practices in Mental Health: An International Journal*, 2(2), 43–57.

Case Study (n.d.) Jerome. Substance Abuse Counseling. COUN 8728.

Stevens, P. & Smith, R. L. (2009). *Substance abuse counseling: Theory and practice* (4th Ed.) Pearson. Upper Saddle River, New Jersey.

Treatment Plans

Tomas Ferraro

Walden University

Treatment Plans

Description of Problem

Sharon was referred at the suggestion of her lawyer after her second DWI. She confides that she feels her drinking is out of control and that she frequents Willy's bar as a place to see friends and those who are fans of the same sports' teams she is. However, it is at this sports bar that the majority of her drinking takes place and she ususally leaves the bar "smashed."

Though she does acknowledge a desire to quit drinking shw is determined to keep her bar and its associates a part of her life. She also feels lonely and would like to meet friends and a man but feels socially awkward.

Current Symptoms or Indicators

Alcohol abuse and possible social anxiety are the two areas that need more investigating. Indicators of a problem are her two DWIs, obsessive drinking at a particular bar, lonliness and the feelings of social awkwardness.

As Dr. Cargiulo states, the first thing a person needs is a good evaluation process to determine the level of addiction (Laureate, 2012). As Sharon is dealing with alcohol issues, the AUI (Alcohol Use Inventory) would provide extensive clarification as it also helps determine levels of social relstionships (Stevens & Smith, 2009).

Goals: Long and Short Term

Once the evaluation has helped determine symptoms and indicators, long and short term goals can be applied. The theories apllied here would be Behavioral therapy (Miller, 2005) in an effort to help Sharon change her behaviors when routing for her team in her chosen bar. As she has stated (Sharon, 2012) she has no desire to leave her friends or her bar where she finds comraderie. Behavior therapy also allows the client to have an active say in treatment goals. This way Sharon can determine the success of her therapy as she applies it within the bar setting.

Short term goals for Sharon would include group therapy for her alcohol abuse including outpatient DUI/DWAI/DUID programs such as Alcoholics Anonymous (Stevens & Smith, 2009) and individual counseling to determine the level of her social anxiety and how that can be overcome to allow Sharon the skills needed to pursue her goal of making new friends.

Objectives/Outcome Criteria

The objectives and outcomes for Sharon would be a new found self-confidence which allows her the opportunity to meet new friends and quit her drinking. An objective might be to explore other avenues of sports viewing that incorporate her team, but in anther venue besides a bar. This would go hand in hand with the making of new friends.

Methods (Stevens & Smith, 2009)

Aversion therapy- a form of behavioral therapy, it pairs an unpleasant stimuli with an individuals craving for a particular drug, his approach has often been paired with acoholics (Stevens $ Smith, 2009).

Harm Reduction- once used in needle exchange for intravenous drug users, it now applies to alcoholics in the reduction of abusive drinking habits. It can also be used to include interlock devices installed on the cars of those arrested for DUIs.

Social Skills Training- Since many ATOD-abusing individuals report that use of substances eases the way in social situations, learning social skills through modeling, role-play and demonstration are available in treatment and an important concept in learning coping techniques.

Services (Stevens & Smith, 2009)

Outpatient Groups and Community Care- group treatment is ideally suited to meeting a client's needs along the continuum of care. Groups provide the means of treatment planning, effective participation, feedback and evaluation, and discharge or graduation.

Self-help Groups- the major self-help groups are based on 12-step programs of the traditional Alcoholics Anonymous. Self-help groups provide an opportunity to demonstrate a commitment to recovery.

With these services, methods and goals in place, the prognosis for Sharon looks successful. However, success can only be determined by the client's commitment to the therapeutic alliance and overcoming addictive and debilitating behaviors herself.

References

Case Study (n.d.) Sharon. Substance Abuse Counseling. COUN 8728.

Miller, G. (2005). *Learning the language of addiction counseling.* Hoboken, NJ: John Wiley & Sons, Inc

Stevens, P. & Smith, R. L. (2009). *Substance abuse counseling: Theory and practice* (4th Ed.) Pearson. Upper Saddle River, New Jersey

The Elderly

Substance and Alcohol Abuse

Substance use, abuse, and dependence are elusive constructs when it comes to assessing problem behavior among individuals who are elderly (defined by Stevens and Smith (2009) as individuals over the age of 65). While it is clear that drug and alcohol use, abuse, and dependence occur among this age group, the extent, types and outcome of use, abuse, and dependence are speculative, at best. According to Benshoff, Harrawood and Koch (2003), individuals over the age of 65 make up roughly 12.4% of the total U.S. population (about 35 million people) and they represent the fastest growing age group; by 2030 this group will nearly double in size to over 70 million individuals and will represent 20% of the U. S. population. However, virtually no data exist to quantify drug use, abuse, and dependence patterns. The sheer size of this population cohort will mean that the size of potential problems will grow. Moreover, there is some suggestion that the baby-boom generation is more likely than earlier generations to have been exposed to drug and alcohol use and may drink or consume drugs at greater rates after age 65. If so, the need for treatment and rehabilitation services will multiply.

The rehabilitation, substance abuse, and literature as it applies to the aging (Benshoff, et al., 2003), pay little attention to alcohol problems of the elderly and largely ignore drug problems all together. Several reasons have been suggested for this lack of information and attention. First, drug abuse/dependence research tends to be driven by the federal agenda and the popularity of drugs at a given time, to the exclusion of other drugs and other drug related behaviors. Initially, research centered on the problems created by dependence on illicit narcotic drugs with recent shifts in attention to cocaine and elicits stimulant drugs. As aging individuals are thought to be among the least likely to use these drug types, little information is known about incidence or prevalence or about the effects of these drug on the elderly population.

Second, as individuals "age out of" drug use and relatively few individuals maintain illicit drug use beyond his or her thirties or forties, individuals who begin substance abuse after age 65 are more likely to abuse alcohol and rarely turn to illicit drugs.

Third, stemming from the massive drug problems that began in the 60s, the emphasis in the literature and treatment has been on drug and alcohol problems presented by adolescents and young adults. Indeed, some have argued that the substance abuse treatment system and treatment literature have been strongly biased towards young males to the neglect of not only the elderly, but women, some minorities, and people with disabilities. As a consequence, little is known or empirically reported about the unique needs presented by individuals who are elderly and experiencing drug and alcohol problems.

Finally, substance abuse among older adults is an "invisible epidemic" noting that older adults, relatives, and caregivers tend to downplay the existence of substance abuse problems in this population. The symptoms of alcohol and drug abuse are often mistaken for the symptoms of aging problems such as dementia, depression, or other problems commonly seen in older adults (Benshoff, et al., 2003).

Consumption of Drugs by the Elderly

Although elderly individuals make-up 12.4% of the population, they consume 25% to 30% of all prescription drugs. On a daily basis elderly adults consume more over-the-counter and prescription drugs than any other age group and are more likely to consume psychoactive drugs with a potential for misuse, abuse, and addiction. In 1985 the most frequently used drug types were analgesics (used by 67% of the population), cardiovascular drugs (34%), laxatives (31%), vitamins (29%), antacids (26%), and anti-anxiety medications (22%). More recently it was noted that elderly individuals are 2-3 times more likely than younger individuals to be prescribed psychoactive drugs, most notably benzodiazepines (Benshoff et al., 2003).

Intervention

Many elderly are unaware of the effects of aging in combination with the use of alcohol and other drugs (Stevens & Smith, 2009). Counselors should ask specifically about the frequency and quantity of use, as well as, OTC medications, prescriptions, and alcohol use. Possible symptoms of use should not be ignored. The older adult should be engaged in a social support system as in a 12-step program, though resistance may be high. Other community activities such as a senior citizen groups may provide reinforcement for the individual. In a treatment program, the elderly respond better to more structured program policies, more flexible rules regarding discharge, more comprehensive assessment, and more outpatient mental health care. Older adults who receive appropriate treatment respond well and can successfully return to their previous lifestyle (Stevens & Smith, 2009).

It is important to note that few studies have been undertaken of treatment for substance abuse among the elderly. Our societies generally negative feelings about the elderly may be in part to blame for this (Stevens & Smith, 2009). However, if the problem is acknowledged and treated, older adults have a high success rate. It is getting them into treatment that is difficult.

References

Benshoff, J. J., Harrawood, L. K., and Koch, D. S. (2003). Substance abuse and the elderly: Unique issues and concerns. *The Journal of Rehabilitation* Vol. 69.

Stevens, P. & Smith, R. L. (2009). *Substance abuse counseling: Theory and practice* (4th Ed.) Pearson. Upper Saddle River, New Jersey

Crisis Intervention Strategy

Tomas Ferraro

Walden University

Crisis Intervention Strategy

Selected Population: Elderly

The elderly is a population that has long been overlooked in terms of psychotherapy and its influence over problems of depression, which may resemble forms of dementia. An obvious problem is the typical mental diseases of old age such as the different kinds of dementia. They may however be beyond therapeutic range. However, more important is the clinician's ability to recognize states that look like dementia, and which are not. The other typical mental disease of old age is late-onset late-life depression, which, according to researchers in the field, are social losses, impaired health and a general breakdown of life having nothing to do with genetic origin (Munk, 2010). With the onset of dementia, i.e., Alzheimer's Disease (AD), and depression comes the potential for alcohol and drug abuse to escape these feelings of despair and helplessness.

Substance use, abuse, and dependence are elusive constructs when it comes to assessing problem behavior among individuals who are elderly. According to Benshoff, Harrawood and Koch (2003), individuals over the age of 65 make up roughly 12.4% of the total U.S. population (about 35 million people) and they represent the fastest growing age group; by 2030 this group will nearly double in size to over 70 million individuals and will represent 20% of the U. S. population. However, virtually no data exist to quantify drug use, abuse, and dependence patterns. Although elderly individuals make-up 12.4% of the population, they consume 25% to 30% of all prescription drugs. On a daily basis elderly adults consume more over-the-counter and prescription drugs than any other age group and are more likely to consume psychoactive drugs with a potential for misuse, abuse, and addiction. More recently it was noted that elderly individuals are 2-3 times more likely than younger individuals to be prescribed psychoactive drugs, most notably benzodiazepines (Benshoff et al., 2003).

Intervention

As with all substance abusers initial screening must take place to determine as to the level of consumption and if the abuser is aware of the problem and a willingness to be involved in the treatment plan. The CAGE is perhaps the simplest and best known screen, consisting of four questions, and although the typical cutoff for a positive score is two positive answers, some authors suggest lowering the threshold to one for the elderly (Menninger, 2002). The MAST is a longer screening instrument for which a 24-item geriatric (MAST-G) has been developed that includes elderly specific consequences. Both the CAGE and MAST-G are sensitive to capturing alcohol use disorders in the elderly, but the MAST-G's length may hinder routine use, especially with those also suffering from AD. Hence, depending upon the agitation levels of the individual, would predetermine what assessment tool to be used.

Brief intervention is more effective than no intervention and typically consists of two or three 10-15 minute counseling sessions which may include motivation-for-change strategies, patient education, assessment and direct feedback, behavioral modification techniques, and the use of written materials such as self-help manuals (Mennigner, 2002).

Psychotherapy and/or Pharmacotherapy

Older adults suffer disproportionately from substance abuse disorders, but few older adults seek and/or receive psychotherapy, and few mental health services are provided for older adults (Zivian, Larsen, Gekoski, Knox and Hatchette, 1994). The literature on geriatric psychotherapy indicates that a) many older clients are receptive to therapeutic suggestion, b) older clients are often more realistic and more compliant than younger clients and c) older adults appear to benefit from many different kinds of psychotherapy, including supportive, psychodynamic, cognitive, and Gestalt therapy.

Nonalcohol substance disorders in the elderly can be divided into illicit drug abuse and prescription drug abuse. Benzodiazeprines remain the mainstay of pharmacological management (Menninger, 2002), and although long-acting ones provide for a smoother withdrawal, they also pose a risk of excess sedation for the elderly.

Reasons for substance abuse need to be established to determine if the abuse started prior to 55 years of age and is a continuation of the abuse started earlier in life, or if the abuse began as a way to deal with the onset of old age and the diseases which accompany the aging process, especially that of depression. Over the past 20 years, numerous studies have investigated the efficacy of psychotherapy for treating late life depression and, to a lesser degree, the efficacy of psychotherapy combined with antidepressant medication. Of the intervention studies, cognitive-behavioral therapy and interpersonal psychotherapy combined with antidepressant medication have the largest base of evidence in support of their efficacy for late life depression (Arean & Cook, 2002). With regard to clinical practice, data suggests that, when available, both kinds of interventions can be offered to depressed older adults, as long as there are no contraindications. The available data suggest that treatment choice for all depressive conditions should be based on contraindications, treatment availability, costs, and preferences of the older adults (Pinquart, Duberstien & Lyness, 2006).

Intervention Strategy

Based on the data presented above, an intervention plan would take on the following components:

- Initial interview and the CAGE screening test to predetermine when abuse began and reasons surrounding substance abuse, including depression.

- Consultation with primary physician for prescription medications used (if unavailable during intake).

- Begin with brief intervention strategies, especially if individual suffers from AD.

- Use of Behavioral and Person-centered therapies.

- Potential use of pharmacotherapy if warranted.

The reasoning behind the therapies chosen is two fold. Within person-centered therapy, the clinician can establish a therapeutic alliance with the patient, whereby more information may be forthcoming after intial trust has been established; and behavioral therapy to begin the treatment of modifying abusive behaviors to curb and end the substance abuse.

Caution in replacing one substance with another needs to be seriously considered (See paragraph 2), as if the pharmacotherapy is not monitored, the therapist may end up treating the client for a new abusive situation.

Ethical and Legal Considerations

Ethical considerations, as decribed in the ACA's Code of Ethics, must always be adhered to as well as the conscript of doing no harm, or in substance abuse cases, no further harm. Legal considerations may center around the elderly individuals coherence as to reasons for the psychotherapy and use of prescribed medications, especially those suffering from AD.

Alzheimer disease is the most common disorder causing cognitive decline in old age and exacts a substantial cost on society. Although the diagnosis of AD is often missed or delayed, it is primarily one of inclusion, not exclusion, and usually can be made using standardized clinical criteria (Small, Rabins, Barry, Buckholtz, DeKosky, Ferris, Finkel, Gwyther, Khachaturian, Lebowitz, McRae, Morris, Oakley, Schneider, Streim, Sunderland, Teri, Tune, 1997). Most cases can be diagnosed and managed in primary care settings, yet some patients with atypical presentations, severe impairment, or complex comorbidity benefit from specialist referral. Alzheimer disease is progressive and irreversible, but pharmacologic therapies for cognitive impairment and nonpharmacologic and pharmacologic treatments for the behavioral problems associated with dementia can enhance quality of life. Hence a close relationship with the patients primary physician is imperative so legal and ethical issues surrounding polysubstance abuse or overdosing to not occur.

References

Arean, P. A. & Cook, B. L. (2002). Psychotherapy and combined psychotherapy/pharmacotherapy for late life depression. *Biological Psychiatry*. Vol. 52, Issue 3, 293-303.

Benshoff, J. J., Harrawood, L. K., and Koch, D. S. (2003). Substance abuse and the elderly: Unique issues and concerns. *The Journal of Rehabilitation* Vol. 69.

Menninger, J. A. (2002). Assessment and treatment of alcoholism and substance-related disorders in the elderly. *Bulletin of the Menniger Clinic*. Vol. 66(2), 166-183.

Munk, K. P. (2010). New aspects of late life depression. *Nordic Psychology* Vol. 62 (2), 1-6.

Pinquart, M., Duberstein, P.R. & Lyness, J. M. (2006). Treatments for later-life depressive conditions: A meta-analytic comparison of pharmacotherapy and psychotherapy. *The American Journal of Psychiatry*. Vol. 163, No. 9, 1493-1501.

Small, G.W., Rabins, P. V., Barry, P. P., Buckholtz, N. S., DeKosky, S. T., Ferris, S. H., Finkel, S. I., Gwyther, L. P., Khachaturian, Z. S., Lebowitz, B.D., McRae, T. D., Morris, J.C., Oakley, F., Schneider, L.S., Streim, J. E., Sunderland, T., Teri, L. A., Tune, L. E. (1997). Diagnosis and treatment of Alzheimer disease and related disorders. *The Journal of the American Medical Association*. Vol. 278 (16), 1363-1371.

Zivian, M. T., Larsen, W., Gekoski, W., Knox, V. J., Hatchette, V. (1994). Psychotherapy for the elderly: Public opinion. *Psychotherapy: Theory, Research, Practice, Training*. Vol. 31 (3), 492-502.

Family Based Interventions

Tomas Ferraro

Walden University

Family Based Interventions

Family Roles

Within the context of "family," I will be discussing the two generations most represented; Julie and her sisters and Julie's children. These current roles include (Stevens & Smith, 2009):

- Mary- Since Mary lives in another town and has a successful career, she may be a non-player in this scenario. There is no mention (Case study, n.d.) of the three women's father abusing alcohol when they were children, there may not be a need to explore roles within the contxt of the first generation present.

- Cathy- this is when the middle child steps up to the role of hero. She understands what is happening within the family dynamic at all levels. She has also gained recognition outside of the family with her job which is within the caretaker genre running a daycare business.

- Julie- playing the part of the scapegoat, she masks the dysfunction at all levels through her abuse of alcohol, possibly not recognizing her own dysfunction as a part of the family dymnamic.

- Alexis- modeling her aunt Cathy, she too is taking the role of hero, helping her mom to bed and doing well in school to save her mother from herself (Case study, n.d.)

- Joshua- taking the role heshares with his mother, Joshua becomes the scapegoat hoping his problems at school will take away the negative attention being paid to his mother. He cries for attention as he sees success all around him, but mixed with dysfunction.

It is important to note, that Cathy is the one who approached the substance abuse center and according to the case study (n.d.) there is no mention of Julie seeking, or wanting to seek treatment of any kind. It may or may not be significant that Cathy still refers to her father as "daddy,' perhaps indicating that if there was dysfunction within the first generation, she may have played the role of the mascot.

Intervention

Should Julie decide that intervention is warranted for herself, a cognitive-behavioral approach (Miller, 2005) would be warranted as she needs to not only change her behavior, but any thought processes that place her there. "Daddy" might be encouraged to do the same depending upon his age as older adults are harder to get into therapy (Benshoff, Harrawood & Koch, 2003).

Ethical and Legal Considerations

Since Julie still has custody of her children, and trying to get them into a program would bring ethical and legal isues into play, most notabley ethical standards B.4.a. and B.5.b. (ACA, 2000). However, should Julie decide that therapy would benefit herself and her family, an outpatient care family week would be in order.

Impact of Therapy

As Julie begins her cognitive-behavioral therapy, the children could engage in play thereapy, acting out how they see their mother in her intoxicated state. This might help to awaken Julie (a kind of "shock" therapy, if you will) as to how her own children see her and their concerns for her. This might also help herfather see what a negative influence he is being on her and on his grandchildren.

As we progressed I would introduce the family to feedback loops and the concept of balancing feedback and positive feedback as the goal is to bring the family back together and create a sense of wholeness and support among its members (Stevens & Smith, 2009).

With the family unit beginning to become whole and more attention paid to those who need it, i.e., Joshua, we may find him beginning to settle down as his own family becomes less chaotic.

Once again and in conclusion, Julie has to start the process by being open to therapy and understanding what her drinking is doing to her family, both syblings and offspring.

References

American Counseling Association (2005) *ACA Code of Ethics*. Retrieved from http://www.counseling.org/Resources/CodeOfEthics/TP/Home/CT2.aspx

Benshoff, J. J., Harrawood, L. K., and Koch, D. S. (2003). Substance abuse and the elderly: Unique issues and concerns. *The Journal of Rehabilitation* Vol. 69.

Case Study (n.d.) Julie. Substance Abuse Counseling. COUN 8728.

Miller, G. (2005). *Learning the language of addiction counseling*. Hoboken, NJ: John Wiley & Sons, Inc

Stevens, P. & Smith, R. L. (2009). *Substance abuse counseling: Theory and practice* (4th Ed.) Pearson. Upper Saddle River, New Jersey

Substance Abuse Assessment and Intervention Plan

Tomas Ferraro

Walden University

Substance Abuse Assessment and Intervention Plan

Substances Abused and Their Implications

Marijuana- A psychoactive substance, acute intoxication results from the resin found in cannabis, tetrahydrocannabinol (THC). Affects include lower motor skills, coordination, impaired judgment, and other behavioral and psychological changes. Heavy use may burn the lungs as cannabis burns 16 times hotter than tobacco (APA, 2000; Schatzberg, Cole and DeBattista, 2010; Stevens and Smith, 2009).

Alcohol- Known as ethanol and a psychoactive drug, it is an unstable CSN depressant which produces euphoria and disinhibition. Every major organ in the human body is affected by alcohol abuse, including the cardiovascular system. Blood Alcohol Levels (BALs) are higher in women than in men (Stevens & Smith, 2009).

Cocaine- Produced from the coca plant, this stimulant is highly addictive as it creates intense central nervous system (CNS) arousal. It is a tremendous mood elevator giving the user a sense of exhileration and and well-being while reducing feelings on inferiority and loosening inhibitions. Due to the short half–life of cocaine (30-50 minutes), frequent dosing is needed to maintain the "high" (APA, 2000; Stevens & Smith, 2009).

Heroin- A semisynthetic opiate, effects may include euphoria, drowsiness, possible respiratory distress, coma and death. The tolerance of dependence appears to be receptor-site specific and tolerance can develop quickly with the user increasing the dosage to the point where regular usage is needed to maintain a normal state without the high (APA, 2000; Schatzberg, et al., 2010; Stevens & Smith, 2009).

Methamphetamines- A class II stimulant, due to its greater potent form of amphetamine, they increase CNS arousal and rapidly increase dopamine levels. Amphetamines mimic cocaine but due to the increased potency of methamphetamines, users can experience reduced motor speed, and functional changes in the brain affecting emotion and memory. They also act on the sympathetic nervous system (SNS) eliciting a fight or flight response (APA, 2000; Stevens & Smith, 2009)

Biological Predispositions

Lisa's father was a frequent user of heroin and died of an overdose (Case study, n.d.). Research suggests that drug abuse may be predisposed by inherited behavioral temperaments. Personalities are shaped through these inherited predisositions, and interaction with physical and social environments (Tarter, 1988). There is evidence linking certain personality characteristics to antisocial and neurotic traits, with the risk of substance abuse.

Biological and chemical factors greatly affect how the drug interacts with the body (pharmacodynamics) and how the body interacts with the drug (pharmacokinetics). Since each person is chemically different, it is hard to project how a drug will interact with the body or the brain (Stevens and Smith, 2009).

Family Considerations

Substance initiation occurs during preadolescence when family exerts a strong influence and this early initiation has been linked to later problems of abuse (Catalano, Morrison, Wells, Gillmore, Iritani and Hawkins, 1992). Parental drug use increases the risk of drug use in offspring as children often model the behavior of parents, which also implies approval and tolerance of substance use.

In a largely Hispanic population where neighborhoods had a high toughness rating (Catalano, et al., 1992), family approval of alcohol was a factor in drug involvement. Children raised in families where there was little supervision or severe or inconsistent discipline were found to be at risk for later substance abuse.

This coorelates with Lisa's case study (Case Study, n.d.) and her father's wishes that she grow up tough fighting her male cousins which lead to gang involvement.

Cultural Considerations

Within the hierarchy of the Hispanic family, the father is seen as the family leader, the one with power. Traditionally, men are supposed to be strong and dominant while the women are self-sacrificing and submissive (Stevens & Smith, 2009). However, in Lisa's case, growing up tough may have confused her as to that cultural role, or at least a compromise, creating the anger and hostility she has toward her boyfriend, Charlie (Case study, n.d.).

According to Galvan and Caetano (2003), patterns of alcohol use vary among ethnic groups, which incorporate cultural factors and drinking norms and attitudes. A risk factor for Hispanic women is unemployment. Lisa's case study (Case Study, n.d.) does not indicate if she is employed now or ever was employed. Research from the 1992 National Longitudinal Alcohol Epidemiologic Survey (NLAES) found, though Hispanic women drink less often than their other ethnic counterparts, they consume more when they do drink. It was also found that heterogeneity was a factor in drinking patterns. Hispanic women from Mexico drink more than other Hispanic women from Central or South America.

Therapy Model

To gain perspective on her life, Lisa is in need of a variety of models (Miller, 2005).

These include:

- Cognitive Behavior Therapy- this will challenge Lisa to confront faulty beliefs with condratictory eveidence. For example her need to be tough (Case study, n.d.). Therapy will also give Lisa an opportunity to confront her own beliefs and become aware of her thought patterns in regards to her actions, drug usage and the potential of incarceration and losing her children.

- Psychoanalytic Therapy- Lisa needs to confront her demons in regards to her fathers abusive relationship with heroin and her mother (Case study, n.d.) and her father's insistence that she fight her cousins to become tough. Psychoanalytic therapy will help her relive earlier experinces and work through repressed conflicts.

- Existential Therapy- though Lisa situation growing up was one of violence, drug use and poverty (Case study, n.d.), she needs to take responsibility for the choices she makes for herself and her children in the present and future. Existential therapy will challenge her to recognize that responsibility and that events are not just happening to her.

Assessment and Diagnosis

One of the most important aspects of any assessment of substance abuse is the diagnostic interview (Stevens & Smith, 2009). A carefully planned and conducted interview is the corner stone of the diagnostic process, and given the prevalence of denial from substances abusers, it is important during the first interview to gain permission to interview family members, friends and co-workers. Though in itself, the interview may not be considered an actual assessment, it will give validity to the assessments chosen by the clinician and a scope of how honest the client is being with the therapist and especially with him/herself.

Based on the conditions a therapist finds a perspective client would predetermine what techniques and instruments to use. For example, if the substance abuse therapy was court ordered, and the client truly believed there was no abuse or addiction, then a CAGE interview followed by SMAST might be more effective (Stevens & Smith, 2009).

The CAGE questionnaire is easily incorporated into the diagnostic interview. A four item questionnaire, it encompasses (C) an attempt to "cut down" on alcohol intake; (A) annoyance to criticism about abusive behaviors; (G) guilt about addictive behaviors; and (E) the "eye-opener," drinking in the morning to relieve withdrawal anxiety. This interview followed by another assessment can help the therapist determine, one, if there is a chemical abuse issue, and two, if there is, what level the addiction has attained. The SMAST is a Short Michigan Alcoholism Screening Test which can be administered verbally. It contains 13 of the 25 questions from the MAST and is easy to score allowing the therapist a quick determination of the extent, if any, of alcohol abuse within the client.

Another assessment tool is the SASSI-3 is single page paper and pencil questionnaire. On one side are 52 true/false questions while on the other side are 26 items that allow clients to self-report the negative effects of any alcohol or drug use (Stevens & Smith, 2009). Depending on the client's state of denial and reluctance to therapy, as mentioned above, due to court order, or an insistence by family and/or friends and the desire by the client to "prove them wrong," the SASSI-3 is effective in uncovering abuse patterns that are hidden.

Since substance abuse almost always occurs within the context of other problems, the therapist must also diagnose the contributing factors that may have lead to the abuse, or recognition that the substance may be exacerbating a current behavioral problem (Stevens & Smith, 2010).

As a general rule, a drug or alcohol problem exists if the substance abuse continues after and despite significant interference in one of the six major areas of a person's life:

- Job or school
- Relationships with family
- Social relationships
- Legal problems
- Financial problems
- Medical problems

Lisa (Case study, n.d.) falls into at least two of these areas. Her volatile relationship with Charlie, and her legal problems.

Treatment Plan and Intervention Strategies

Unfortunately, Hispanics underuse mental health services and tend to terminate after one contact (Stevens & Smith, 2009). Since Lisa's therapy is at the suggestion of her attorney rather than court ordered, it is up to the counselor to establish the beginnings of a therapeutic alliance as quickly as possible, as ineffective and inappropriate counseling approaches to the values held by Hispanics are often reasons for termination.

However, in Lisa's case, the fact that she is in therapy may be a positive factor in the eyes of the court, allowing her a substance abuse program rather than incarceration, and allowing her continued custody of her children.

Psychotherapy should initially be the first choice in helping Lisa. Though pharmacotherapy may be appealing in helping her off methamphetamines, there is the possibility that one drug could replace another futher antagonizing the addiction cycle. One on one counseling sessions with group therapy, e.g., AA, or other 12-step programs, would be helpful in assuring her that she is not alone in her efforts for therapy, though no mention of her willingness to want to quit was presented in her case sudy (Case study, n.d.).

Once Lisa is becoming "clean and sober," then other diagnoses can be made as to possible disorders brought on my substance abuse as in her hearing her father's voice when attacking Charlie.

Ethical and Legal Considerations

The first ethical consideration given Lisa is her ability to understand and give her informed consent in the counseling relationship (ACA Standards A.2.a-d, 2005) taking into account her culture and comprehension level. As with all clients, Standards A.4.a & b (ACA, 2005) need to be observed by the counselor. Though we may need to engage CPA at some point (ACA, 2005, Standard B.2.a.), a thourough diagnosis of Lisa's willingness to change her abusive patterns and lifestyle may even prevent that from happening.

With Lisa going to court, there may be an order to disclose certain information from therapeutic sessions (Standard B.2.c.) which clients must be made aware of, though Lisa's attorney, after consulting her therapist, may want to place the counselor on the stand as a witness in favor of Lisa's prognosis and rehabilitative efforts.

References

ACA Code of Ethics (2005). American Counseling Association. Retrieved from http://www.counseling.org/Files/FD.ashx?guid=ab7c1272-71c4-46cf-848c-f98489937dda

APA (2000). *Diagnostic and statistical manual of mental disorders.* (4th Ed.). American Psychiatric Association, Washington, D.C.

Case Study (n.d.) Lisa. Substance Abuse Counseling. COUN 8728.

Catalano, R. F., Morrison, D. M., Wells, E. A., Gillmore, M. R., Iritani, M. A. & Hawkins, J. D. (1992). Ethnic differences in family factors related to early drug initiation. *Journal of Studies on Alcohol and Drugs.* Vol. 53(3) 208-217.

Galvan, F. H. & Caetno, R. (2003). Alcohol use and related problems among ethnic minorities in the united states. *Alcohol Research & Health.* Vol. 27.

Miller, G. (2005). *Learning the language of addiction counseling* (2nd ed., chap. 2, pp. 16ñ31). Hoboken, NJ: John Wiley & Sons, Inc

Schatzberg, A.F., Cole, J.O. & DeBattista, C. (2010). *Manual of clinical psychopharmacology* (7th ed.). Washington, DC: American Psychiatric Publishing, Inc.

Stevens, P. & Smith, R. L. (2009). *Substance abuse counseling: Theory and practice* (4th Ed.) Pearson. Upper Saddle River, New Jersey

Tarter, R. E. (1988). Are there inherited behavioral traits that predispose to substance abuse? *Journal of Consulting and Clinical Psychology.* Vol. 56(2), 189-196.

Relapse Prevention Models

The major goal of relapse prevention (RP) is to address the problem of relapse and to generate techniques for preventing or managing its occurrence. Based on a cognitive-behavioral framework, RP seeks to identify high-risk situations in which the patient is exposed to relapse and use both cognitive and behavioral coping strategies to prevent future relapses (Marlett & Donovan, 2005).

The Cognitive-Behavioral Model of Relapse

The cognitive-behavioral model centers on an individual's response in a high-risk situation. The components include the interaction between the person (affect, coping, self-efficacy, outcome expectancies) and environmental risk factors (social influences, access to substance, cue exposure). If the patient lacks an effective coping response and/or confidence to deal with the situation, the tendency is to "give in to temptation."

If the client views a lapse as internal and uncontrollable, then the relapse risk is heightened. If, however, the client views the lapse as external and controllable, the risk factor is decreased (Marlett & Donovan, 2005). If the patient looks at a lapse as a learning experience, he more likely to experiment with alternative coping strategies.

A Self-Regulation Model of Relapse Prevention

Self-regulation consists of the internal and external processes that allow a client to engage in goal-directed actions over time and in different contexts (Ward & Hudson, 2000). This includes the initial selection of goals, planning, monitoring, evaluation, and modification of behavior to accomplish one's goals in an optimal and satisfactory manner. It is clear that self-regulation is not solely concerned with inhibiting or suppressing behavior but can include the enhancement, maintenance, or elicitation of behavior as well.

Similarities and Differences

Though both are goal oriented and are concerned with the outcomes of those goals as set by the patient, CBT is more therapist driven having the patient follow the parameters as set down by the cognitive-behavioral theory. Self-regulation is client driven forcing himself to stay with the goals he has made. The latter seems to make more sense to me as the goal of therapy is to wean the client away from it and the therapist while taking responsibility for himself. Though not mentioned, I would follow up with a 12-step program, as the client may need a support system.

Reference

Marlett, G. A. & Donovan, D. M. (Eds.)(2005). *Prevention relapse: Maintenance strategies in the treatment of addictive behaviors.* The Guilford Press. New York.

Ward, T. & Hudson, S. M. (2000). *A self-regulation model of relapse prevention.* Sage Publications, Thousand Oaks, CA.

Expanding the Role of Psychology: Prescription Privileges

Though psychotherapy and psychological testing are the roles more attributed to clinical psychologists, more have begun advocating for legally sanctioned prescription authority in their professional roles. This is partly due to the decline in reimbursement as more psychiatric disorders require medications (Walker, 2002). As psychology has become more ingrained in dealing with the problems of society, it may become necessary to rethink limitations that are fundamental to its scope of practice (DeLeon, Folen, Jennings, Willis & Wright, 1991). Psychologists usually are not trained in psychopharmacology and there is considerable disagreement as to whether the profession should enter the prescription arena. This may be an evolving issue as legislation at the state and federal levels move forward. However, as the debate continues, state legislatures agree with the psychiatrists, whereby, though psychologists agree that post-graduate training in physiology and pharmacology are needed, psychiatrists insist that medical school or nurse practitioner training is needed to be knowledgeable enough to prescribe medications (Holmes, 2003). Currently, however, and in anticipation of legislative law permitting such practices, the APA is offering training through a series of Educational DVD series to train psychologists in psychopharmacology (APA, 2006).

This 14-hour series is designed for psychologists who wish to gain prescription privileges, to prepare for the PEP (Psychopharmacology Examination for Psychologists) test. The DVD series also help to keep counselors up to date in the area of psychopharmacology, as many therapists see clients who may currently be on medication for various disorders.

Meanwhile, the APA makes an argument for prescription practices citing various psychological disorders that require, or will require, a combination of pharmacotherapy and psychotherapy, depressive disorders taking the lead. According to Williams-Nickelson (2000), depression with psychological etiology will be the second leading cause of non-fatal disabling effects of disease by 2020. CAPP (Committee for the Advancement of Professional Practice) identifies the following prerequisites to participate in post-doctoral training in psychopharmacology:

1. A doctoral degree in psychology.
2. Current state license as a psychologist.
3. Five years of practice as a "health service provider" psychologist as defined by state law or the APA.

Then actual training, which includes 300 hours in the following didactic and clinical components:

1. Neuroscience

2. Clinical and Research Pharmacology and Psychopharmacology

3. Physiology and Pathophysiology

4. Physical and Laboratory Assessment

5. Clinical Pharmacotherapeutics

The psychologist-trainee should see a minimum of 100 patients. Currently there are three different programs for a psychopharmacology certificate or degree (Levant & Shapiro, 2002):

1. Postdoctoral programs that award certificates and/or continuing education credit

2. Postdoctoral programs that award master's degrees in psychopharmacology

3. A predoctoral program that awards joint psychology and nursing degrees

Hence, due to the above argument, as a mental health counselor who will undoubtedly come in contact with clientele who may be in need of pharmaceuticals, I would advocate for prescription privileges to be given to trained psychologists. The more knowledge we have as a society about the cognitive behaviors of substance abuse, and the more resources to help those abandon the practice through psychotherapy and pharmacotherapy, the sooner we may bring the epidemic of abuse to an end.

References

APA (2006). Division 55: Training and continuing education. *American Society for the Advancement of Psychopharmacology*. Retrieved from http://www.division55.org/

DeLeon, P. H., Folen, R. A., Jennings, F. L., Willis, D. J. & Wright, R. H. (1991). The case for prescription privileges: A logical evolution of professional practice. *Journal of Clinical Child Psychology*. Vol. 20, Issue 3, 254-267.

Holmes, L. (2003). Should psychologists prescribe medications? *Health's Disease and Condition*. Retrieved from **http://mentalhealth.about.com/cs/psychopharmacology/a/prescribe.htm**

Levant, R. F. & Shapiro, A. E. (2002). Training psychologists in clinical psychopharmacology. *The Journal of Clinical Psychology*. Vol. 58, No. 6, 611-615.

Walker, K. (2002). An ethical dilemma: Clinical psychologists prescribing psychotropic medications. *Issues In Mental Health Nursing*. Vol. 23, No. 1, 17-29.

Williams-Nickelson, C. (2000). Prescription privileges for psychologists: Implications for students. *Prescription Privileges Fact Sheet: What Students Should Know About the APA's Pursuit of Prescription Privileges for Psychologists (RxP).* APAGS N

Prevention Approaches

This particular concern, though nationwide, needs to be addressed by the communities each preventative program serves. In this case the community concern would be teen use of drugs.

Now, with D.A.R.E. (Drug Abuse Resistance Education), a program that targets elementary school students, and Project TND (Towards No Drug Abuse), which targets high school seniors, and other drug prevention programs available, there seems to be a need for preventative services to better communicate with each other. Albee and Ryan-Finn (1993) point out that "the greatest deficiency in the field stems from the lack of communication and cooperation among those working in the various areas of prevention, both within and outside the field of psychology." This would not only include programs already in place, but the communities they serve, including teachers, administrators and parents.

One of the reasons for a lack of success in prevention programs is the refusal of the community to admit there is a problem, or parents in denial that their child is participating in drug use. The "not my child" mantra has been heard by every teacher who knows better, and, often, knows the child better than the parents.

As Kidd and Kral (2005) explain, PAR is about bringing the community together to research the problem. Once the community has proven to itself that there is a problem, then it empowers itself to do something about it. PAR is a process in which researchers and participants, teachers, parents and students, develop goals, gather an analyze data, then implement the results in a way that will raise the consciousness of the community and promote change in the lives of those involved. Research takes time depending upon the needs of the community and how fast data is collected and evaluated; but having the community involved with the research is a way to have the community involved with the development of preventative programs that might work better than the "one size fits all" approach national preventative programs offer.

During the research phase of examining the data and finally coming to terms with the fact that a community does have a drug problem that encompasses elementary through high school, the community can begin to research the preventative programs already in place and begin to choose the ones that will be most successful, even if it means a "mix and match" approach, taking the best each has to offer and creating programs that will effectively serve the uniqueness of the community.

D.A.R.E. might serve the needs of elementary school children, but what viable programs will effectively serve the Junior High community that students will buy into, and then, the High school community. This is why PAR is so effective. It allows students, especially those involved in the drug culture, to participate in helping select or create programs that will be successful in the community's goal of prevention and intervention (Kidd & Kral, 2005). For if those who will benefit from a program, helping design the program, and buying into the program is done during its very creation.

References

Albee, G. W., & Ryan-Finn, K. D. (1993). An overview of primary prevention. *Journal of Counseling & Development, 72*(2), 115-123.

Kidd, S., & Kral, M. (2005). Practicing participatory action research. *Journal of Counseling Psychology*, 52(2), 187–195.

Psychopharmacology

Psychopharmacology

Psychopharmacology is the study of the use of medications in treating mental disorders. The complexity of this field requires continuous study in order to keep current with new advances. Psychopharmacologists, psychiatrists, psychologists and counselors need to understand all the clinically relevant principles of pharmacokinetics (what the body does to medication) and pharmacodynamics (what the medications do to the body). This includes an understanding of:

- Protein binding (how available the medication is to the body)
- Half-life (how long the medication stays in the body)
- Polymorphic genes (genes which vary widely from person to person)
- Drug-drug interactions (how medications affect one another)

Since the use of these medications is to treat mental disorders, an extensive understanding of basic neuroscience, basic psychopharmacology, clinical medicine, the differential diagnosis of mental disorders, and treatment options is required (ASCP, 2008)

Psychopharmacology in Treatment

Pharmaceuticals play an important role in clinical psychology and the counseling profession. They can cure, and destroy, so it is important to know what types of drugs a client is taking upon the intake evaluation.

Over prescription can come in the guise of wanting to tame children, especially in the school setting. SSRIs (Selected Serotonin Reuptake Inhibitors) are prescribed for depression, while Ritalin is usually prescribed for ADHD (Attention Deficit Hyperactive Disorder). There is rising concern that Ritalin is over prescribed as a way to subdue children who have discipline problems, who are fidgety, or not focused on the assignment.

Before prescribing drugs for children, many other factors should be weighed.

References

ASCP (2008). American Society of Clinical Psychopharmacology. Retrieved from http://www.ascpp.org/pages.aspx?PanelID=1&PageName=What_is_Psychopharmacology

Pharmacodynamics and Pharmacokinetics

Pharmacodynamics and Pharmacokinetics

Psychodynamics is the manner in which a drug affects the body and the processes, which are activated once the drug has reached its target area. As Pharmacodynamics is described as what the drug does to the body, pharmacokinetics is what the body does to the drug (Rivas-Vasquez, 2001).

Drugs are distributed throughout the body through systemic circulation. The extent of the distribution depends on the blood flow and how well it adheres to plasma proteins. If two or more drugs are administered, there may be a displacement of one of the drugs in its capability to bind to proteins. When this occurs this can create a free faction. With free drug availability comes the increased potential of side effects (Rivas-Vasquez, 2001).

Dosage forms (e.g., tablets, capsules, solutions), consisting of the drug plus other ingredients, are formulated to be given by various routes (e.g., oral, buccal, sublingual, rectal, parenteral, topical, inhalational). Regardless of the route of administration, drugs must be in solution to be absorbed (Kopacek, 2007).

As described in Schatzberg, Cole and DeBattista (2010), most antidepressants are taken orally, sometimes twice a day, with an increase in dosage should it become necessary. Most orally administered drugs are absorbed through the small intestine, undergo presystemic metabolism by the liver, then enter systemic circulation, traversing the blood brain barrier to access the central nervous system. Due to the pH of the bowels, this can limit absorption rates and the impact of the drug to the target area (Rivas-Vazquez, 2001).

The job of metabolism is to remove drugs from systemic circulation while turning them into compounds that will be more readily excreted. Therefore, drugs need to become more water soluble to have more of the medication absorbed easily and the major dosage to reach its target area (Rivas-Vasquez, 2001). A drug's water solubility allows for renal clearance and excretion.

In conclusion, there is little doubt that pharmacodynamics and pharmacokinetics will play a viable and increasing role as new drugs are discovered, created and administered.

References:

Kopacek, K. B. (2007). Drug absorption. Retrieved from http://www.merckmanuals.com/professional/clinical_pharmacology/pharmacokinetics/drug_absorption.html

Rivas-Vazquez, R. A. (2001). Understanding drug interactions. *Professional Psychology: Research and Practice,* Vol. 32, No. 5, 543-547

Schatzberg, A.F., Cole, J.O., DeBattista, C. (2010). *Manual of clinical psychopharmacology* (7th ed.). Washington, DC: American Psychiatric Publishing, Inc.

Antidepressants

Not only are antidepressants the most commonly prescribed medication in the United States, but their availability has steadily increased. Though the general wisdom is that all antidepressants are equally suitable for the treatment of depression, it is too heterogeneous to suggest that all medications will work equally for all types of depression (Schatzberg, Cole, DeBattista, 2010).

Antidepressants are categorized in two primary groups, typical antidepressants and MAO inhibitors. Anxiety, agitation, irritability, aggression and pronounced suicidality SSRIs are usually the first treatment strategy. The side effect factor is key in choosing an antidepressant. Some side effects are common within the first week or two as considerations of pharmacodynamics and pharmacokinetics play out. This is referred to as activation and can include increased anxiety, restlessness and insomnia (Preston and Johnson, 2012).

Since most patients are prescribed antidepressants due to hopelessness and pessimism, they are prone to discontinuing treatment prematurely; however, if treatment is not affective, dosage may increase and perhaps not by prescription as many OTC products have efficacy in treating depression (Preston and Johnson, 2012). This could lead to overdosing.

According to Preston and Johnson (2012) and Schatzberg et al. (2010) treatment for the following conditions to include:

Condition	Symptoms	Antidepressant
Bipolar disorder	Decreased need for sleep Rapid, pressured speech High levels of energy Intense irritability Racing thoughts	MAOIs
Dysthymic disorder	Daytime fatigue Negative, pessimistic thinking Low self-esteem Low motivation, lack of enthusiasm Decreased capacity for joy	MAOIs or SSRIs
OCD	Repetitive behavior Intrusive impulse or thought leading to anxiety	SSRIs

Geriatrics	Depression	SSRIs but limited to escitalopram, citolopram and sertraline due age considerations and renal clearance
PTSD	Startle responses Memory/concentration problems Sleep disturbance Guilt about surviving Avoidance of stimuli that mimic the event	SSRIs paroxetine sertraline

In prescribing antidepressants to patients, age, diet, medications, and other factors must be taken into account. Since each patient's chemical make up is different, how a drug reacts to the body (pharmacodynamics) and how the body reacts to the drug (pharmacokinetics) must be taken in strict consideration.

References:

Preston, J. & Johnson, J. (2012) *Clinical psychopharmacology made ridiculously simple* (7th ed.). Miami, FL: Medmaster, Inc.

Schatzberg, A.F., Cole, J.O., DeBattista, C. (2010). *Manual of clinical psychopharmacology* (7th ed.). Washington, DC: American Psychiatric Publishing, Inc.

Depression and Manic-depression

Many people experience brief episodes of depression. The death of a loved one, the loss of a job, an auto accident, or just the stress of everyday life, especially in this economy can lead people into feelings of depression. However, depression is eventually overcome with out therapy or the use of psychotropic drugs. According to the DSM-IV (2000), Major Depressive Episodes are characterized by a period of at least 2 weeks during which there is depressed mood characterized by: Reactive sadness, grief, medical illness and medications that can cause depression, and clinical depression (Preston & Johnson, 2012).

A Manic Episode is defined by a distinct period during which there is an abnormally and persistently elevated, expansive or irritable mood (DSM-IV, 2000). Manic Episodes are characterized by: Grandiosity, decreased need for sleep, rapid speech, racing thoughts, distractibility, increased activity, expansiveness and poor judgment (Preston & Johnson, 2012).

The most important guideline in prescribing antidepressants is the attribute of sustained psychological symptoms. Occasional sleep disturbance or loss of appetite does not warrant medication. However, if the symptoms persist and grow in seriousness over time, then antidepressants are indicated (Preston & Johnson, 2012).

Since it is better to err on the side of caution, antidepressants are started at low dosages and steadily increased to meet the target need. However, the mistake family practitioners make is to under-medicate (Preston & Johnson, 2012). The treatment of major depression involves three phases:

- Acute Treatment- From the first dose until the patient is asymptomatic.
- Continuation Treatment- Continued treatment for 6 months.
- Maintenance Treatment- For patients having recurrent episodes.

Primary symptoms of clinical depression may be caused by a dysregulation of certain neurotransmitters. Antidepressants are able to restore normal neurochemical functioning in key limbic structures in the brain (Preston & Johnson, 2012). Many depressed patients become easily discouraged if there is no relief in a few days. Therefore, monitoring is essential in the first week of the prescription.

References:

DSM-IV (2000). *Diagnostic and statistical manual of mental disorders.* (4th Ed.) American Psychiatric Association. Washington, D.C.

Preston, J. & Johnson, J. (2012) *Clinical psychopharmacology made ridiculously simple* (7th ed.). Miami, FL: Medmaster, Inc

Psychotropic Medication in Children and Adolescents: Ethical Concerns

Perhaps nowhere is the science-to-service gap more pronounced than in the delivery of services to individuals and families suffering from the effects of behavioral health disorders (Graff, Springer, Bitar, Gee and Arrendondo, 2010). Behavioral health disorders (e.g., substance use disorders, depression, suicide, ADHD) account for more deaths, illnesses, and disabilities than any other preventable health condition (New Freedom Commission on Mental Health, 2003). These disorders are often associated with many of the nation's most serious and tragic problems, including homelessness, violence, injury, HIV infection, cardiovascular disease, and cancers. Left untreated, these disorders place enormous economic strains on our society with estimated annual costs at more than $414 billion (Haack & Hoover, 2001).

Primary care providers are uniquely positioned to help improve the availability, accessibility, and quality of behavioral health care services. While these providers currently provide about half the care for common behavioral health disorders and prescribe the majority of psychotropic medication (New Freedom Commission on Mental Health, 2003), these professionals often do not identify and diagnose behavioral health disorders with the same degree of accuracy as they do other preventable diseases. As a result, the role of these front-line health professionals in prevention, early identification, and referral remains largely untapped. For this reason, many adolescents with behavioral health disorders go unidentified; for others, the disorder goes unrecognized far too long and becomes more difficult and more costly to treat (Graff, et al., 2010).

Due to the fact that children and adolescents are not immune to depression or manic episodes, counselors are given strict ethical guidelines when it comes to all clients. The ACA Code of Ethics (2005) clearly states that counselors will avoid harm (Standard A.4.a.). In the last 2 decades, there has been an awareness that mental, behavioral, and emotional disorders that afflict adults and adolescents also can strike and devastate the lives of prepubertal children and their families. While severe developmental disorders such as autism and mental retardation have been well established, only recently has more information emerged about the diagnosis of other emotional and behavioral disorders in this young age group. Thus, we now know that attention-deficit hyperactivity disorder (ADHD) and oppositional defiant disorder (ODD) can be described and reliably diagnosed in young children (Jensen, 1998).

Unfortunately, however, in the United States, very few psychotropic agents approved by the Food and Drug Administration (FDA) for use in adults have been tested and approved for use in younger children. Therefore, of all of the psychotropic agents used in preschool children, only some antipsychotic agents have received testing sufficient for the FDA to allow labeling their use for child mental and behavioral disorders.

The lack of childhood safety and efficacy data for medications developed and tested principally in adults is actually a very widespread problem that applies to 80% of all medications (including antibiotics and anesthetics) currently available in the US formulary. Children have often been termed "therapeutic orphans" because the kind of research needed to demonstrate the safety and efficacy of various therapeutics in children has been left largely undetermined. Consequently, parents and clinicians have had to make difficult treatment decisions, relying principally on sporadic case reports, small pilot studies, or downward extrapolations of adult data to make assumptions about apparent benefits, safety, and efficacy of these agents in children (Jensen, 1998). Another factor to be considered is the fact that the central nervous system and the neurotransmitters and receptors on which psychotropic agents act are in a period of substantial growth, development, and refinement through childhood and adolescence.

While the possibility of side effects, lack of efficacy data, and availability of alternative therapies do not comprise a universal proscription against the use of medication in young children, they do suggest the need for caution and an in-depth evaluation of the possible alternatives for each child.

This is the core component of ethical clinical practice, namely, ensuring a process that allows the clinician to provide the best therapeutic strategy for each child based on the particular needs of that child and family.

Anything that compromises that process, whether it be a shortened assessment period that curtails the evaluation or fiscal pressures to use a less effective or less safe form of treatment over another, should be regarded as unethical (Jensen, 1998).

References:

Graff, C. A., Springer, P., Bitar, G. W., Gee, R. & Arredondo, R. (2010). A purveyor team's experience: Lessons learned from implementing a behavioral health care program in primary care settings. *Family, Systems & Health.* Vol. 28, No. 4, 356-368

Haack, M. R., & Hoover, A. (2001). Strategic plan for interdisciplinary faculty development: Arming the nation's health professional workforce for a new approach to substance use disorder. In Graff, C. A., Springer, P., Bitar, G. W., Gee, R. & Arredondo, R. (2010). A purveyor team's experience: Lessons learned from implementing a behavioral health care program in primary care settings. *Family, Systems & Health.* Vol. 28, No. 4, 356-368

Jensen, P. S. (1998). Ethical and pragmatic issues in the use of psychotropic agents in young children. Retrieved from **https://ww1.cpaapc.org/French_Site/Publications/Archives/CJP/1998/Aug/jensen.html**

Generic/Brand

Low

Chlorpromazine/ Thorazine

Thioridazine/ Mellaril

Clozapine* /Clozaril & FazaClo

Mesoridazine/ Serentil

Quetiapine* /Seroquel

High

Molindone/ Moban

Perphenazine/ Trilafon

Lozapine /Loxitane

Trifluoperazine/ Stelazine

Fluphenazine /Prolixin**

Thiothixene /Navane

Haloperidol /Haldol **

Olanzapine* /Zyprexa

Pimozide /Orap

Risperidone*/ Risperdal**

Ziprasidone* /Geodon

Aripiprazole* / Abilify

Paliperidone* / Invega

Iloperidone* / Fanapt

Asenapine* / Saphris

Lurasidone / Latuda

Psychotropic Medication in Children and Adolescents: Ethical Concerns

Perhaps nowhere is the science-to-service gap more pronounced than in the delivery of services to individuals and families suffering from the effects of behavioral health disorders (Graff, Springer, Bitar, Gee and Arrendondo, 2010). Behavioral health disorders (e.g., substance use disorders, depression, suicide, ADHD) account for more deaths, illnesses, and disabilities than any other preventable health condition (New Freedom Commission on Mental Health, 2003). These disorders are often associated with many of the nation's most serious and tragic problems, including homelessness, violence, injury, HIV infection, cardiovascular disease, and cancers. Left untreated, these disorders place enormous economic strains on our society with estimated annual costs at more than $414 billion (Haack & Hoover, 2001).

Primary care providers are uniquely positioned to help improve the availability, accessibility, and quality of behavioral health care services. While these providers currently provide about half the care for common behavioral health disorders and prescribe the majority of psychotropic medication (New Freedom Commission on Mental Health, 2003), these professionals often do not identify and diagnose behavioral health disorders with the same degree of accuracy as they do other preventable diseases. As a result, the role of these front-line health professionals in prevention, early identification, and referral remains largely untapped. For this reason, many adolescents with behavioral health disorders go unidentified; for others, the disorder goes unrecognized far too long and becomes more difficult and more costly to treat (Graff, et al., 2010).

Due to the fact that children and adolescents are not immune to depression or manic episodes, counselors are given strict ethical guidelines when it comes to all clients. The ACA Code of Ethics (2005) clearly states that counselors will avoid harm (Standard A.4.a.). In the last 2 decades, there has been an awareness that mental, behavioral, and emotional disorders that afflict adults and adolescents also can strike and devastate the lives of prepubertal children and their families. While severe developmental disorders such as autism and mental retardation have been well established, only recently has more information emerged about the diagnosis of other emotional and behavioral disorders in this young age group. Thus, we now know that attention-deficit hyperactivity disorder (ADHD) and oppositional defiant disorder (ODD) can be described and reliably diagnosed in young children (Jensen, 1998).

Unfortunately, however, in the United States, very few psychotropic agents approved by the Food and Drug Administration (FDA) for use in adults have been tested and approved for use in younger children. Therefore, of all of the psychotropic agents used in preschool children, only some antipsychotic agents have received testing sufficient for the FDA to allow labeling their use for child mental and behavioral disorders.

The lack of childhood safety and efficacy data for medications developed and tested principally in adults is actually a very widespread problem that applies to 80% of all medications (including antibiotics and anesthetics) currently available in the US formulary. Children have often been termed "therapeutic orphans" because the kind of research needed to demonstrate the safety and efficacy of various therapeutics in children has been left largely undetermined. Consequently, parents and clinicians have had to make difficult treatment decisions, relying principally on sporadic case reports, small pilot studies, or downward extrapolations of adult data to make assumptions about apparent benefits, safety, and efficacy of these agents in children (Jensen, 1998). Another factor to be considered is the fact that the central nervous system and the neurotransmitters and receptors on which psychotropic agents act are in a period of substantial growth, development, and refinement through childhood and adolescence.

While the possibility of side effects, lack of efficacy data, and availability of alternative therapies do not comprise a universal proscription against the use of medication in young children, they do suggest the need for caution and an in-depth evaluation of the possible alternatives for each child. This is the core component of ethical clinical practice, namely, ensuring a process that allows the clinician to provide the best therapeutic strategy for each child based on the particular needs of that child and family. Anything that compromises that process, whether it be a shortened assessment period that curtails the evaluation or fiscal pressures to use a less effective or less safe form of treatment over another, should be regarded as unethical (Jensen, 1998).

References:

Graff, C. A., Springer, P., Bitar, G. W., Gee, R. & Arredondo, R. (2010). A purveyor team's experience: Lessons learned from implementing a behavioral health care program in primary care settings. *Family, Systems & Health.* Vol. 28, No. 4, 356-368

Haack, M. R., & Hoover, A. (2001). Strategic plan for interdisciplinary faculty development: Arming the nation's health professional workforce for a new approach to substance use disorder. In Graff, C. A., Springer, P., Bitar, G. W., Gee, R. & Arredondo, R. (2010). A purveyor team's experience: Lessons learned from implementing a behavioral health care program in primary care settings. *Family, Systems & Health.* Vol. 28, No. 4, 356-368

Jensen, P. S. (1998). Ethical and pragmatic issues in the use of psychotropic agents in young children. Retrieved from https://ww1.cpaapc.org/French_Site/Publications/Archives/CJP/1998/Aug/jensen.html

Psychotic Disorders

According to Preston and Johnson (2012), the three major psychotic disorders are categorized as:

1.Schizophrenia- A recurring illness, prone to repeated psychotic episodes.

The two types are Positive and Negative.

Positive symptom is broken into two subtypes. Positive, itself, is described as active, florid delusions and hallucinations; agitation and emotional dyscontrol. The two subtypes are:

   Schizophreniaform disorder- This looks like schizophrenia but remits quicker and often does not recur.

Negative symptom- This is a neuro-development disorder which includes a social aloofness/withdrawal, the absence of florid delusions and hallucinations. Negative symptom schizophrenia tends to have an earlier and more insidious onset. Children are often seen as odd or aloof.

2. Psychotic Mood Disorders- Both mania and depression can present with poor reality testing and other psychotic symptoms.

3. Psychosis Associated with Neurological Conditions- Head injuries produce transient psychotic behavior and degenerative diseases like Alzheimer's can produce periods of agitated confusion. It is important to distinguish these from schizophrenia or mood disorders (Preston & Johnson, 2012) and a brief mental status exam may be useful.

Antipsychotic Use

Patients presenting psychotic disorders should be referred to a psychiatrist, as these patients could be very hard to treat. Though patient can be treated in an out patient setting, hospitalization may be required.

Antipsychotic medication is usually prescribed in low doses then titrated up until there is a reduction in the more disruptive aspects of the psychosis. Broken doses are advisable to start but then gradually switching to a once-a-day bedtime dosage. Assuming a good response and if it is a first episode, dosages should be decreased to a maintenance level dosage and the patient treated for one year. Repeat episodes should be treated for 2-3 years with, owing to the risk of TD, the lowest possible dose that provides relief should be administered (Preston & Johnson, 2012).

Generic/Brand

Low

Chlorpromazine/ Thorazine

Thioridazine/ Mellaril

Clozapine * /Clozaril & FazaClo

Mesoridazine/ Serentil

Quetiapine* /Seroquel

High

Molindone/ Moban

Perphenazine/ Trilafon

Lozapine /Loxitane

Trifluoperazine/ Stelazine

Fluphenazine /Prolixin**

Thiothixene /Navane

Haloperidol /Haldol **

Olanzapine* /Zyprexa

Pimozide /Orap

Risperidone*/ Risperdal**

Ziprasidone* /Geodon

Aripiprazole* / Abilify

Paliperidone* /Invega

Iloperidone* /Fanapt

Asenapine* /Saphris

Lurasidone /Latud

Antipsychotic Medication II

Mental illness can affect up to 10% of pregnant women, and women with a pre-existing psychiatric condition are more likely to experience a relapse of symptoms during pregnancy. Antipsychotic drugs are an important part of the treatment of psychotic illnesses; however, their safety with pregnant or breastfeeding women has not been fully established (Usher, Foster & McNamara, 2005). The only large controlled studies of antipsychotics in pregnancy have been conducted on women with hyperemesis gravidarum. Much lower doses of medication (generally drugs such as phenothiazines) are used for these patients than for patients with schizophrenia, and residual confounding is commonplace. Conclusions are therefore limited. A meta-analysis reported that exposure to low potency antipsychotics during the first trimester was associated with a small additional risk of congenital anomalies. Antipsychotics can also produce toxic effects in newborn infants medicated in the womb, including respiratory depression and neonatal behavioral abnormalities such as extrapyramidal movements and difficulty with oral feeding, although these effects usually resolve within days (Howard, L., Webb, R. & Abel, K. 2004).

Despite being frequently prescribed in the elderly, antipsychotic medications are commonly associated with adverse effects in this population, including sedative, orthostatic and extrapyramidal adverse effects. Growing evidence suggests that antipsychotics can also cause deleterious cognitive effects in some elderly patients.

Preclinical and growing clinical evidence indicates that inhibitory effects on dopaminergic, cholinergic and histaminergic neurochemical systems may account for antipsychotic-associated cognitive impairment in the elderly (Byerly, Weber, Brooks, Snow, Worley & Lescouflair, 2001).

The use of atypical antipsychotics in children has been consistently associated with weight gain and moderate prolactin elevation, while only a few case reports address the issue of glucose dysregulation and dyslipidaemia. The risk of weight gain and hyperprolactinaemia might be higher in younger children. Other risk factors have also been associated with antipsychotic-induced metabolic disturbances. These changes seem to be reversible, at least in some cases. Metabolic side effects of atypical antipsychotics could lead to serious complications in children who are prescribed these medications (Fedorowicz & Fombonne, 2005).

Hyponatremia and Polydipsia

Hyponatremia is a frequent electrolyte disorder. A hyponatremia is called acute severe when the duration has been 36 to 48 hours. Such patients often have advanced symptoms as a result of brain edema. Acute severe hyponatremia is a medical emergency. It should be corrected rapidly to prevent permanent brain damage. In contrast, in chronic severe hyponatremia, there is no brain edema and symptoms are usually mild (Gross, Reimann, Henschkowski & Damian, 2001).

Polydipsia is the intake of more than three liters of fluids per day. Primary polydipsia occurs when excessive drinking cannot be explained by an identified medical condition, and is not secondary to polyuria. The prevalence of this problem in psychiatric inpatients has been estimated at between 6 and 17%. It can hinder standard care and be a highly disabling, even life-threatening condition (Brookes & Ahmed, 2009).

Side effects include: confusion, lethargy, psychosis, and seizures or death (Illowsky & Kirch, 1988).

Neurotransmitters

Research suggests that inhibition of central dopamine functions may be a common basic property of antipsychotic drugs (Carlsson, 1978). Emerging knowledge about the interactions between different neurotransmitters in complex neurocircuits opens up possibilities for achieving antipsychotic activity by interfering with many different neurotransmitters. Most intriguing is the finding in animal experimental models, indicating that it should be possible to alleviate psychotic conditions by stabilizing rather than paralyzing neurocircuits, thus avoiding the risk of motor and mental side effects of the currently used drugs (Carlsson, Waters & Carlsson, 1999).

References

Brookes, G. & Ahmed, A. G. (2009). Pharmacological treatments for psychosis-related polydipsia. DOI: 10.1002/14651858.CD003544.pub2

Byerly, M. J., Weber, M. T., Brooks, D. L., Snow, L. R., Worley, M. A., Lescouflair, E. (2001). Antipsychotic medications and the elderly: Effects on cognition and implications for use. Retrieved from **http://www.ingentaconnect.com/content/adis/dag/2001/00000018/00000001/art00004**

Carlsson, A. (1978). Antipsychotic drugs, neurotransmitters, and schizophrenia. *The American Journal of Psychiatry.* Vol. 135, No. 2, 164-173.

Carlsson, A., Waters, N. & Carlsson, M. L. (1999). Neurotransmitter interactions in schizophrenia—therapeutic implications. *Biological Psychiatry.* Vol. 46, No. 10, 1388-1395.

Fedorowicz, V. J. & Fombonne, E. (2005). Metabolic side effects of atypical antipsychotics in children: A literature review. *Journal of Psychopharmacology.* Vol. 19, No. 5, 533-550.

Gross, P., Reimann, D., Henschkowski, J., Damian, M. (2001). Treatment of severe hyponatremia: Conventional and novel aspects. *Journal of the American Society of Nephrology.* 12:S10-S14.

Howard, L., Webb, R. & Abel, K. (2004). Safety of antipsychotic drugs for pregnant and breastfeeding women with non-affective psychosis. Retrieved from http://www.bmj.com/content/329/7472/933.short

Illowsky, B. P. & Kirch, D. G. (1988). Polydipsia and hyponatremia in psychiatric patients. *The American Journal of Psychiatry.* Vol. 145, No. 6, 675-683.

Usher, K., Foster, K. & McNamara, P. (2005). Antipsychotic drugs and pregnant or breastfeeding women: the issues for mental health nurses. *Journal of Psychiatric and Mental Health Nursing.* Vol. 12, Issue 6. DOI: 10.1111/j.1365-2850.2005.00903.x

Antipsychotic Medication II, pt 2

Off Label Use

Antipsychotic medications have long been a cornerstone of effective treatment for schizophrenia. Most second-generation antipsychotics have also been approved to treat bipolar disorder, and in late 2007 aripiprazole was approved for the adjunctive treatment of major depressive disorder. However, once a drug has been approved by the Food and Drug Administration (FDA), clinicians are free to prescribe it as they see fit. The benefits of such off-label use are usually unclear because there has not been a high level of published clinical research evaluating the safety and efficacy of these drugs for non-FDA-approved indications.

Although some off-label use of second-generation antipsychotics may be appropriate, these drugs are expensive and have serious side effects (including weight gain, diabetes mellitus, tardive dyskinesia, and extrapyramidal symptoms), and their off-label use may therefore represent significant risk and cost with undemonstrated clinical benefit and potential harm (Leslie, Mohamed & Rosenheck, 2009).

Several studies have investigated the extent to which antipsychotic medications have been used off label. A previous Department of Veterans Affairs (VA) study found that 33.5% of patients who received a prescription for an antipsychotic medication in the VA health care system during a four-month period in 1999 did not have a diagnosis of either schizophrenia or bipolar disorder. A more recent study by Domino and Swartz, using data from the Medical Expenditure Panel Survey (MEPS), found rates of off-label use of 18%–19% in 1996–1997 and 2004–2005. A report by the Agency for Healthcare Research and Quality (AHRQ) found that the most common off-label uses of second-generation antipsychotics reported in the literature were treatment of agitation in dementia and treatment of depression, obsessive-compulsive disorder, posttraumatic stress disorder (PTSD), personality disorders, Tourette's syndrome, and autism; however, there was very little strong evidence in the literature that these drugs were effective in treating these disorders.

Despite the fact that most antipsychotics have only been formally evaluated for the treatment of schizophreniform disorder, schizophrenia, mania, and schizoaffective disorder, antipsychotics are widely used for the treatment of a broad range of symptoms and disorders. Patients most often stated that they took antipsychotics as a tranquilizer or an anxiolytic. Neither gender, education, duration of treatment, nor efficacy of treatment showed an influence on the prescription practices for antipsychotics. In older patients (49-70 years), antipsychotics were almost exclusively used for off-label indications (Weiss, Hummer, Koller, Ulmer, Fleischhacker, 2000).

Medication Switching

Approximately half of all treated depressed patients fail to show adequate response to their initially prescribed antidepressant medication. Switching to another medication represents one possible next-step approach for nonresponsive or partially responsive patients. However, specific techniques for switching between antidepressants have not been well studied (Wohlreich, Mallinckrodt, Watkin, Wilson, Greist, Delgado & Fava, 2005). In controlled studies of acute therapy, less than 50% of patients with major depressive disorder remit during the initial course of antidepressant medication. For those who do not obtain adequate benefit from an initial course of pharmacotherapy, a wide variety of next-step strategies are available, including switching within and between classes of antidepressants, various augmentation and antidepressant combination strategies, and adding or switching to psychotherapy. Although the efficacy of most of these strategies has been established in randomized controlled trials, few comparative studies are available to help determine which of these options should be considered the preferred next step for patients who do not benefit adequately from an initial course of pharmacotherapy (Thase, Friedman, Biggs, Wisniewski, Trivedi, Luther, Fava, Nierenberg, McGrath, Warden, Niederehe, Hollon & Rush, 2007).

Typical/Atypical Antipsychotic Medications

Effective treatment of psychosis involves the use of antipsychotic medication. Yet, reported rates of nonadherence (noncompliance) to antipsychotics range from 20%–89%, with an average rate of approximately 50%. In patients with schizophrenia, nonadherence to antipsychotic maintenance treatment leads to psychotic relapse, rehospitalization, and more frequent clinic and emergency room visits. The improved side effect profile of atypical antipsychotics (i.e., lower incidences of extrapyramidal symptom and tardive dyskinesia, compared with the incidences for typical antipsychotics) has led investigators to speculate that patients receiving these medications will show greater adherence. There are, however, of only a few published reports comparing typical and atypical antipsychotics in terms of medication adherence (Dolder, Lacro, Dunn & Jeste, 2002).

Clozapine, an antipsychotic agent of the dibenzodiazepine class, is characterized by relatively weak central dopaminergic activity and displays atypical pharmacological and clinical properties in relation to the classic antipsychotics. Clinical studies have shown clozapine to be effective in suppressing both the positive and negative symptoms of schizophrenia and to be associated with an extremely low incidence of extrapyramidal side effects.

Clozapine has been shown to be of comparable, or on some criteria superior, therapeutic efficacy to perphenazine, levomepromazine, haloperidol and chlorpromazine in several short term comparative studies in patients with schizophrenia of predominantly acute symptomatology.

Moreover, clozapine is effective in a substantial proportion (30 to 50%) of schizophrenic patients who are refractory to or intolerant of classic antipsychotic therapy. Despite its promising therapeutic potential, the relatively high incidence of clozapine-induced agranulocytosis (1 to 2% of patients) is a major factor restricting the drug's wider use in psychiatric practice (Heel, 1990). Olanzapine is a serotonin-dopamine-receptor antagonist indicated for use in the treatment of schizophrenia and other psychotic disorders. The affinity of olanzapine for neuroreceptors is similar to that of clozapine. The drug is well absorbed from the GI tract; food has no effect. However, unlike typical dopamine-receptor antagonists used for antipsychotic therapy, olanzapine is more effective in reducing the negative symptoms of schizophrenia. Unlike clozapine, olanzapine does not cause agranulocytosis. No cases of tardive dyskinesia or neuroleptic malignant syndrome have been reported. Olanzapine has been associated with slight increases in hepatic transaminases. More study is needed to determine whether olanzapine interacts significantly with other drugs (Bever & Perry, 1998).

References

Bever, K. A., Perry, P. J. (1998). Olanzapine: a serotonin-dopamine-receptor antagonist for antipsychotic therapy. *American Journal of Health-System Pharmacy*. Vol. 55, Issue 10, 1003-1016.

Dolder, C. R., Lacro, J. P., Dunn, L.B., & Jeste, D. V. (2002). Antipsychotic medication adherence: Is there a difference between typical and atypical agents? The American Journal of Psychiatry. Vol. 159, No. 1, 103-108.

Heel, F. A. (1990). Clozapine. A review of its pharmacological properties, and therapeutic use in schizophrenia. *Drugs*. Vol. 40. No.5, 722-747.

Leslie, D. L., Mohamed, S., Rosenheck, R. A. (2009). Off-label use of antipsychotic medications in the department of veterans affairs health care system. *Psychiatric Services*. Vol. 60, No. 9, 1175-1181.

Thase, M. E., Friedman, E S., Biggs, M. M., Wisniewski, S. R., Trivedi, M. H., Luther, J. F., Fava, M., Nierenberg, A. A., McGrath, P. J., Warden, D., Niederehe, G., Hollon, S. D., & Rush, A. J. (2007). Cognitive therapy versus medication in augmentation and switch strategies as second-step treatments. The American Journal of Psychiatry. Vol. 164, No. 5, 739-752.

Weiss, E., Hummer, M., Koller, D., Ulmer, H., Fleischhacker, W. W. (2000). Off-label use of antipsychotic drugs. *Journal of Psychopharmacology*. Vol. 20, Issue 6, 695-698.

Wohlreich, M. M., Mallinckrodt, C. H., Watkin, J. G., Wilson, M. G., Greist, J. H., Delgado, P. L. & Fava, M. (2005). Immediate switching of antidepressant therapy: results from a clinical trial of duloxetine. *Official Journal of the American Academy of Clinical Psychiatrists*. Vol. 17, No. 4, 259-269.

Acute Antipsychotic Treatment

With the availability of SGAs (Second Generation Agents) it has become more complex as to which antipsychotic agent to administer first for a first break of psychosis or in an emergency room setting. In general SGAs are now the first-line antipsychotics in the treatment of most psychotic episodes (Schatzberg, Cole & DeBattista, 2010). However, evidence suggests that first generation drugs are underutilized in favor of the more expensive, but no more efficacious SGAs. First generation agents are more inclined to be used rather than SGAs as first intervention in some situations, such as, management of acutely agitated psychotic patients.

Choosing among the SGAs is a matter of best matching patient characteristics to the side effect profiles of the various agents. This also works well in prescribing first generation antipsychotics (Schatzberg, et al., 2010) as antipsychotic drugs differ in dosages and formulations in which they are available. For instance, the dosage for fluphenazine decanote is 0.25 cc/month, while chloropromazine and thioridazine are both prescribed at 100 mgs.

There is no evidence how long to continue antipsychotic therapy for a patient recovering from a first psychotic episode. Clearly stopping treatment too soon after initial signs of recovery will undoubtedly have the patient returning to the psychosis while tapering off over a three month period might be better tolerated by many patients without relapse ensuing. Antipsychotic drugs are effective in preventing relapse of schizophrenia. Unfortunately, 25 – 50% of patients will experience a relapse in 2 years. At this time, SAGs are the drugs of choice for maintenance therapy of schizophrenia. Unfortunately these second-generation agents produce significant weight gain as opposed to their first-generation counterparts (Schatzberg, et al., 2010).

Antipsychotics can be used to treat other psychiatric disorders. They include:

Bipolar Disorder- Research is showing that antipsychotics are helping patients to remain stable in the community. Aripiprazole has demonstrated its utility in maintenance treatment. SGAs, except clozaphine, have had two trials supporting their efficacy in treating acute mania. Another application of antipsychotics is in the treatment of bipolar depression, while SGAs are far more commonly used to treat mood disorders than they are in the treatment of schizophrenia.

Unipolar Depression- In psychotic depression there is good evidence that the pairing of an antipsychotic and an antidepressant is quite effective. So far perphenazine and amitriptyline has been the pairing of choice.

Anxiety Disorder- GADs (General Anxiety Disorders) can be treated by SGAs. Studies have shown that quetiapine is comparably beneficial to other FDA approved SGAs. Antipsychotics have long been used in the treatment of PTSD and are useful with patients exhibiting OCD.

Personality Disorders- Antipsychotics and SGAs have long played a role in the treatment of BPD having a stabilizing effect on irritability, mood lability, impulsivity and a decrease in anxiety.

Other States include, delirium, Alzheimer's dementia, and mental retardation with varying degrees of benefit. Sometimes, due to side effects, antipsychotics can cause more harm than good, and their use is strictly empirical (Schatzberg, et al., 2010).

Reference

Schatzberg, A.F., Cole, J.O., DeBattista, C. (2010). *Manual of clinical psychopharmacology* (7th ed.). Washington, DC: American Psychiatric Publishing, Inc.

Mood Stabilizers and Mood Disorders

According to Preston and Johnson (2012), the diagnosis of bipolar disorder is based upon two sources of data: the current clinical picture of depression and mania, and a clear history of both episodes. Bipolar disorder is divided into several groups. Bipolar l clearly recognizes depressive and manic episodes, while Bipolar ll has defined episodes of depression with the manic episodes so mild as to be unrecognizable to the patient. Typical bipolar episodes may last for several weeks or months. Should a patient experience two or more episodes (e.g., depression-mania-depression-mania-depression), this is referred to rapid cycling bipolar disorder. Substance abuse or treatment with antidepressants are common factors in provoking RC. Dysphoric Mania, or Mixed Mania, is a diagnostic term which describe patients who have concurrent manic and depressive symptoms, as increased activity, agitation, suicidal ideas and feelings of worthlessness.
It is interesting to note that in Preston and Johnson (2012) that although still encouraged in the use of lithium as having the best track record in providing long-term mood stabilization and a significant reduction in suicides, despite such side effects as tremor and weight gain, Schatzberg, Cole and DeBattista (2010) offer a derivative of valproic acid and divalproex sodium for the treatment of acute mania, and since 1994, it has surpassed lithium in the treatment of bipolar disorder offering advantages of a superior therapeutic index with less toxicity.

Pharmacokinetics and Pharmacodynamics

Lithium is readily and nearly completely absorbed in the gastrointestinal tract, however it is not metabolized and approximately 95% is renally excreted. Though with use of diuretics may reduce renal clearance, it can lead to toxicity. Lithium overdoses can be fatal (Keck & McElroy, 2002). The effects of lithium on depolarization-provoked and calcium-dependent release of dopamine from nerve terminals in the central nervous system, neuronal second messenger signaling pathways and across neuronal membranes have contributed to its therapeutic effects.

Potentiators

Alterations in signaling pathways represent a likely source of pathogenesis. Dynamic regulation of complex signaling pathways plays a critical role in higher order brain functions, which include the regulation of mood, cognition, and sense of self and reality; thus implicating their involvement in mood disorder pathophysiology and pathogenesis. Impairments in neuroplasticity in the brains of patients suffering from mood disorders suggest that novel medications designed to attenuate impairments in these processes may have efficacy in their treatment (Gould & Manji, 2007).

Off-label Uses

The off-label prescription of mood stabilizers is very common in psychiatry and such usage benefits patients. When prescribing off-label, psychiatrists should consider the evidence that the drug is likely to be effective for the unlicensed indication. Where there is limited evidence of benefit, a trial of the drug, with clinical monitoring, may be indicated. Patients should be fully informed about their medication, and this includes information that the prescription is off-label. Pharmacists can assist this process. The off-label concept may be difficult for some patients to understand (Haw & Stubbs, 2005).

References

Gould, T. D., Manji, H. K. (2007). Targeting neurotrophic signal transduction pathways in the treatment of mood disorders. *Current Signal Transduction Therapy*. Vol. 2, No. 2, 101-110.

Haw, C., Stubbs, J. (2005). A survey of the off-label use of mood stabilizers in a large psychiatric hospital. *Journal of Psychopharmacology*. Vol. 19, No. 4, 402-407.

Keck, P. E., McElroy, S. L. (2002). Clinical pharmacodynamics and Pharmacokinetics of anti-manic and mood-stabilizing medications. *Journal of Clinical Psychiatry*. Vol. 63, No 4, 3-11.

Preston, J. & Johnson, J. (2012) *Clinical psychopharmacology made ridiculously simple* (7th ed.). Miami, FL: Medmaster, Inc

Schatzberg, A.F., Cole, J.O., DeBattista, C. (2010). *Manual of clinical psychopharmacology* (7th ed.). Washington, DC: American Psychiatric Publishing, Inc.

Mood Stabilizers and Disorders, Disc 2

Tardive dyskinesia is a socially stigmatizing and potentially irreversible long-term adverse effect of treatment with first-generation antipsychotic medications that has been linked with poor quality of life and increased medical morbidity and mortality. In long-term studies, first-generation antipsychotics have been associated with an incidence of tardive dyskinesia of approximately 5% per year in adults and 25%–30% in elderly patients (Correll, Leucht and Kane, 2004). Tardive dyskinesia is also a movement disorder affecting 20%-40% of patients treated chronically with neuroleptic drugs (Tsai, Goff, Chang, Flood, Baer & Coyle, 1998), There are elevated levels of oxidative stress and glutamatergic neurotransmission in tardive dyskinesia, both of which may be relevant to the pathophysiology of tardive dyskinesia.

Based on lower rates of acute extrapyramidal side effects associated with second-generation antipsychotics, compared to first-generation antipsychotics, and based on preliminary data, second-generation antipsychotics are expected to cause less tardive dyskinesia than first-generation antipsychotics (Correll, et al.). Mainly due to their shared feature of reduced liability for acute extrapyramidal side effects, compared to first-generation antipsychotics, the second-generation antipsychotics, including clozapine and antipsychotics developed after the introduction of clozapine, have quickly become the preferred treatment for psychotic and various nonpsychotic disorders across age groups. Moreover, since data suggest that early extrapyramidal side effects are an important and potentially modifiable risk factor for tardive dyskinesia, it is hoped that the use of second-generation antipsychotics will also lead to less tardive dyskinesia, compared to first-generation antipsychotics

Lithium therapy may induce a confusional state when serum levels are in toxic or therapeutic ranges. Lithium can also cause nonconvulsive status epilepticus (NCSE), which may clinically resemble a nonictal encephalopathy. Therefore patients taking lithium or other neuroleptic drugs, and who have intercurrent illnesses, pose diagnostic challenges in determining the primary cause of confusion (Kaplan & Birbeck, 2006).

Lithium also affects a number of monoamine neurotransmitters. It reduces the excretion of norepinephrine in patients with mania, but increases it in patients with depression (Schatzberg, Cole & DeBattista, 2010). These effects are consistent with lithium's beneficial actions. Because lithium affects a number of neurotransmitters, researchers have postulated that the principal action of the drug on the postsynaptic signal that the number of neurotransmitters generate. In the past two decades attention has been paid to the use of anticonvulsant medications, mainly to promote mood stabilization. Valproate may be the most convenient general term all these formulations and the most commonly used drug in the treatment of bipolar disorder as well as aggression, agitation, and impulsivity in patients with a number of disorders; while Carbamazepine has drug interaction and side effect profiles that make it more cumbersome to use (Schatzberg, et al., 2010). The major concern with carbamazepine is the threat of agranulocytosis or aplastic anemia, both potentially lethal conditions. Still many patients experience positive results with carbamazepine who do not do well with lithium or valproate.

References

Correll, C. U., Leucht, S. and Kane, J M. (2004). Lower risk for tardive dyskinesia associated with second-generation antipsychotics: A systematic review of 1-year studies.
The American Journal of Psychiatry. Vol. 161, No. 3, 414-425.

Kaplan, P. W. & Birbeck, G. (2006). Lithium-induced confusional states: Nonconvulsive status epilepticus or triphasic encephalopathy? *Epilepsia.* Vol. 47, Issue 12, 2071-2074.

Schatzberg, A.F., Cole, J.O., DeBattista, C. (2010). *Manual of clinical psychopharmacology* (7th ed.). Washington, DC: American Psychiatric Publishing, Inc.

Tsai, G., Goff, D. C., Chang, R. W., Flood, J., Baer, L. and Coyle, J. T. (1998). Markers of glutamatergic neurotransmission and oxidative stress associated with tardive dyskinesia. *The American Journal of Psychiatry.* Vol. 155, No. 9, 1207-1213.

Anxiolytic (anti-anxiety), Sedative, & Hypnotics I

Anxiolytic agents are the most commonly used psychotropic drugs (Schatzberg, Cole, & DeBattista, 2010). Anxiolytics are prescribed for a wide variety of patients who do not have a primary anxiety disorder, as anxiolytics (e.g., benzodiazepines) are indicated for muscle tension, insomnia, myoclonic epilepsy, and alcohol withdrawal. Anxiety disorders also include: panic disorders, phobias, obsessive-compulsive disorder, PTSD, generalized anxiety disorder and social anxiety.

The anxiolytic benzodiazepines are commonly divided into three subclasses on the basis of structure. The pharmacokinetic properties vary among these classes reflecting differences in metabolic rate. The 2-keto drugs are oxidized in the liver giving these compounds relatively long half-lives. The 3-hydroxy compounds are metabolized rapidly and have shorter half-lives, while the triazolo compounds are also oxidized and have shorter half-lives.

Several SSRIs have been approved for one or more anxiety diagnoses (e.g. paroxetine for social anxiety, GAD, OCD, panic disorder, PMDD and PTSD; sertraline for panic disorder, OCD, PMDD, social anxiety disorder and PTSD).

Since SSRIs show no notable differences in treating specific anxiety disorders, the consensus (Schatzberg, et al., 2010) is all SSRIs are reasonably effective across the whole range of anxiety disorders. Clinically, most, if not all, TCAs and SSRIs exert similar antipanic effects. The MAOI, phenelzine, is a potent antipanic agent and MAOIs have been found to be effective in social anxiety disorders.

Assessment challenges, differential diagnoses and psychopharmacological treatment (see above) of the following anxiety disorders (APA, 2000):

Panic disorders- characterized by recurrent unexpected panic attacks about which there is persistent concern. A panic attack is a discrete period in which there is a sudden onset of in tense apprehension, fearfulness, or terror often associated with feelings of impending doom. During these attacks, symptoms such as shortness of breath, palpitations, chest pain or discomfort, choking or smothering sensations, and fear of "going crazy" or losing control are present. Panic disorder is not diagnosed if the panic attacks are judged to be a direct physiological consequence of a general medical condition.

Phobias- Characterized by persistent fear of clearly discernible, circumscribed objects or situations. Specific phobias differ from most other anxiety disorders. Typically, individuals with specific phobias do not present with pervasive anxiety because their fear is limited to specific, circumscribed objects or situations. However, generalized anxious anticipation may emerge under conditions in which encounters with the phobic stimulus become more likely (e.g. a fear of snakes ignited by a walk in a desert region).

OCD- Characterized by obsessions (which cause marked anxiety or distress) and/or by compulsions (which serve to neutralize anxiety). OCD is not diagnosed if the content of the thoughts or the activities is exclusively related to another mental disorder (e.g., preoccupation with appearance in Body Dysmorphic Disorder, preoccupation with a feared object or situation in Specific or Social Phobia, or hair pulling in Trichotillomania). An additional diagnosis of OCD may be warranted if there are obsessions or compulsions whose content is unrelated to the other mental disorder.

PTSD- Characterized by the re-experiencing of an extremely traumatic event accompanied by symptoms of increased arousal and avoidance stimuli associated with the trauma. In PTSD, the stressor must be of an extreme (i.e., life-threatening) nature. Not all psychopathology that occurs in individuals exposed to an extreme stressor should be attributed to PTSD. Symptoms of avoidance, numbing, and increased arousal that are present before the stressor do not meet the criteria for the diagnosis of PTSD.

GAD- Characterized by at least 6 months of persistent and excessive anxiety and worry. The diagnosis of GAD should only be made when the focus of the anxiety and worry is unrelated to another disorder, that is, the excessive worry is not restricted to a panic attack (Panic Disorder), being embarrassed in public (Social Phobia), or being contaminated (OCD).

Social anxiety- Characterized by exposure to certain types of social or performance situations, often leading to avoidance behavior. Individuals with panic attacks and social anxiety a potentially diagnostic problem. Panic disorder may develop from fear of being seen having a panic attack, while social anxiety may bring on a panic attack due to the fear of social situations (e.g. speaking in public), though when social anxiety attacks occur they take the form of situationally bound or situationally predisposed panic attacks.

References:

APA (2000). *Diagnostic and statistical manual of mental disorders.* (4th Ed.). American Psychiatric Association, Washington, D.C.

Schatzberg, A.F., Cole, J.O. & DeBattista, C. (2010). *Manual of clinical psychopharmacology* (7th ed.). Washington, DC: American Psychiatric Publishing, Inc.

Sleep Disorders and Sedative Hypnotics and Anxiolytics

Sleep disorders are organized into four major sections according to presumed etiology.

The following sleep disorders are noted by the DSM-IV (APA, 2000):

- Primary Sleep Disorders- These are subdivided into Dyssomnias, characterized by abnormalities in the amount, quality, or timing of sleep; and Parasomnias, characterized by abnormal behavioral or psychological events occurring in association with sleep, specific sleep stages, or sleep-awake transitions.
- Sleep Disorder Related to Another Mental Disorder- Characterized by complaint of sleep disturbance that results in the diagnosis of mental disorder often a Mood or Anxiety disorder but is sufficiently severe to warrant independent clinical attention.
- Sleep Disorder Due to a General Medical Condition- Characterized by a prominent complaint of sleep disturbance resulting from a direct physiological effect of a general medical condition on the sleep-wake system.
- Substance-Induced Sleep Disorder- This involves complaints of sleep disturbance that results from the concurrent use, or recent discontinuation of use, of a substance, including medications.

The benzodiazepines are still among the most widely prescribed sedative-hypnotics in the United States today (Schatzberg, Cole & DeBattista, 2010). Although most benzodiazepines have hypnotic properties, only five have an FDA-approved indication as a hypnotic: flurazepam, temazepam, estazolam, quazepam, and triazolam. Four nonbenzodiazepines, zolpidem, zaleplon, eszopiclone, and ramelteon, are also FDA approved as hypnotics.

Some clinicians argue that a non-long-acting compound (e.g., temazepam or zolpidem) offer great advantages over longer-acting agents, although one study has pointed to the safe use of trilolam for inducing sleep on transatlantic flights and preventing jet lag, there may be disadvantages associated with very short-acting hypnotics, primarily rebound insomnia and anterograde amnesia (Schatzberg, et al., 2010).

The side effects of the sedative-hypnotic benzodiazepines are similar to those of their anxiolytic counterparts. They include sedation, ataxia, anterograde amnesia, slurred speech, and nausea. One possible problem with longer-acting benzodiazepine (e.g., flurazepam) is the potential of withdrawal once switch to a shorter-acting hypnotic as with temazepam. The nonbenzodiazepines have a reputation of being less addictive though high doses may induce euphoria, with side-affects being drowsiness and dizziness. The specific hypnotic effects of these drugs have distinct disadvantages with some patients. The muscle relaxing properties of benzodiazepine may compromise the airways of patients with sleep apnea.

Zolpidem, the most prescribed hypnotic in the United States is also the most addicting with 40% of the prescribed population developing a tolerance for it and ingesting more and becoming dependent upon it. The availability of ramelteon, a melatonin agonist, does not have the habit-forming potential of traditional hypnotics and is not sedating (Schatzberg, et al., 2010).

However, ramelteon may not be as effective in addressing the spectrum of sleep difficulties as benzodiazepine and nonbenzodiazepines hypnotics, while producing side-affects that include headache, somnolence, fatigue, dizziness and nausea, which seem to improve after several weeks of treatment.

References:

APA (2000). *Diagnostic and statistical manual of mental disorders.* (4th Ed.). American Psychiatric Association, Washington, D.C.

Schatzberg, A.F., Cole, J.O. & DeBattista, C. (2010). *Manual of clinical psychopharmacology* (7th ed.). Washington, DC: American Psychiatric Publishing, Inc.

Anxiolytic (anti-anxiety), Sedatives, Hypnotics II

Six different anxiety disorders are seen in clinical practice (Preston and Johnson, 2012). These include:

1. G.A.D.- This is usually long-term with no apparent life stressors. Daily living provides anxiety. Though many physicians treat G.A.D. with benzodiazepines, this presents two problems. Fist, benzodiazepines can cause depression in some patients, and second, patients can develop tolerance/dependence problems. The SSRIs venlafaxine and buspirone have been shown effective without the tolerance/dependence problems.

2. Stress-related anxiety- The patient functions fairly well and experiences stress in the face of major life stressors such as divorce and serious illness. Minor tranquilizers are helpful in reducing anxiety symptoms. It is important to consider if the stress is acute or of short duration. If it is just one in a series of life crisis, then benzodiazepines should not be recommended.

3. Panic disorder- Characterized by repeated episodes of full-blown panic with the development of phobias. One isolated attack is usually sufficient evidence of panic disorder and may accompany other types of disorders. Some, however, do not.

4. Medical illness presenting with anxiety disorders- In almost all instances the treatment of choice is to treat the primary medical illness or to discontinue the offending drug. Caution is advised when abruptly discontinuing some drugs, as discontinued use of coffee may mimic anxiety.

5. Social phobias- Anxiety is experienced when a person is in a social setting, e.g., public speaking, or social gatherings. Social phobias are generally not treated medically but rather with psychotherapy and behavioral approaches. In some cases beta-blockers, MAOIs or SSRIs have been helpful.

6. Anxiety disorders as part of a primary mental disorder- Anxiety frequently accompanies many mental disorders. Treating the primary disorder is usually sufficient.

Some degree of anxiety and stress is a common part of every day living (Preston & Johnson, 2012). Medication should only be recommended if anxiety symptoms are so severe as to interfere with everyday living.

In the past two decades there has been a significant increase in patients seeking complementary and alternative medicine (CAM). Recent surveys show that 40% of Americans have turned to CAM for the treatment of many illnesses, as there are many OTC products have been shown to be as effective. Five have research support for efficacy in treating depression: St. John's Wort, SAMe, 5-HTP, Omega-3 fatty acids and folic acid. The first three have been used to treat depression in monotherapy, while folic acid and omega-3 acids are used to augment antidepressants.

Studies suggest a complex relationship between cognitive-behavior therapy (CBT) and pharmacotherapy for the combined treatment of mood disorders and anxiety disorders (Otto, Smits & Reese, 2006). Combined treatment for depression may have beneficial effects when applied to patients with chronic depression and in cases to prevent relapse.

In bipolar disorder there is evidence for a strong effect of psychosocial treatment on the course of the disorder.

In the anxiety disorders, there are some benefits in the short term, but combined treatment may limit the maintenance of treatment gains offered by CBT alone. Combined treatment should not be considered the default treatment for mood and anxiety disorders, with the possible exception of bipolar disorder.

Instead, decisions whether combined treatment is worth the added cost and effort should be made in relation to the disorder under treatment, the level of severity or chronicity, and the stage of treatment (e.g., acute vs. relapse prevention).

Reference

Otto, M. W., Smits, J. A. J. and Reese, H. E. (2006). Combined psychotherapy and pharmacotherapy for mood and anxiety disorders in adults: review and analysis. *Clinical Psychology: Science and Practice Vol.* 12, Issue 1, 72-86.

Preston, J. & Johnson, J. (2012) *Clinical psychopharmacology made ridiculously simple* (7th ed.). Miami, FL: Medmaster, Inc

Professional and Ethical Issues

Informed consent has become increasingly important in psychotherapy and in medicine. Standard practice has long called for informing the patient of the benefits and risks of various psychopharmacological medications (Schatzberg, Cole & DeBattista, 2010). Some courts have judged that physicians, clinicians and therapist be held liable if they do not tell their patient about every side effect. Most clinicians do not for several reasons, including the time involved and unnecessarily frightening the patient.

Once a diagnosis is made, the clinician should tell the patient about treatment options. This is a part of "informed consent" in which the therapist must share with patients their available treatment options (mentioning those treatments that are empirically supported). Thus even if a therapist is not especially fond of pharmacological treatments, it behooves them to share information regarding drug treatments. At the heart of informed consent is a respect for our clients in terms of allowing them to be the final judge in opting for certain treatments (Preston, 2010).

A continued discussion should include:

- Medication side effects
- The likely or common positive benefits of drug treatments (i.e. what kinds of symptoms are likely to be improved with medications)
- The length of time that it may take for medications to begin to show clinical effects.
- Limitations of medication treatments
- The importance of collaborative treatment, e.g. the value in having both the therapist and the prescribing doctor share information about the course of treatment (e.g. improvement, lack of improvement, emergent side effects, etc.)

There is one case in which a non-medical clinician was found to be unethical and this was due to the fact that this person only recommended an over-the-counter produce but failed to talk about other available treatment options. Some over-the-counter products do have empirical support for efficacy in treating some psychiatric disorders, and can be mentioned to patients as options. However, this must be done in the context of presenting all available empirically validated treatment options.

Due to the impact of managed care, many patients are receiving prescriptions for psychotropic medications from primary care physicians who have very limited time to spend with the patients both initially (when the diagnosis is made and treatment is initiated) and in follow-up. This is a significant problem and psychotherapists can provide enormous help to patients by monitoring their medication treatment and providing support and information regarding drug treatments, and be able to do so in ethical and legal ways.

References

Preston, J. (2010). *Introduction to psychopharmacology: A practical clinician's guide.* Retrieved from

http://www.continuingedcourses.net/active/courses/course015.php

Schatzberg, A.F., Cole, J.O. & DeBattista, C. (2010). *Manual of clinical psychopharmacology* (7th ed.). Washington, DC: American Psychiatric Publishing, Inc.

Pharmacology in Special Situations

Pediatrics

Most standard psychiatric drugs have not received FDA approval for use in children, and since there are few data on the long-term consequences of psychiatric drug therapy in children, the decision to use a drug treatment must be based on a clear clinical need (Schatzberg, Cole & DeBattista, 2010). Prepubescent children have relatively efficient livers, allowing them to metabolize drugs rapidly and enabling them to tolerate higher doses of psychiatric drugs than adults. Drugs should be reserved for clearly distressed or dysfunctional conditions for which psychosocial treatments have either failed or are likely to be of short-term benefit.

Unfortunately, however, in the United States, very few psychotropic agents approved by the FDA for use in adults have been tested and approved for use in younger children. Therefore, of all of the psychotropic agents used in preschool children, only some antipsychotic agents have received testing sufficient for the FDA to allow labeling their use for child mental and behavioral disorders (Jensen, 1998).

The lack of childhood safety and efficacy data for medications developed and tested principally in adults is actually a very widespread problem that applies to 80% of all medications.

Children have often been termed "therapeutic orphans" because the kind of research needed to demonstrate the safety and efficacy of various therapeutics in children has been left largely undetermined. Consequently, parents and clinicians have had to make difficult treatment decisions, relying principally on sporadic case reports, small pilot studies, or downward extrapolations of adult data to make assumptions about apparent benefits, safety, and efficacy of these agents in children.

Adult ADHD

The issue of the existence of ADHD in adults has received more attention in the last few years. Attention-Deficit/Hyperactivity Disorder is the only condition, other than narcolepsy and weight reduction for which stimulants are approved by the FDA (Schatzberg, et al., 2010). Some individuals who have had clear clinical benefit from stimulants in childhood continue to require and benefit from stimulant medication well into adult life. The interesting and clinically useful aspect of stimulant therapy in treating adults with ADHD is that the clinical effects are often clear and dramatic within a day or two of reaching the appropriate dosage. Various treatment options such as bupropion, antidepressants and stimulant therapy are explored depending upon abusive issues with other drugs or the prescribed drug itself.

Substance use, abuse, and dependence are elusive constructs when it comes to assessing problem behavior among individuals who are elderly. According to Benshoff, Harrawood and Koch (2003), individuals over the age of 65 make up roughly 12.4% of the total U.S. population (about 35 million people) and they represent the fastest growing age group; by 2030 this group will nearly double in size to over 70 million individuals and will represent 20% of the U. S. population. However, virtually no data exist to quantify drug use, abuse, and dependence patterns. Although elderly individuals make-up 12.4% of the population, they consume 25% to 30% of all prescription drugs. On a daily basis elderly adults consume more over-the-counter and prescription drugs than any other age group and are more likely to consume psychoactive drugs with a potential for misuse, abuse, and addiction. More recently it was noted that elderly individuals are 2-3 times more likely than younger individuals to be prescribed psychoactive drugs, most notably benzodiazepines (Benshoff et al., 2003).

Pregnant Women

Pregnancy, unfortunately, does not protect patients against the occurrence, recurrence, or exacerbation of psychiatric conditions. At least 10% of patients meet criteria for a depressive order during pregnancy, which appears to increase OCD and other anxiety disorders. All psychotropic drugs cross the placenta to some degree and while gross physical malformations are easy to detect and the possibility of drugs given during pregnancy may affect brain function and behavior years later, there is no clear evidence that it actually occurs (Schatzberg, et al., 2010). However, not treating mental illness during pregnancy has significant risks. Severely depressed pregnant women do not take care of themselves optimally and conflicting reports suggest a higher risk of birth weight and preterm deliveries in untreated women. Children born to mothers taking first-generation antipsychotics showed no significant differences in motor development, growth or intellect up to age 4. A study done by the Stanford group suggests that there may be mild motoric differences in children exposed to anti depressants in utero but no effects on mental development. These studies while important are insufficient to answer the question of whether in utero exposure to psychotropics has negative behavioral effects.

Polypharmacy

Multiple drug use is common in older people, and may give rise to drug related problems. Elderly patients use more medications than younger patients and the trend of increasing drug use continues through 80 years of age. Studies conducted in a variety of settings have shown that patients over 65 years of age use an average of 2 to 6 prescribed medications and 1 to 3.4 non-prescribed medications. Most research resulting in the development and marketing of these medications has been directed at proving the efficacy and safety of single drug products. Little research has been directed to determine the safety and efficacy of combining multiple medications to treat concurrent conditions in a single patient (Stewart & Cooper, 1994). It is known that the use of multiple medications increases the risks of adverse drug reactions, drug-drug interactions, and makes compliance with medication regimens more difficult. Methods to reduce the risks of polypharmacy include patient education, physician education, such as education and feedback systems, and regulatory intervention.

References:

Benshoff, J. J., Harrawood, L. K., and Koch, D. S. (2003). Substance abuse and the elderly: Unique issues and concerns. *The Journal of Rehabilitation* Vol. 69.

Jensen, P. S. (1998). Ethical and pragmatic issues in the use of psychotropic agents in young children. *Canadian Journal of Psychiatry* 43:585588.

Schatzberg, A.F., Cole, J.O. & DeBattista, C. (2010). *Manual of clinical psychopharmacology* (7th ed.). Washington, DC: American Psychiatric Publishing, Inc.

Stewart, R. B. & Cooper, J. W. (1994). Polypharmacy in the aged: Practical solutions. *Drugs & Aging*. Vol. 4, No. 6, 449-461.

Psychotherapy and the Elderly

Solely Psychotherapy

The elderly is a population that has long been overlooked in terms of psychotherapy and its influence over problems of depression, which may resemble forms of dementia. An obvious problem is the typical mental diseases of old age such as the different kinds of dementia. They may however be beyond therapeutic range. However, more important is the clinician's ability to recognize states that look like dementia, and which are not. The other typical mental disease of old age is late-onset late-life depression, which, according to researchers in the field, are social losses, impaired health and a general breakdown of life having nothing to do with genetic origin (Munk, 2010). Older adults suffer disproportionately from psychiatric disorders, but few older adults seek and/or receive psychotherapy, and few mental health services are provided for older adults (Zivian, Larsen, Gekoski, Knox and Hatchette, 1994). It is not simply that older adults are poor candidates for psychotherapy.

The literature on geriatric psychotherapy indicates that a) many older clients are receptive to therapeutic suggestion, b) older clients are often more realistic and more compliant than younger clients and c) older adults appear to benefit from many different kinds of psychotherapy, including supportive, psychodynamic, cognitive, and Gestalt therapy.

Medicating the Elderly for Alzheimer's Disease

Alzheimer disease is the most common disorder causing cognitive decline in old age and exacts a substantial cost on society. Although the diagnosis of AD is often missed or delayed, it is primarily one of inclusion, not exclusion, and usually can be made using standardized clinical criteria (Small, Rabins, Barry, Buckholtz, DeKosky, Ferris, Finkel, Gwyther, Khachaturian, Lebowitz, McRae, Morris, Oakley, Schneider, Streim, Sunderland, Teri, Tune, 1997). Most cases can be diagnosed and managed in primary care settings, yet some patients with atypical presentations, severe impairment, or complex comorbidity benefit from specialist referral. Alzheimer disease is progressive and irreversible, but pharmacologic therapies for cognitive impairment and nonpharmacologic and pharmacologic treatments for the behavioral problems associated with dementia can enhance quality of life. Psychotherapeutic intervention with family members is often indicated, as nearly half of all caregivers become depressed.

Psychotherapy and Medications

Over the past 20 years, numerous studies have investigated the efficacy of psychotherapy for treating late life depression and, to a lesser degree, the efficacy of psychotherapy combined with antidepressant medication. Of the intervention studies, cognitive-behavioral therapy and interpersonal psychotherapy combined with antidepressant medication have the largest base of evidence in support of their efficacy for late life depression (Arean & Cook, 2002). With regard to clinical practice, data suggests that, when available, both kinds of interventions can be offered to depressed older adults, as long as there are no contraindications. The available data suggest that treatment choice for all depressive conditions should be based on contraindications, treatment availability, costs, and preferences of the older adults (Pinquart, Duberstien & Lyness, 2006).

References

Arean, P. A. & Cook, B. L. (2002). Psychotherapy and combined psychotherapy/pharmacotherapy for late life depression. *Biological Psychiatry.* Vol. 52, Issue 3, 293-303.

Munk, K. P. (2010). New aspects of late life depression. *Nordic Psychology* Vol. 62 (2), 1-6.

Pinquart, M., Duberstein, P.R. & Lyness, J. M. (2006). Treatments for later-life depressive conditions: A meta-analytic comparison of pharmacotherapy and psychotherapy. *The American Journal of Psychiatry.* Vol. 163, No. 9, 1493-1501.

Small, G.W., Rabins, P. V., Barry, P. P., Buckholtz, N. S., DeKosky, S. T., Ferris, S. H., Finkel, S. I., Gwyther, L. P., Khachaturian, Z. S., Lebowitz, B.D., McRae, T. D., Morris, J.C., Oakley, F., Schneider, L.S., Streim, J. E., Sunderland, T., Teri, L. A., Tune, L. E. (1997). Diagnosis and treatment of Alzheimer disease and related disorders. *The Journal of the American Medical Association.* Vol. 278 (16), 1363-1371.

Zivian, M. T., Larsen, W., Gekoski, W., Knox, V. J., Hatchette, V. (1994). Psychotherapy for the elderly: Public opinion. *Psychotherapy: Theory, Research, Practice, Training.* Vol. 31 (3), 492-502.

Herbals, Dietary Supplements, Complementary Approaches

There has been a significant increase in the number of patients seeking complementary and alternative medicine (CAM in the past two decades. Forty percent of Americans have turned to CAM for the treatment of illnesses. However, 70% whom are taking these products never mention it to their doctors which can be problematic when it relates to drug-drug interactions (Preston & Johnson, 2012).

There are, however, three concerns addressed by Preston and Johnson (2012) concerning the use of CAMs. These are:

- Consumers' misinterpretation of what is "natural." Many people think that natural means safe. Some OTC products are known for producing dangerous drug-drug interactions; most notably: St. Johns Wort, which effects liver metabolism, inhibiting some liver-enzymes while inducing others.

- FDA does not have oversight of dietary supplements. Many of these products are not quality controlled and in many cases do not contain the amount of drug advertised on the label while containing contaminants such as lead, mercury and arsenic.

- No medical supervision. Many people self-diagnose taking OTC medications without their physicians' knowledge or approval. Should the supplement bring about an episode of depression, they begin self-treating for that, which in turn could turn the episode manic. In those with bipolar disorder use of OTC medications which treat depression can provoke manic episodes.

There are several OTC products that have been shown to be effective in treating depression and anxiety.

Anxiety

Anxiety is a state of uncertainty and fear caused by anticipation or the realization of danger. Anxiety and fear are common occurrences and serve an adaptive function driving us to maintain an even balance in our lives. Pathologic anxiety or fear concerning unspecified danger interferes with our ability to deal with life as we are unable to develop productive plans to deal with unknown and unreal dangers (Gable, 1998).

Herbal remedies for Anxiety include:

Chamomile- all varieties have been used in related part to the chemical constitutes of the volatile oil of which the chamomile flower contains 1 to 2 percent. In doses up to 30 mg it has an antianxiety effect without demonstrating muscle relaxing, sedating or anticonvulsant activity. At doses between 30 and 100 mg, a mild sedation is produced.

Valerian- considered a very potent tranquilizer; indications for its use include insomnia and anxiety. Though the active ingredients of valerian are unknown, current research is focused on chemicals in the volatile oils. The effectiveness of valerian in anxiety and insomnia may result from the interaction with the inhibitor neurotransmitter GABA.

Kava-Kava- potent sedation and central muscular relaxant effects have been attributed to kava, which acts on GABA and benzodiazepine binding sites in the brain. Therapeutically, the uses for this herb include anxiety, stress and restlessness. Due to its CNS profile, kava is not recommended for use in patients with depression.

Depression

Depression is the most common psychiatric problem among American adults with a lifetime prevalence of 5.8%. Symptoms include decreased interest in activities that are usually pleasurable, decreased activity levels, agitation, decreased sleep and appetite and the inability to concentrate.

Herbal remedies for Depression include:

St. John's Wort- effective in the treatment of mile to moderate depression, current investigations indicate hypericin's ability to inhibit serotonin reuptake and may be its primary mechanism of action. Side effects include fatigue, weight gain, emotional instability and the potential for photosensitivity.

SAMe- a naturally occurring bio-molecule, it is just as effective to standard antidepressants. Most people have no side effects, but if side effects due occur, they include nausea, diarrhea, headaches, restlessness and insomnia.

5-HTP- derived from tryptophan, it is an effective and well tolerated antidepressant treating major depression, however, should not be combined with prescription antidepressants.

Insomnia

Melatonin- though use as a sleeping pill is discouraged, melatonin helps to cool the body down allowing entry to slow wave (deep) sleep. 0.5 mg four hours prior to sleep is recommended as higher levels, though producing drowsiness may also cause depression.

Chamomile, Valerian and Kava are also recommended for insomnia.

References:

Gable, T. L. (1998). Herbal medications, nutraceuticals, and anxiety and depression. In Miller, L. G. & Murray, W. J. (Eds). *Herbal medicinals: A clinician's guide.* Pharmaceutical Products Press, The Hawthorne Press, Inc. Binghamton, NY.

Preston, J. & Johnson, J. (2012) *Clinical psychopharmacology made ridiculously simple* (7th ed.). Miami, FL: Medmaster, Inc.

Holistic Approaches for Anxiety and Depression

The use of complementary and alternative medicine (CAM) is widespread. Those with psychiatric disorders are more likely to use CAM than those with other diseases (Mamtani & Cimino, 2002). There are both benefits and limitations to CAM. Many controlled studies have yielded promising results in the areas of chronic pain, insomnia, anxiety, and depression. There is sufficient evidence, for example, to support the use of a) acupuncture for addiction problems and chronic musculoskeletal pain, b) hypnosis for cancer pain and nausea, c) massage therapy for anxiety, and the use of d) mind-body techniques such as meditation, relaxation, and biofeedback for pain, insomnia, and anxiety. Large doses of vitamins, herbal supplements, and their interaction with conventional medications are areas of concern.

Mind-body medicine encompasses a wide range of practices and therapies designed to facilitate the mind's capacity to affect health. Based on national survey data, relaxation techniques, guided imagery, hypnosis, and biofeedback are the most popular mind-body therapies in the United States (Wolsko, Elsenberg, Davis & Phillips, 2004).

While use of many mind–body techniques predates modern biomedicine, they have received increased attention as biomedical research identifies mechanisms by which the mind and body influence each other. Despite widespread popular interest in mind–body therapies and their potential as useful medical treatments, many questions about their use remain unanswered. For instance, while mind–body therapies are clearly efficacious in the treatment of chronic pain and insomnia; it is not known whether persons with these conditions routinely use these effective and inexpensive therapies. Conversely, it is not known whether persons are using mind–body therapies while not supervised by a physician for conditions that might best be treated with other, more effective, therapies. The evidence base for the efficacy of the majority of complementary and alternative interventions used to treat anxiety and depression remains poor though evidence for the use of acupuncture in treating anxiety disorders is becoming stronger. There is currently minimal empirical evidence for the use of aromatherapy or mindfulness-based meditation. Recent systematic reviews all point to a significant lack of methodologically rigorous studies within the field (van der Watt, Laugharne & Janca, 2008). This lack of evidence does not diminish the popularity of such interventions within the general Western population. The issue of possible harm associated with the use of all complementary therapies has been high in the minds of consumers, physicians, and policy makers.

While herbs and supplements have received the most attention, with some clearly causing harm through direct toxicity and drug/herb interactions, inappropriate use of mind-body therapies may also result in direct harm. For instance, use of specific mind-body therapies by persons with unstable psychiatric conditions (such as posttraumatic stress disorder) may worsen psychiatric symptoms, especially if the patient does not have appropriate oversight (Wolsko, et al., 2004). Another type of harm is indirect, caused by forgoing or delaying more effective treatments in favor of mind-body therapies. This may happen when a patient has excessive expectations for the benefits of a mind-body therapy, choosing this route without ever consulting a physician or unwisely choosing mind-body therapy as the primary mechanism of treatment despite discussions with their caregiver.

Personally, I favor alternative sources of herbal medicines and supplements. Unfortunately, HMOs are inundated with pharmaceutical companies and the dollars they represent. Health insurance agencies have yet to see the benefits of paying for preventative care, being reactive rather than proactive. Hence, if we take care of ourselves through diet, exercise and more "natural" medications and supplements, our proactive approach to our own mental and physical health just may benefit us now and in later years as well.

References

Mamtani, R. & Cimino, A. (2002). A primer of complementary and alternative medicine and its relevance in the treatment of mental health problems. *Psychiatric Quarterly*. Vol. 73, No. 4, 367-381.

van der Watt, G., Laugharne, J., Janca. A. (2008). Complementary and alternative medicine in the treatment of anxiety and depression. *Current opinion in Psychiatry*. Vol. 21, Issue 1, 37-42.

Wolsko, P. M., Elsenberg, D. M., Davis, R. B. & Phillips, R. S. (2002). Use of mind-body medical therapies. Journal of General Internal Medicine. Vol. 19, Issue 1, 43-50.

Expanding the Role of Psychology: Ethics and Legal Issues

New Mexico has become the first state granting prescription privileges to psychologists (Holmes, 2002). This is due to the fact that New Mexico is primarily a rural state with few opportunities to access medical care. Psychologists, after proper training, receive a "conditional prescription certificate" allowing them to prescribe psychotropic medications for two years under the supervision of a licensed physician. After the initial two years, psychologists can apply for a "prescription certificate" allowing them to prescribe without supervision.

As long as laws are passed permitting psychologists' prescription privileges within the state of practice, there will be no legal issues as far as prescribing goes. Psychologists may need additional liability and malpractice insurance and client confidentiality may take on a different scope as well, as courts may subpoena records indicating what types of medications were prescribed, and if those drugs attributed to a clients behavior as to make them end up in court in the first place. Ethical concerns surface over the level of training required as both the ACA (2005) and the APA (2010) subscribe to the ethical principles of beneficence and nonmaleficence. Psychologists will need access to a patient's medical records in order to determine poly-substance intake or abusive behaviors with medications in the past and drug-drug efficacy.

As with all human beings there will be temptations to abuse the prescription privilege, as there obviously have been therapists who violated Standards A.5.a.and b., hence the need for those ethical standards (ACA, 2000). If the ACA didn't foresee the potential for abuse, there would be no need for the ethical standard in the first place. Since most legislation is still pending in most states, abusive psychologists in states that prescribe to prescription privileges may undo the underpinnings of the APA in their efforts in obtaining prescription privileges for all psychologists interested in having that additional resource for their clientele.

References

American Counseling Association (2005) *ACA Code of Ethics*. Retrieved from http://www.counseling.org/Resources/CodeOfEthics/TP/Home/CT2.aspx

American Psychological Association (2010). *Ethical Principles of Psychologists and Code of Conduct*. Retrieved from **http://www.apa.org/ethics/code/index.aspx**

Holmes, L. (2002). New Mexico allows psychologists to prescribe. *Mental Health*. Retrieved from http://mentalhealth.about.com/library/weekly/aa031202a.htm

Final Project

Tomas Ferraro

Walden University

Final Project

Legal and Ethical Issues of Psychologists Prescribing Medications

Though psychotherapy and psychological testing are the roles more attributed to clinical psychologists, more have begun advocating for legally sanctioned prescription authority in their professional roles. This is partly due to the decline in reimbursement as more psychiatric disorders require medications (Walker, 2002). As psychology has become more ingrained in dealing with the problems of society, it may become necessary to rethink limitations that are fundamental to its scope of practice (DeLeon, Folen, Jennings, Willis & Wright, 1991). Psychologists usually are not trained in psychopharmacology and there is considerable disagreement as to whether the profession should enter the prescription arena. This may be an evolving issue as legislation at the state and federal levels move forward. However, as the debate continues, state legislatures agree with the psychiatrists, whereby, though psychologists agree that post-graduate training in physiology and pharmacology are needed, psychiatrists insist that medical school or nurse practitioner training is needed to be knowledgeable enough to prescribe medications (Holmes, 2003).

New Mexico has become the first state granting prescription privileges to psychologists (Holmes, 2002). This is due to the fact that New Mexico is primarily a rural state with few opportunities to access medical care. Psychologists, after proper training, receive a "conditional prescription certificate" allowing them to prescribe psychotropic medications for two years under the supervision of a licensed physician. After the initial two years, psychologists can apply for a "prescription certificate" allowing them to prescribe without supervision.

As long as laws are passed permitting psychologists' prescription privileges within the state of practice, there will be no legal issues. Ethical concerns surface over the level of training required as both the ACA (2005) and the APA (2010) subscribe to the ethical principles of beneficence and nonmaleficence.

Pharmacodynamics and Kinetics of Specific Antidepressants

In selecting an antidepressant, clinicians must take into account the patient's age, sex and medical condition (Schatzberg, Cole & DeBattista, 2010) as well as the subtype of depression. Though the claim is made that all antidepressants are effective, this is unlikely as depression is too heterogeneous to assume that all medications will work equally well for all depression types.

Mirtazapine is an effective and well-tolerated medication for the treatment of patients with moderate to severe major depression. It has the equivalent efficacy to tricyclic antidepressants while being as effective as trazodone and a faster onset of action than SSRIs (Holm & Markham, 1999).

It is a rapidly and well-absorbed medication entering the blood stream from the gastrointestinal tract after oral administration (Timmer, Sitsen & Delbressine, 2000). The pharmacokinetics of mirtazapine are dependent on gender and age as females and the elderly show higher plasma concentrations than males and young adults.

Anticholinergic events including tremors and indegestion are less common with Mirtazapine than with tricyclic antidepressants. Increased appetite and body weight are the only reported side effects when compared to other antidepressants. Mirtazapine has a low potential for negative interaction with other drugs including antipsychotics, which is of major benefit for

It is also useful in patients who suffer from anxiety symptoms and sleep disturbance (Holm & Markham, 1999). In addition, mirtazapine does not appear to be associated with sexual dysfunction or adverse cardiovascular effects (Fawcett & Barkin, 1998).

Mirtazapine is a unique addition to antidepressant medications as first-line therapy in patients with major depression and symptoms of anxiety, agitation or complaints of insomnia and as a useful alternative in depressed patients who do not adequately respond to or are intolerant of tricyclic antidepressants or SSRIs.

MAOIs and Diet

Though MOAIs were met with great anticipation as the first treatment of depression in the 1950s, that excitement quickly diminished after reports of fatal interactions with foods containing tyramine, a naturally occurring compound in cheese and other foods (Gardner, Shulman, Walker & Tailor, 1996). Seventy different foods and beverages have been identified as offending agents. Over inclusive dietary restrictions can have consequences as patients discover that some restricted foods produce no ill effects resulting in the experimentation of other foods that are dangerous such as aged cheese and tap beer.

These diets have served as an obstacle to the ready use of MAOIs, yet very little critical review of the basis for food restriction has been undertaken. An international survey of MAOI diets was conducted and foods were categorized according to frequency of restriction on the diet lists. According to this survey it was determined that only four foods warranted absolute prohibition: aged cheese, pickled fish (herring), concentrated yeast extracts and broad bean pods. While there is insufficient evidence to prohibit alcohol completely (even chianti wine) true moderation must apply (Sullivan & Shulman, 1984).

Recently, confidence in handling such reactions and in MAOI usage has increased. MAOIs treat anxiety and depression by supposedly inhibiting the inactivation of neurotransmitters. A side effect is the failure to inactivate tyramine, a potent blood vessel constrictor. Consumption of 6 mg of tyramine may produce a mild crisis whereas 10 to 25 mg may produce severe headaches with intracranial hemorrhaging and its consequences. Any food rich in aromatic amino acids can become high in tyramine if aged, contaminated, subjected to prolonged storage, or should spoilage occur (McCabe, 1986).

Managing Patients on Mood Stabilizers

Valproate is the among the most commonly used drug in the treatment of bipolar disorder as well as symptoms of aggression, agitation, and impulsivity (Schatzberg, et al., 2010). Valproate showed good efficacy relative to lithium and a number of open-label studies indicate that valproate is an effective prophylactic medication in the treatment of bipolar disorder.

It is recommended that liver tests be taken every 6-12 months, though the better the patient's response to the drug might offset the abnormal liver tests. Side effects may include pancreatitis, weight gain, thrombocytopenia (slow bleeding into the tissue causing bruising) and platelet dysfunction, sedation and alopecia (baldness in areas where the body normally grows hair). Serious drug interactions are uncommon with valproate, though it has been associated with increased serum levels of a variety of drugs (Schatzberg, et al., 2010).

Management care and patient compliance can be monitored by the use of psychotherapy in addition to pharmacotherapy. It has been demonstrated that patients receiving bipolar therapy responded quicker and with less reoccurrence both acutely and preventatively in a stable program that includeds both medication and counseling (Frank, Swartz, Mallinger, Thase, Weaver & Kupfer, 1999).

A recent study suggested that there is a linear relationship between serum valproate levels and therapeutic efficacy. However, there have also been concerns that maintenance therapy with valproate is associated with increased incidence of polycystic ovary syndrome and an erosion of bone density (Yatham, Kennedy, O'Donovan, Parikh, MacQueen, McIntyre, Sharma & Beaulieu, 2006). Therefore close monitoring of a female patient would be necessary, and medications changed should these affects occur.

Medications and Treatment for PTSD

Acute stress disorder (a precursor to PTSD) describes posttraumatic stress reactions that occur between 2 days and 4 weeks following a trauma (Bryant, Sackville, Dang, Moulds & Guthrie, 1999). A major use of this diagnosis is that it can identify many individuals in the acute phase who will subsequently develop chronic posttraumatic stress disorder (PTSD). For example, between 78% and 82% of motor vehicle accident survivors who satisfy the criteria for acute stress disorder suffer PTSD 6 months posttrauma. These patterns contrast with evidence that whereas 94% of rape victims meet the symptomatic criteria shortly after their assaults, only 47% still meet these criteria 3 months after the trauma. It appears that the specific diagnostic criteria in acute stress disorder permit a more accurate identification of those individuals who will not naturally recover from the adverse effects of their traumatic experience.

PTSD is quite common, yet often unrecognized, and leads to significant morbidity or mortality. Effective treatment often entails use of psychotropic medication. Only recently has this become apparent, and awareness of the role of drug therapy in PTSD remains limited. A number of studies have indicated efficacy for antidepressant, mood stabilizing, anticonvulsant and antianxiety medications (Davidson, 1992).

There is no guide to determine the choice of medication for PTSD; rather medications should be taken into consideration with other types of therapy and interventions such as cognitive-behavioral therapy, psycho-education, supportive therapy, and family therapy (Friedman, Donnelly and Mellman, 2003). A decision to use pharmacotherapy should be specific to the patient's individual needs, influences, concerns and preferences.

Reviews have supported the efficacy of psychotherapy for PTSD, particularly cognitive behavior therapy and, more recently, eye movement desensitization and reprocessing (Bradley, Greene, Russ, Dutra & Western, 2005). Although the short-term treatments tested in clinical trials (primarily cognitive behavior therapy) are clearly effective in reducing PTSD symptoms, research has yet to determine which patients are most likely to respond, although a combination of pharmacotherapy and psychotherapy seems to be most effective in immediate results and in short and long-term management.

Typical and Atypical Antipsychotics: Side Effects and Potency Levels

Effective treatment of psychosis involves the use of antipsychotic medication. In patients with schizophrenia, nonadherence to antipsychotic maintenance treatment leads to psychotic relapse, rehospitalization, and more frequent clinic and emergency room visits. The improved side effects of atypical antipsychotics (i.e., lower incidences of extrapyramidal symptom and tardive dyskinesia, compared with the incidences for typical antipsychotics) have led researchers to speculate that patients receiving these medications will show greater adherence. There are, however, of only a few published reports comparing typical and atypical antipsychotics in terms of medication adherence (Dolder, Lacro, Dunn & Jeste, 2002).

Clinical studies have shown clozapine to be effective in suppressing both the positive and negative symptoms of schizophrenia and to be associated with an extremely low incidence of extrapyramidal side effects. Moreover, clozapine is effective in a substantial proportion of schizophrenic patients who are intolerant of classic antipsychotic therapy. Despite its promising therapeutic potential, the high incidence of clozapine-induced agranulocytosis (a break down of white blood cells promoting vulnerability of infection) is a major factor restricting the drug's wider use in psychiatric practice (Heel, 1990). Olanzapine is a serotonin-dopamine-receptor antagonist indicated for use in the treatment of schizophrenia and other psychotic disorders. The affinity of olanzapine for neuroreceptors is similar to that of clozapine. The drug is well absorbed from the GI tract; food has no effect. However, unlike typical dopamine-receptor antagonists used for antipsychotic therapy, olanzapine is more effective in reducing the negative symptoms of schizophrenia. Unlike clozapine, olanzapine does not cause agranulocytosis. No cases of tardive dyskinesia or neuroleptic malignant syndrome have been reported. Olanzapine has been associated with slight increases in hepatic transaminases (Bever & Perry, 1998).

Pharmacotherapy and Psychotherapy in Panic Attacks and Length of Treatment

Panic disorder is common and associated with significant morbidity and dysfunction. The pharmacologic treatment of panic disorder is aimed at reducing or eliminating panic attacks, avoidance behavior, anticipatory anxiety, and comorbid conditions, and substantially improving and normalizing overall function and quality of life. Antidepressants and benzodiazepines remain the current drugs of choice of pharmacotherapy for panic disorder, although other novel medications and strategies are becoming available and may increase effective alternatives to therapeutic resources (Pollack, 2005). There has been substantial research in determining efficacious treatments for panic disorder. Pharmacotherapy and cognitive behavior therapy (CBT) have shown efficacy for panic disorder as both have enduring effects (Milrod, Leon, Busch, Rudden, Schwalberg, Clarkin, Aronson, Singer, Turchin, Klass, Graf, Teres & Shear, 2007). Psychodynamic psychotherapy is a form of psychotherapy related to psychoanalysis and though both treatments share common theoretical underpinnings, psychodynamic psychotherapy is a recognizably different treatment. Panic-focused psychodynamic psychotherapy is a brief, panic-focused psychodynamic intervention. Psychoanalytic psychotherapy has existed for more than a century, during which successful psychoanalytic treatments of patients with panic disorder have been reported (Milrod, et al., 2007). Panic-focused psychodynamic psychotherapy is a 24-session, twice-weekly (12 week), manualized psychoanalytic psychotherapy.

Pharmacodynamics and Kinetics in Stimulant Use for ADHD

Attention-deficit/hyperactivity disorder (ADHD) is the most common neurobehavioral disorder affecting children and adolescents, with persistence into adulthood causing significant lifelong impairments in academic, career, and social functioning. Neurobiological studies show that dysregulation of largely dopaminergic and noradrenergic systems in the brain stem, striatum, cerebellum, and front-cortical regions appear operant in ADHD (Wilens, 2006). Stimulant medications, such as amphetamines, have been used to treat children (those under the age of 18) with symptoms ADHD for more than 30 years. Because stimulants are drugs of potential abuse and ADHD remains a descriptive syndrome without diagnostic biological markers, controversy continues to plague the use of these medications drugs, especially for preschool-age children (Zuvekas, Vitiello & Norquist, 2006).

Short-acting stimulants control symptoms only for a few hours, creating the need for multiple daily doses of the medication. For school-age children, this make sit necessary to administer medication during school hours. Longer-acting medications often control symptoms for up to 8 hours with only one daily dose of the medication, eliminating the need for in-school administration. Some long-acting stimulants are designed to control symptoms for up to 10 to 12 hours. Although stimulants are effective in most cases, some children are unable to tolerate these medications (Lopez, 2006). Efficacy for ADHD appears related to the pharmacokinetics of the medications, which in turn is related to their pharmacodynamics.

Detox Plan for Alcohol Withdrawal

The symptoms of alcohol withdrawal range from minor symptoms as insomnia and tremors to severe complications such as withdrawal seizures and delirium. Although the alcoholic history and physical examination usually are sufficient to diagnose alcohol withdrawal syndrome, other conditions may present with similar symptoms. Most patients undergoing alcohol withdrawal can be treated safely and effectively as outpatients (Bayard, McIntyre, Hill & Woodside, 2004).

Alcohol enhances the GABA inhibitory effects on signal-receiving neurons, thereby lowering neuronal activity, leading to an increase in excitatory glutamate receptors. Over time, tolerance occurs as GABA receptors become less responsive to neurotransmitters, and more alcohol is needed to produce the same inhibitory effect. When alcohol is suddenly removed, the number of excitatory glutamate receptors remains, but without the suppressive GABA effect. This situation leads to the signs and symptoms of alcohol withdrawal (Asplund, Aaronson & Aaronson, 2004). Pharmacologic treatment involves the use of medications that are cross-tolerant with alcohol. Benzodiazepines may be administered on a fixed or symptom-triggered schedule. Carbamazepine is an appropriate alternative to a benzodiazepine in the outpatient treatment with mild to moderate alcohol withdrawal symptoms. Treatment of alcohol withdrawal should be followed by treatment for alcohol dependence.

Benzodiazepines are preferred medications for alcohol withdrawal, with choices among different drugs as guided by duration of action, rapidity of onset, and cost. Dosage should be individualized, based on withdrawal severity measured by withdrawal scales, and history of withdrawal seizures (Mayo-Smith, 1997).

Symptom-triggered therapy individualizes treatment, and decreases both treatment duration and the amount of benzodiazepine used. It is as efficacious as standard fixed-schedule therapy for alcohol withdrawal.

Patients with mild to moderate alcohol withdrawal symptoms and no serious psychiatric or medical comorbidities can be safely treated in the outpatient setting while patients with moderate withdrawal should receive pharmacotherapy to treat their symptoms and reduce their risk of seizures and delirium during outpatient detoxification (Alspund et al., 2004). Benzodiazepines are the treatment of choice for alcohol withdrawal, however, healthy individuals with mild-to-moderate alcohol withdrawal, carbamazepine has many advantages making it a first-line treatment for properly selected patients.

Lamotrigine

Lamotrigine is an antiepileptic drug which is believed to suppress seizures by inhibiting the release of excitatory neurotransmitters. Efficacy has been demonstrated for lamotrigine as add-on therapy to existing treatments in patients with resistant partial seizures. Secondarily generalized tonic and clonic spasms respond well to lamotrigine, and there is first-hand evidence of improvement in patients with primary genralized seizures. Seizure control has been maintained in patients who have continued to receive lamotrigine as monotherapy after discontinuation of other medications (Goa, Ross, Chrisp, 1993). Lamotrigine also inhibits the onset of new mood episodes in the treatment of bipolar disorder and there is evidence that it may also be effective in the treatment of bipolar depression (Schatzberg, et al., 2010).

Lamotrigine appears well tolerated in the longer term, in fact, compared to other approved maintenance treatments of bipolar, lamotrigine is less likely to be attributed to weight gain. Common side effects include dizziness, headaches, double vision, unsteadiness, sedation, and rash in up to 10% of patients. Influences of valproic acid and enzyme-inducing anti-epileptics on lamotrigine eliminate necessary dosage modifications as lamotrigine has little apparent influence on the pharmacokinetics of other drugs, although it may increase plasma concentrations of the active metabolite of carbamazepine during co-administration. Thus, lamotrigine permits improved seizure control in some patients with resistant partial seizures, and may prove to be especially effective in secondarily generalized tonic and clonic spasms (Goa et al., 1993).

Like all mood stabilizers, Lamotrigine should be gradually tapered rather than suddenly discontinued. Although no symptoms have been attributed with the discontinuation of lamotrigine, seizures are occasionally reported as with the abrupt stoppage of any anticonvulsant. Alcohol can worsen the sedation of lamotrigine, however, the interactions of OTC drugs are unknown (Schatzberg, et al., 2010).

References

Alspund, C. A., Aaronson, J. W., Aaronson, H. E. (2004). 3 Regimens for alcohol withdrawal and detoxification. *The Journal of Family Practice*. Vol. 53, No. 7.

American Counseling Association (2005) *ACA Code of Ethics*. Retrieved from http://www.counseling.org/Resources/CodeOfEthics/TP/Home/CT2.aspx

American Psychological Association (2010). *Ethical Principles of Psychologists and Code of Conduct*. Retrieved from **http://www.apa.org/ethics/code/index.aspx**

Bayard, M., McIntyre, J., Hill, K. R. & Woodside, J. (2004). Alcohol withdrawal syndrome. *American Family Physician*. Vol. 69, No. 6, 1443-1450.

Bever, K. A., Perry, P. J. (1998). Olanzapine: a serotonin-dopamine-receptor antagonist for antipsychotic therapy. *American Journal of Health-System Pharmacy*. Vol. 55, Issue 10, 1003-1016.

Bradley, R., Greene, J., Russ, E., Dutra, L., Western, D. (2005). A Multidimensional Meta-Analysis of Psychotherapy for PTSD. *American Journal of Psychiatry*. Vol. 162, 214-227.

Bryant, R. A., Sackville, T., Dang, S. T., Moulds, M. & Guthrie, R. (1999). Treating acute stress disorder: An evaluation of cognitive behavior therapy and supportive counseling techniques. *The American Journal of Psychiatry*. Vol. 156, No. 11 1780-1786.

Davidson, J. (1992). Drug therapy of post-traumatic stress disorder. *The British Journal of Psychiatry*. Vol. 160, 309-314.

DeLeon, P. H., Folen, R. A., Jennings, F. L., Willis, D. J. & Wright, R. H. (1991). The case for prescription privileges: A logical evolution of professional practice. *Journal of Clinical Child Psychology*. Vol. 20, Issue 3, 254-267.

Dolder, C. R., Lacro, J. P., Dunn, L.B., & Jeste, D. V. (2002). Antipsychotic medication adherence: Is there a difference between typical and atypical agents? *The American Journal of Psychiatry.* Vol. 159, No. 1, 103-108.

Fawcett, J. & Barkin, R. L. (1998). Review of the results from clinical studies on the efficacy, safety and tolerability of mirtazapine for the treatment of patients with major depression. *Journal of Affective Disorders.* Vol. 51, Issue 3, 267-285.

Frank, E., Swartz, H. A., Mallinger, A. G., Thase, M. E., Weaver, E. V. & Kupfer, D. J. (1999). Adjunctive psychotherapy for bipolar disorder: Effects of changing treatment modality. *Journal of Abnormal Psychology.* Vol. 108, No. 4, 579-587.

Friedman, M. J., Donnelly, C. L., Mellman, T. A. (2003). Pharmacotherapy for PTSD. *Psychiatric Annals.* Vol. 33, No 1.

Gardner, D. M., Shulman, K. I., Walker, S. E. & Tailor, S. A. N. (1996). The making of a user friendly MAOI diet. *Journal of Clinical Psychiatry.* Vol. 57, 99-104.

Goa, K. L., Ross, S. R. Chrisp, P. (1993). Lamotrigine, a review of its pharmacological properties and clinical efficacy in epilepsy. *Drugs.* Vol. 46, No. 1, 152-176.

Heel, F. A. (1990). Clozapine. A review of its pharmacological properties, and therapeutic use in schizophrenia. *Drugs.* Vol. 40. No.5, 722-747.

Holm, K. J. & Markham, A. (1999). Mirtazapine: A review of its use in major depression. *Drugs.* Vol. 57, No. 4, 607-631.

Holmes, L. (2002). New Mexico allows psychologists to prescribe. *Mental Health.* Retrieved from http://mentalhealth.about.com/library/weekly/aa031202a.htm

Holmes, L. (2003). Should psychologists prescribe medications? *Health's Disease and Condition.* Retrieved from

Lopez, F. (2006). ADHD: New pharmalogical treatments on the horizon. *Journal of Developmental & Behavioral Pediatrics.* Vol. 27, Issue 5, 410-416.

Mayo-Smith, M. F. (1997). Pharmalogical management of alcohol withdrawal. *Journal of the American Medical Association.* Vol. 278, No. 2, 144-151.

McCabe, B. J. (1986). Dietary tyramine and other pressor amines in MAOI regimens: a review. *Journal of American Diet Association.* Vol. 86, No. 8, 1059-1064.

Milrod, B., Leon, A. C., Busch, F., Rudden, M., Schwalberg, M., Clarkin, J., Aronson, A., Singer, M., Turchin, W., Klass, E. T., Graf, E., Teres, J. J. & Shear, M. K. (2007). A randomized controlled clinical trial of psychoanalytic, psychotherapy for panic disorder. *The American Journal of Psychiatry.* Vol. 164, No. 2, 265-272.

Pollack, M. H. (2005). The pharmacotherapy of panic disorder. *The Journal of Clinical Psychiatry.* Vol. 66, Suppl 4, 23-27.

Schatzberg, A.F., Cole, J.O. & DeBattista, C. (2010). *Manual of clinical psychopharmacology* (7th ed.). Washington, DC: American Psychiatric Publishing, Inc.

Sullivan, E. A. & Shulman, K. I. (1984). Diet and monoamine oxidase inhibitors: A re-examination. *Canadian Journal of Psychiatry.* Vol. 29, No. 3, 707-711

Trimmer, C. J., Sitsen, J. M., Delbressine, L. P. (2000). Clinical pharmacokinetics of mirtazapine. *Clinical Pharmacokinetics.* Vol. 38, No. 6, 461-474.

Walker, K. (2002). An ethical dilemma: Clinical psychologists prescribing psychotropic medications. *Issues In Mental Health Nursing.* Vol. 23, No. 1, 17-29.

Wilens, T. E. (2006). Mechanism of action of agents used in attention-deficit/hyperactivity disorder. *The Journal of Clinical Psychiatry.* Vol. 67, Suppl 6, 32-37.

Yatham, L. N., Kennedy, S. H., O'Donovan, C., Parikh, S. V., Macqueen, G., McIntyre, R. S., Sharma, V. & Beaulieu, S. (2006). Canadian network for mood and anxiety treatments guidelines for the management of patents with bipolar disorder: Update 2007. *Bipolar Disorders*. Vol. 8, Issue 6, 721-739.

Zuvekas, S. H., Vitiello, B., Norquist, G. S. (2006). Recent trends in stimulant medication use among U. S. children. *The American Journal of Psychiatry*. Vol. 163, No. 4, 579-585.

Expanding the Role of Psychology: Prescription Privileges

Though psychotherapy and psychological testing are the roles more attributed to clinical psychologists, more have begun advocating for legally sanctioned prescription authority in their professional roles. This is partly due to the decline in reimbursement as more psychiatric disorders require medications (Walker, 2002). As psychology has become more ingrained in dealing with the problems of society, it may become necessary to rethink limitations that are fundamental to its scope of practice (DeLeon, Folen, Jennings, Willis & Wright, 1991). Psychologists usually are not trained in psychopharmacology and there is considerable disagreement as to whether the profession should enter the prescription arena. This may be an evolving issue as legislation at the state and federal levels move forward. However, as the debate continues, state legislatures agree with the psychiatrists, whereby, though psychologists agree that post-graduate training in physiology and pharmacology are needed, psychiatrists insist that medical school or nurse practitioner training is needed to be knowledgeable enough to prescribe medications (Holmes, 2003).

Currently, however, and in anticipation of legislative law permitting such practices, the APA is offering training through a series of Educational DVD series to train psychologists in psychopharmacology (APA, 2006). This 14 hour series is designed for psychologists who wish to gain prescription privileges, to prepare for the PEP (Psychopharmacology Examination for Psychologists) test. The DVD series also help to keep counselors up to date in the area of psychopharmacology, as many therapists see clients who may currently be on medication for various disorders.

Meanwhile, the APA makes an argument for prescription practices citing various psychological disorders that require, or will require, a combination of pharmacotherapy and psychotherapy, depressive disorders taking the lead. According to Williams-Nickelson (2000), depression with psychological etiology will be the second leading cause of non-fatal disabling effects of disease by 2020.

CAPP (Committee for the Advancement of Professional Practice) identifies the following prerequisites to participate in post-doctoral training in psychopharmacology:

1. A doctoral degree in psychology.
2. Current state license as a psychologist.
3. Five years of practice as a "health service provider" psychologist as defined by state law or the APA.

Then actual training, which includes 300 hours in the following didactic and clinical components:

- Neuroscience
- Clinical and Research Pharmacology and Psychopharmacology
- Physiology and Pathophysiology
- Physical and Laboratory Assessment
- Clinical Pharmacotherapeutics

A minimum of 100 patients should be seen by the psychologist-trainee

Currently there are three different programs for a psychopharmacology certificate or degree (Levant & Shapiro, 2002):

1. Postdoctoral programs that award certificates and/or continuing education credit

2. Postdoctoral programs that award master's degrees in psychopharmacology

3. A predoctoral program that awards joint psychology and nursing degrees

References

APA (2006). Division 55: Training and continuing education. *American Society for the Advancement of Psychopharmacology*. Retrieved from http://www.division55.org/

DeLeon, P. H., Folen, R. A., Jennings, F. L., Willis, D. J. & Wright, R. H. (1991). The case for prescription privileges: A logical evolution of professional practice. *Journal of Clinical Child Psychology*. Vol. 20, Issue 3, 254-267.

Holmes, L. (2003). Should psychologists prescribe medications? *Health's Disease and Condition*. Retrieved from **http://mentalhealth.about.com/cs/psychopharmacology/a/prescribe.htm**

Levant, R. F. & Shapiro, A. E. (2002). Training psychologists in clinical psychopharmacology. *The Journal of Clinical Psychology*. Vol. 58, No. 6, 611-615.

Walker, K. (2002). An ethical dilemma: Clinical psychologists prescribing psychotropic medications. *Issues In Mental Health Nursing*. Vol. 23, No. 1, 17-29.

Williams-Nickelson, C. (2000). Prescription privileges for psychologists: Implications for students. *Prescription Privileges Fact Sheet: What Students Should Know About the APA's Pursuit of Prescription Privileges for Psychologists (RxP)*. APAGS Newsletter.

Research

Analyzing Research

There is a saying, "Practice what you preach." In counseling it is more, "Practice what you learn," and if that is the case, what is learned must be data than can be critically analyzed so make sure it is valid to a client's condition. Ethical consideration must be given to all data analyzed, and research compiled. The ACA Code of Ethics (2005) specifically states that all research be done in accordance with ethical principles.

According to Sheperis, Young and Daniels (2010), one of the most serious infractions of unethical behavior is the researcher who designs a study and collects data, then publishes misrepresenting research which can lead to client harm and even death. One of the guiding principles of counseling is nonmaleficence, whether it is in the counseling forum or the research arena. Every client has the right to know what the study entails, what the perceived outcomes are, and more importantly, the risks involved.

Therapy should always adhere to empirically based research and evidence based practice (Laureate, 2010). This makes us more effective as counselors, being able to meet clients where they are. And as counselors, we are driven by the best research and practices available in treatment methods, evidence-based assessment, consultation, education and referral. This can only enhance the therapeutic relationship as clients come to count on our accuracy in defining and diagnosing the concern and treatment plan.

When we think of cultures, it is easy to lump the term into race, or ethnicity. But culture is defined by individuals who share similar characteristics, events, socioeconomic status, environment and more (Sheperis, et al., 2010).

In California, for example, there is the "surfing" culture. Though individually the surfers may come from different socioeconomic standings, and relate to different environmental situations, they all share that same culture when on the sand and water. Hence the term multicultural, which most of us are.

Life's ultimate "multi-task," we share a variety of cultures within our perceived major culture, and trying to place a "colorful" label on it, does not do it, nor ourselves, justice.

References

American Counseling Association. (2005). *ACA Code of Ethics.* Retrieved from http://www.counseling.org/Resources/CodeOfEthics/TP/Home/CT2.aspx

Laureate Education, Inc. (2010). *Research and Program Evaluation.* Baltimore, MD. Author.

Sheperis, C. J., Young, J. S., & Daniels, M. H. (2010). *Counseling research: Quantitative, qualitative, and mixed methods.* Upper Saddle River, NJ: Pearson Education, Inc.

Counselor as Scholar-Practitioner

Tomas Ferraro

Walden University

Counselor as Scholar-Practitioner

The Role of Research

Research has many values and functions within the counseling profession, and none is more prevalent than that of the managed care system. More and more HMOs and other managed health care organizations are demanding prove of treatment before approving payment for such treatment (R. L. Hayes & Dagley, 1996; Kent & Hersen, 2000; Sanchez & Turner, 2003). Therapists must prove that the treatments are researched based and empirically sound (Crane & McArthur, 2002; Kent & Hersen, 2000), and not based solely on the professional "opinion" of the counselor. The treatment offered must be supported by data indicating a desired outcome (S. C. Hayes, Barlow & Nelson-Gray, 1999; Kent & Hersen, 2000).

Counselors are now being trained to be scientist-practitioners in order to better appreciate, understand and interpret the data presented to them (Sexton, 1999), thereby translating it to healthcare organizations in an effort to maintain credibility to treatment programs. This also helps counselors explain diagnoses and treatment plans to clients as a part of the therapeutic alliance. Research helps therapists to better understand the events and challenges of counseling producing better and inclusive ways of working with clients resulting in positive outcomes (Sheperis, Young & Daniels, 2010).

Though research is important to validate treatment with managed care, the most important reason for research is to improve the ability to describe, predict, or explain clients' characteristics and actions to better diagnose and provide treatment plans conducive to the betterment of the clients (Gall, Gall & Borg, 2006; Sexton, 1996). Research, more than likely, would also help

The Scholar-Practitioner

The term scholar is associated with one who learns. According to Dr. Patton (Laureate, 2010), a scholar studies how the world is and takes note of the happenings in the world and why things happen the way they do. Research is more analytical, viewing the world more systematically, and using methodologies to better explain why things happen as they do.

The scholar is involved with research, reviewing it critically asking the question, "How were the findings discovered?" and "What makes those findings valid?" The scholar is also involved in research just as the scientist-practitioner is.

The practitioner (Laureate, 2010) is dedicated to helping people and making a difference in the world based upon the findings of the scholar. This might be interpreted as a "look before you leap" scenario, whereby the credibility of the therapist is knowledge based on the most current and proven findings available. The scholar-practitioner also follows up with the clientele in the effort to understand what changes, if any, have occurred as a result of therapy, and discusses satisfaction rates with the clients.

This, in itself, is another type of research to see if the counselor is being effective with clients, and if diagnoses were accurately targeted, and treatment plans successful.

The scholar-practitioner is dedicated to exploring changes, which are necessary to get better results (Laureate, 2010). And though practitioners may not always be full-time researchers or scholars, they will always be full-time consumers of research, looking for that better and more updated way to help clients achieve greater and more successful outcomes with their treatment plans.

As consumers we research what products are most efficient while being cost effective. We research what foods are nutritious, though in America this research seems to be largely ignored, what technologies will better enhance our lives, and what we find entertaining. Research is a part of everyday life and must be used in counseling as scholar practitioners to enhance our therapeutic skills to the betterment of our clients.

References

Crane, R. D. & McArthur, H. (2002). Meeting the needs of evidence-based practice in family therapy: Developing the scientist-practitioner model. In Sheperis, C. J., Young, J. S., & Daniels, M. H. (2010). *Counseling research: Quantitative, qualitative, and mixed methods.* Upper Saddle River, NJ: Pearson Education, Inc.

Gall, M. D., Gall, P. J., Borg, W. R. (2006). *Educational research: An introduction.* In Sheperis, C. J., Young, J. S., & Daniels, M. H. (2010). *Counseling research: Quantitative, qualitative, and mixed methods.* Upper Saddle River, NJ: Pearson Education, Inc.

Hays, R. L. & Dagley, J. C. (1996). Restructuring school counselor education. In Sheperis, C. J., Young, J. S., & Daniels, M. H. (2010). *Counseling research: Quantitative, qualitative, and mixed methods.* Upper Saddle River, NJ: Pearson Education, Inc.

Hays, S. C., Barlow, D. H. & Nelson-Gray, R. O. (1999). *The scientist-practitioner: Research and accountability in the age of managed care.* In Sheperis, C. J., Young, J. S., & Daniels, M. H. (2010). *Counseling research: Quantitative, qualitative, and mixed methods.* Upper Saddle River, NJ: Pearson Education, Inc.

Kent, A. J. & Hersen, M. (2000). An overview of managed health care: Past, present & future. In Sheperis, C. J., Young, J. S., & Daniels, M. H. (2010). *Counseling research: Quantitative, qualitative, and mixed methods.* Upper Saddle River, NJ: Pearson Education, Inc.

Laureate Education, Inc. (2010). *Research and Program Evaluation.* Baltimore, MD. Author.

Sanchez, L. M. & Turner, S. M. (2003). Practicing psychology in the area of managed care: Implications for practice and training. In Sheperis, C. J., Young, J. S., & Daniels, M. H. (2010). *Counseling research: Quantitative, qualitative, and mixed methods.* Upper Saddle River, NJ:

Sexton, T. L. (1999). *Evidenced based counseling: Implications for counseling practice, preparation and professionalism.* In Sheperis, C. J., Young, J. S., & Daniels, M. H. (2010). *Counseling research: Quantitative, qualitative, and mixed methods.* Upper Saddle River, NJ: Pearson Education, Inc.

Sheperis, C. J., Young, J. S., & Daniels, M. H. (2010). *Counseling research: Quantitative, qualitative, and mixed methods.* Upper Saddle River, NJ: Pearson Education, Inc.

Evidence-Based Practice

Tomas Ferraro

Walden University

Evidence-Based Practice

Case Study

This particular case study presents a 51-year-old African American woman, Annique, who is suffering from major depressive disorder, dating back to adolescence. Her family history includes close relatives who suffer from unipolar and bipolar II mood disorders. She is taking antidepressant medications monitored by a private psychiatrist. She has initiated psychotherapy due to dependent personality disorder and menopausal complaints detracting from the quality of her life and relationships (Norcross, Hogan and Koocher, 2008).

Critical Elements

The critical elements are:

- Major depressive disorder- 296.31 (DSM-IV, p. 369). Major depressive disorder is associated with a high risk of suicide, therefore Standard B.2.a. (ACA Code of Ethics, 2005) must be a consideration within the counseling practice.

- Family History of Bipolar II- 296.89 (DSM-IV, p. 392).

- Dependent Personality Disorder- 301.6 (DSM-IV, p. 721). This disorder is characterized by an excessive need to be taken care of, submissive and clinging behaviors, and fears of separation. The client may have difficulty in making everyday decisions without an excessive amount of advice from others, including the therapist.

- Potential for Drug Abuse with Anti-depressants.

Research Studies

According to Kessler, Berglund, Demler, Merikangas and Walters (2005), approximately 17-18% of the U.S. population experiences a Major Depressive Disorder (MDD). One aspect of MDD is the likelihood for recurrence following each successive episode. Personality disorder is associated with an especially pernicious course of MDD; this course is marked by high levels of functional impairment, high levels of emotional dysregulation, poor social functioning, and low levels of general well being. Additional studies have demonstrated that depressed individuals with comorbid personality disorders compared to depressed individuals without personality disorders have experienced greater rates and more frequent recurrences of MDD (Craighead, Sheets, Craighead and Madsen, (2011).

One of the most consistent and enduring findings in research on major depressive disorder (MDD) is a higher prevalence of MDD in women than in men. This gender difference appears in early adolescence, reaches a rate of approximately 2:1 by mid- adolescence, and persists at least through the end of midlife. Gender differences in rates of MDD have been found cross culturally and cannot be accounted for by differences in treatment seeking (Harkness, Alavi, Slavich, Monroe, Gotlib and Bagby (2010). Investigators have reported that women may experience events that have particular relevance for the etiology of depression. Women's need for affiliation, mediated by hormonal changes at the pubertal transition, renders women particularly vulnerable to developing MDD in the face of interpersonal events. Consistent with this formulation, adult women report higher rates of life events involving their social networks prior to the onset of MDD. The implication here is that the events that cluster in the period prior to MDD onset represent the stressors that were most central in triggering that onset.

Ethical, Legal and Socio-Cultural Considerations

One ethical consideration was already discussed earlier as those with MDD have a higher suicidal rate. Therefore a counselor need take that into consideration when papers are signed regarding confidentiality.

When a counselor is engaged in research he must do so with the utmost responsibility and integrity, taking ethics, laws and cultural differences into account. Research ethics is defined as "the study or science of right and wrong — of what one ought to do when confronted with conflicting values or obligations," (Steneck, 2003, p. 240). Irresponsible conduct, within research, can have adverse and even deadly outcomes. An example is given whereby a counselor is conducting research on clients with depression. She breaks the group in two giving one group traditional counseling and medication, while the other receives only counseling. Though it become apparent that there are those in the counseling only group who need medication, she continues with the experiment, subjecting those clients to a continuous interruption in their lives and the possibility of suicide (Sheperis, Young and Daniels, 2010). Therefore, in Annique's case, and as she is already seeing a psychiatrist about her medications, that should not be interfered with, but rather the counselor should be in communication with the psychiatrist about all phases of her treatment.

As Annique is an African American, certain cultural issues need to be defined in how the counselor will approach this client, gain a therapeutic alliance, and enter into a treatment plan that is mutually acceptable. The first thing a counselor must do is to define what culture is. Sheperis, et al. (2010), define culture as the "totality of the human experience for social

Culture is defined by biological, psychological, historical, and political events; and includes behaviors, attitudes, feelings, and cognitions related to our identities living in the world.

Research designs centered around multicultural populations are defined as qualitative and quantitative. Some of the research may need to be done ahead of time as qualitative research involves large sample sizes and quantification of constructs allowing for statistical control and generalizability across various populations. Qualitative research involves a natural setting to understand the phenomenon of interest and provide rich descriptions to give voice to multiple perspectives (Sheperis, et al., 2010).

Multicultural competence is the ability to understand, identify and relate to the uniqueness of the client and with regard to their individual cultural perspective.

In the case of Annique, we are dealing with culture, gender and age in regards to her conditions of Major Depressive Disorder and Dependent Personality Disorder. We need to keep close watch and accurate records as to how she responds to treatment, encouraging her to add as much input from as to her own diagnosis, to be successful.

References

American Counseling Association. (2005). *ACA Code of Ethics*. Retrieved from http://www.counseling.org/Resources/CodeOfEthics/TP/Home/CT2.aspx

American Psychiatric Association. (2000). *Diagnostic and statistical manual of mental disorders* (4th ed.). Washington, DC: Author.

Craighead, W. E., Sheets, E. S., Craighead, L.W., Madsen, J.W. (2011). Recurrence of MDD: A prospective study of personality pathology and cognitive distortions. *Personality Disorders: Theory, Research and Treatment*. Vol. 2, No. 2, 83-97.

Harkness, K. L., Alvi, N., Slavich, G. M., Monroe, S. M., Gotlib, I. H., Bagby, R. M. (2010). Gender differences in life events prior to onset of major depressive disorder: The moderating effect of age. *Journal of Abnormal Psychology*. Vol. 119, No. 4, 791-803.

Kessler, R. C., Berglund, P., Demler, O., Jin, R., Merikangas, K. R., & Walters, E. E. (2005). Lifetime prevalence and age-of-onset distributions of *DSM–IV* disorders in the National Comorbidity Survey Replication. In Craighead, W. E., Sheets, E. S., Craighead, L.W., Madsen, J.W. (2011). Recurrence of MDD: A prospective study of personality pathology and cognitive distortions. *Personality Disorders: Theory, Research and Treatment*. Vol. 2, No. 2, 83-97.

Norcross, J., Hogan, T., & Koocher, G. (2008). *Clinician's guide to evidence-based practices: Mental health and the addictions*. New York, NY: Oxford Press.

Sheperis, C. J., Young, J. S., & Daniels, M. H. (2010). *Counseling research: Quantitative, qualitative, and mixed methods*. Upper Saddle River, NJ: Pearson Education, Inc.

Steneck, N. H. (2003). The role of professional societies in promoting integrity in research. In Sheperis, C. J., Young, J. S., & Daniels, M. H. (2010). *Counseling research: Quantitative, qualitative,*

Statistics for Counseling and Program Evaluation

Tomas Ferraro

Walden University

Statistics for Counseling and Program Evaluation

The Study

The study I chose was, *Evaluating Expectations About Negative Emotional States of Aggressive Boys Using Bayesian Model Selection* (van de Schoot, Hoijtink, Mulder, Van Aken, Orobio de Castro, Meeus and Romeijn, 2011). Having been a teacher for 30 years, and having witnessed aggressive behavior, especially in boys, this study resonated with me.

The study, itself, had to do with introducing a negative emotional state in aggressive boys who would score higher than non-aggressive boys.

A "null" hypothesis was used when boys were originally tested, but this hypothesis proved that the groups were not tested properly due to inequality constraints between the groups. Hence, the researchers set out, using the Bayesian model to test their own hypothesis for the study.

Statistical Concepts

1. Split-half Reliability: Reliability of a test is measured by splitting the test in half and correlating the scores on each half, then correcting for length (Sheperis, Young & Daniels, 2010). To prove the validity of the hypotheses being used in the above study, van de Schoot, et al. (2011), use this concept to prove that two of the hypotheses used are valid and in conjunction with each other.

2. Types of Distributions: van de Schoot, et al. (2011) then ran analyses for different populations using the following scales to determine what types of populations "housed" the most aggressive boys.

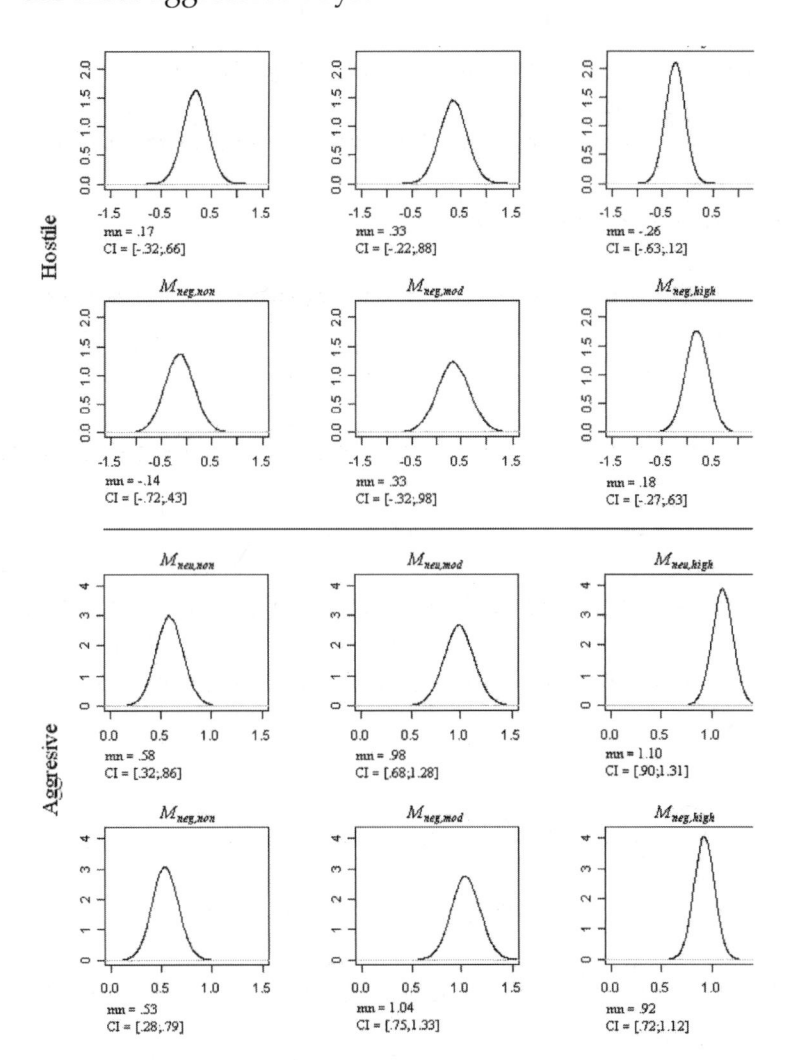

3. Means and Variance: The researchers created data in such a way that the means and variance correspond exactly to the population values.

Rationale for Selecting the Identified Statistical Concepts

Within the research it is shown that utilizing and comparing different hypotheses and statistical concepts can help prove the accuracy of the research. Using the three statistical concepts above, not only do the researchers help to prove the reliance of the data gathered, but the accurate conclusions of the hypotheses presented.

The rationale for the selections are based on the need for accuracy within the reliability of using the split-half procedure, as longer tests are more reliable (Lee, 2010). Depending on what is being researched, distribution can play an enormous role on the outcome and reliability of the research. See Ethical, Legal and Socio-cultural below.

Finally, the data needs to come to terms with the mathematical equations presented my mean and variance to see if the research is applicable to a majority of the population within the distribution.

Appropriateness for Counseling Research and Program Evaluation

In this article, the researchers show that using comparative statistics and a diverse population spread, they can accurately draw to conclusions about aggressive boys and their behavior. This research will benefit school counselors as they evaluate their programs to offset such behavior at school and within the classroom.

Ethical, Legal and Socio-cultural Considerations

Though legal considerations for the research could not be found, consideration for socio-cultural factors must be taken into account. Within the research article, the exact population of the disbursement was not noted. Hence, it is not known if the research was conducted on a cross-cultural population, or on a particular set where race, and socio-economic conditions were similar. Ethical considerations must be taken into account (Standard A.2.c., and B.1.a., ACA Code of Ethics, 2005), when gathering and interpreting data in this type of research. Socio-economics, race, environment, and culture would play an important role in the outcome of the data.

References

American Counseling Association. (2005). *ACA Code of Ethics.* Retrieved from

http://www.counseling.org/Resources/CodeOfEthics/TP/Home/CT2.aspx

Lee, S. M. (2010). Basic Statistical Concepts and Descriptive Statistics. In Sheperis, C. J., Young, J. S., & Daniels, M. H. (2010). *Counseling research: Quantitative, qualitative, and mixed methods.* Upper Saddle River, NJ: Pearson Education, Inc.

Sheperis, C. J., Young, J. S., & Daniels, M. H. (2010). *Counseling research: Quantitative, qualitative, and mixed methods.* Upper Saddle River, NJ: Pearson Education, Inc.

van de Schoot, R., Hoijtink, H., Mulder, J., Van Aken, M. A. G., Orobio de Castro, B., Meeus, W. & Romeijn, J. W. (2011). Evaluating expectations about negative emotional states of aggressive boys using Bayesian model selection. *Developmental Psychology.* Vol. 47, No. 1, 203-212.

Quantitative Designs

Tomas Ferraro

Walden University

Quantitative Designs

Pretest-Posttest Control Group

Participants in the study are randomly assigned a treatment group. All groups, treatment and control, are given a pretest. The treatment group receives some kind of intervention, while the control group receives none. A posttest is given after the intervention and all groups are compared based on the posttest. The primary benefit for giving a pretest to both groups is to assure equality at the beginning of the research.

Solomon Four Group

Again, the participants are randomly assigned to one of four groups; two control groups, one of which gets both a pre and posttest, and two treatment groups, one of which gets both tests. After the intervention given to only the treatment groups, a posttest is given to all four groups and all four are compared accordingly.

Similarities and Differences

All participants from both research groups were randomly assigned to a group and received a posttest. Not all received a pretest or intervention before being administered the posttest.

Strengths and Weaknesses

The strength of the pretest-posttest model is the assurance of equality at the onset of the study between treatment and control groups. The weakness comes whereby the participants who took the pretest may have some knowledge as to how to answer the posttest so progress appears to have been made.

The Solomon Four model is a strong design because it ensures equality of groups, and the researcher can determine whether or not a pretest is affecting change as opposed to the actual intervention.

Insight and/or Conclusion

Though participants may gain some insight as to what may be on the posttest, the researcher needs to make sure that all participants have been measured prior to treatment. Measurement of growth can only occur if one knows where the beginning was. Initial random selection for groups is fine, but modifications may need to be made after the pretest as to guarantee that proper intervention is reaching the right participants; otherwise the study may be skewed.

Ethical, Legal and Socio-cultural Considerations

Counselors and researchers must abide by the ethical codes as set down by the ACA Code of Ethics (2005). In regards to research, this includes Standards G.1.a., b., d., e., f., g., all of G.2. and 3. Some incorporate legal issues when working with minors and/or the handicapped. Consideration must be given to those with limited education, income or cultural differences.

A limited education may need further and detailed explanations of the research and the participants' role in it. A limited income may be a precursor of a participant involved in research for the wrong reasons and potentially skewing the results while thinking that is what the head counselor wants. Finally, cultural considerations in regards to the overall understanding and language of the research, as well as, moral, religious, and other cultural concerns as addressed in Standard B.1.a. (ACA Code of Ethics, 2005).

References

American Counseling Association. (2005). *ACA Code of Ethics*. Retrieved from
    http://www.counseling.org/Resources/CodeOfEthics/TP/Home/CT2.aspx

Sheperis, C. J., Young, J. S., & Daniels, M. H. (2010). *Counseling research: Quantitative, qualitative, and mixed methods*. Upper Saddle River, NJ: Pearson   Education, Inc.

Survey Development

Tomas Ferraro

Walden University

Survey Development

Self-efficacy

Since the working definition of efficacy is the ability to produce an intended or desired outcome, my working definition of self-efficacy will be a person's perception of their own abilities in relationship to online versus land-based counseling graduate degree programs.

According to Lent, Hoffman, Hill, Treistman, Mount and Singley (2006), research on counselor self-efficacy (CSE) has become an important part of counselor training and development over the past two decades. Hence developing a survey to measure the confidence levels a student has about themselves and their relationship to the educational program they are involved in, will help professors understand the concerns and confidence students have of land-based and electronic instruction.

The Survey

The following 10 item survey was constructed to measure the self-efficacy of counseling students involved in one of the afore mentioned programs. The design chosen was the Cross-Sectional Survey Design. Data from this survey is collected at only one point in time (Sheperis, Young & Daniels, 2010), and includes surveys comparing two or more groups, and surveys to evaluate programs. As the survey is designed to evaluate the self-efficacy between two groups and their respective programs, a survey designed to reflect both seems appropriate.

Self-administered questionnaires will be used for both groups; however, the land-based groups will be given a pencil and paper questionnaire, while online students will be given an

The Questionnaire

The questionnaire is a 10 item construct with a scale from 1 to 5. 1 = Strongly disagree, 2 = Disagree, 3 = Neutral, 4 = Agree, and 5 = Strongly Agree. The questions range from ease of access, to instructor interaction, to time spent on assignments.

The questionnaire is as follows:

Name: _____ Class: _____

1. I have enough time to research and write my assignments. 1 2 3 4 5
2. I have adequate interaction with my instructor. 1 2 3 4 5
3. I understand the assignments given and how to complete them. 1 2 3 4 5
4. I am confident my questions will be answered thoroughly. 1 2 3 4 5
5. I am confident in my ability to turn my assignments in on time. 1 2 3 4 5
6. I have the resources I need to help me succeed. 1 2 3 4 5
7. I enjoy the program I have chosen. 1 2 3 4 5
8. I still have time for a personal life. 1 2 3 4 5
9. The program gives me the opportunity to interact with classmates. 1 2 3 4 5
10. The program is designed to help me succeed. 1 2 3 4 5

Data Design and Analysis

In this design, I felt it was appropriate to ask for names, as if too may 1s and 2s began to appear for a student, the instructor may want to do some counseling as to the problem this specific student is having. The questions were designed to be positive in nature, allowing the

- That all online students have computers and internet access in good operating condition so as to meet the demands and requirements of an online program.
- That all land-based students have adequate transportation as to get to classes in a timely manner.
- That all students have access and the ability to retrieve information from various sources as required by the program, classes and instructors.
- That all students know and practice APA formatting for papers.

Since the land-based survey will be pencil and paper and the online survey will come in electronically, I did not see the need to distinguish between them on the survey itself.

Rationale

Students worry about getting assignments in on time, if their questions are being addressed and answered in a timely manner by the instructor, and if resources are adequate and readily available to help them succeed. Hence many of the questions center on those concerns.

Challenges

The challenge in constructing a survey of this nature is in the limitation of the items. Reliability of a measurement tool, including surveys, can come from the length of the instrument (Laureate, 2010). If the survey was longer, the results could explore more specifically where students were high in self-efficacy and where they might be questioning themselves and their lack of self-efficacy.

For example, I would give myself high marks in self-efficacy when it comes to the art, and counselor/client therapeutic relationship of counseling, but lower when it comes to the research and statistical knowledge of counseling.

References

Laureate Education, Inc. (Executive Producer). (2010). *Assessment in counseling and education.* Baltimore, MD: Author.

Lent, R. W., Hoffman, M. A., Hill, C. E., Treistman, D., Mount, M., Singley, D. (2006). Client-specific counselor self-efficacy in novice counselors: Relation to perceptions of session quality. *Journal of Counseling Psychology.* Vol. 53. No. 4, 453-463.

Sheperis, C. J., Young, J. S., & Daniels, M. H. (2010). *Counseling research: Quantitative, qualitative, and mixed methods.* Upper Saddle River, NJ: Pearson Education, Inc.

Conducting Time Series Research

Tomas Ferraro

Walden University

Conducting Time Series Research

Research Problem

The initiating problem with this study is:

- It does clarify the type of school Kaya attends, e.g., public, private, charter, etc.
- It does not specify what grade level Kaya is in.
- It does not specify if Kaya has the same teacher all day, or if there is a rotation schedule.

Therefore, the following observational report is based on the only information given, not taking into account the child's age, how long the problem has persisted throughout her education, nor any information about Kaya's actions at home, or a physician's diagnosis or report.

Time Series Design

The type of behavior Kaya is exhibiting lends itself to Momentary Time Sampling. According to Sheperis, Young, and Daniels (2010), MTS is advantageous as it does not take away from observation time and that interval behavior can be recorded at anytime it occurs. MTS can be calculated as a percent of intervals.

Through observation, Kaya's behavior could be noted at various intervals throughout the time period while also observing the possibility of contributing factors such as, how other children react to her, the environment in which her acting out takes place and how the teacher deals with it.

Multiple Baseline Design

A multiple baseline design across behaviors would be appropriate in the case of a student exhibiting several disruptive behaviors. This type of design is also effective, as the treatment would involve all behaviors instead of focusing on one at a time (Sheperis, et al., 2010).

The chart below clearly identifies the levels of behavior as they relate to the days of the week. Since the activities differ, it is hard to calculate if the exact activity is a contributing factor to the behavior.

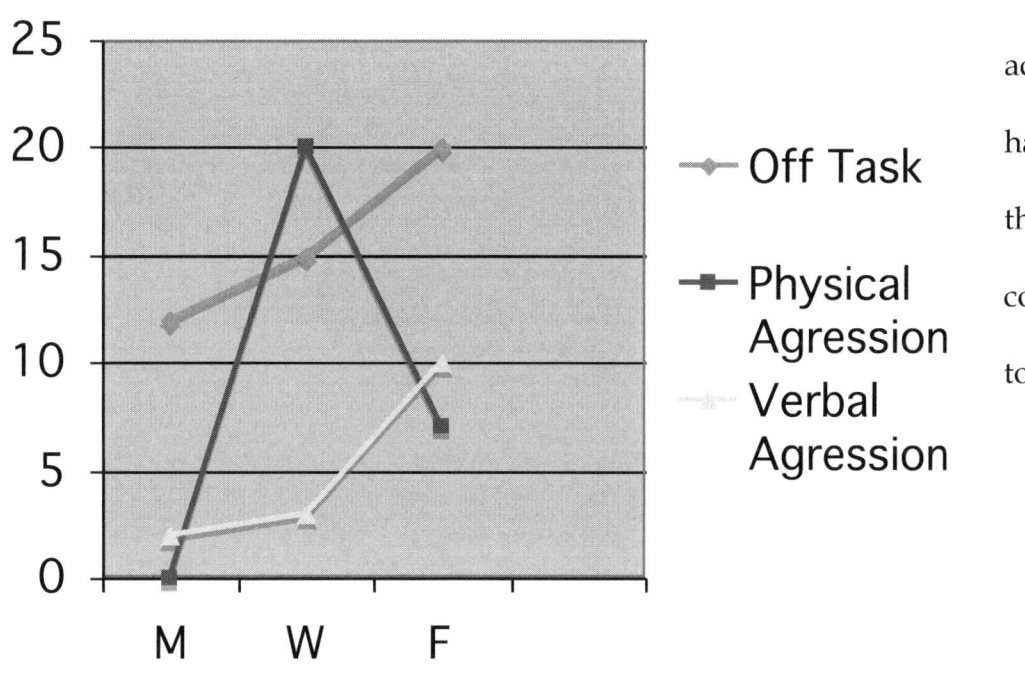

Data Analyzed

Off task and verbal aggression seem to correlate and increase as the week progresses. Kaya seems to be off task during those times during group activities or when unsupervised as in recess. Her verbal and physical aggression correlate with being off task. The lowest points are during structured math time when the lessons may be more task oriented and individualized.

Narrative Analysis

During unstructured times of group activities and recess, where there may be limited adult interaction, is when Kaya exhibits behaviors that are out of control. During more structured activities, her behaviors subside due to a more controlled environment. Therefore, it would seem reasonable that Kaya be placed into those environments that are more structured and possibility tailored to her academic achievement level.

Reference

Sheperis, C. J., Young, J. S., & Daniels, M. H. (2010). *Counseling research: Quantitative, qualitative, and mixed methods.* Upper Saddle River, NJ: Pearson Education, Inc.

Conducting Quantitative Research

Tomas Ferraro

Walden University

Conducting Quantitative Research

Phenomenological Research

Phenomenological research focuses on everyday human experiences and the interaction and perceptions of the individual or group experiencing them (Sheperis, Young & Daniels, 2010). Phenomenological research is interactive and relies on the relationship between researcher and participant. Phenomenologists seek to understand the individual's life-worlds at a deep level, then describe it applies to a particular experience.

The Study and Design

The Gregorc Style Delineator (GSD) is a self-report non-cognitive inventory, which assists in identifying dominant styles of processing information. Styles vary between two dimensions: perception (abstract vs. concrete) and sequence (sequential vs. random). A phenomenological rather than an empirical approach was taken to test development (Benton & Ferro, 1993). The GSD seems closely related to the Gregorc Transaction Ability Inventory (TAI). The words used in the original TAI were presented to 60 adults employed in private industry. The 60 adults then apparently selected 40 words they considered expressive of the four styles. The 40 words fall within four combinations of the two dimensions of style: Concrete Sequential (CS), Abstract Sequential (AS), Abstract Random (AR), and Concrete Random (CR). Respondents must rank order words within each of 10 sets, by assigning the numbers 1 (least descriptive of self) to 4 (most descriptive of self).

Strengths and Limitations

How the adults selected the words is unclear. In addition, no information is provided about the sampling methodology. Some evidence exists for subscale internal consistency and stability, although no standard errors of measurement are reported. Therefore reliability is suspect. The 40 words on the GSD lack parallelism. For example, Set 2 contains the words perfectionist, research, colorful, and risk-taker. This mixture of adjectives and nouns is common throughout all 10 sets. In ranking a word as 4, a respondent must at the same time assign lower ranks to the other three words. Using the words above as examples, this eliminates the possibility that one could equally describe herself as a perfectionist, a researcher, and a risk-taker. However, data collected from interviews with more than 400 individuals were used in the development of the instrument design, attesting to the construct validity of the instrument. Participants in the reviewer's classes and workshops have responded favorably to the instrument and its descriptions of the four channels or styles, thereby establishing its face validity. In their survey of learning style instruments for adults, James and Blank (1993) assess as 'moderate' the evidence of validity, the evidence of reliability, and the strength of the research base and assess as 'strong' the overall usability of the instrument (Benton & Ferro, 1993).

Analysis

There seems to be support for the phenomenological aspect of the research. 400 individuals were used in the development of the study, indicating a level of interaction between the researcher and participants, though there is no accounting of the time spent or the questions the participants were asked in developing the construct of the instrument used. It would appear useful to have a follow up interview to measure each participant's views of the instrument and

References

Benton, S. L. & Ferro, T. R. (2010). Review of Gregorc style delineator. Retrieved from http://web.ebscohost.com.ezp.waldenulibrary.org/ehost/detail?vid=3&hid=25&sid=310b2bb7-1eab-4b94-94f6-907ff4e3725e%40sessionmgr15&bdata=JnNpdGU9ZWhvc3QtbGl2ZSZzY29wZT1zaXRl#db=loh&AN=12091367

James, W. B., & Blank, W. E. (1993). Review and critique of available learning-style instruments for adults. In Benton, S. L. & Ferro, T. R. (2010). Review of Gregorc style delineator. Retrieved from http://web.ebscohost.com.ezp.waldenulibrary.org/ehost/detail?vid=3&hid=25&sid=310b2bb7-1eab-4b94-94f6-907ff4e3725e%40sessionmgr15&bdata=JnNpdGU9ZWhvc3QtbGl2ZSZzY29wZT1zaXRl#db=loh&AN=12091367

Sheperis, C. J., Young, J. S., & Daniels, M. H. (2010). *Counseling research: Quantitative, qualitative, and mixed methods*. Upper Saddle River, NJ: Pearson Education, Inc.

Deconstructing Mixed Methods Research

Tomas Ferraro

Walden University

Deconstructing Mixed Methods Research

Design Type & Data Collection Timing

The Concurrent Transformative design (Hanson, Creswell, Clark, Petska, Creswell, 2005) was used in this research study. Concurrent transformative designs use an explicit advocacy lens (e.g., feminist perspectives, critical theory), which is usually reflected in the purpose statement, research questions, and implications for action and change. In these designs, quantitative data may be collected and analyzed, followed by qualitative data, or conversely, qualitative data may be collected and analyzed, followed by quantitative data. Thus, either form of data may be collected first, depending on the needs and preferences of the researchers. Priority may be unequal and given to one form of data or the other or, in some cases, equal and given to both forms of data. Data analysis is usually connected, and integration usually occurs at the data interpretation stage and in the discussion. These designs are useful for giving voice to diverse or alternative perspectives, advocating for research participants, and better understanding a phenomenon that may be changing as a result of being studied. With this type of design the researcher begins by collecting qualitative data, in this case, conducting interviews to analyze information from semistructured interviews examining Latino intercultural competence (Torres, 2009). The typical interview lasted 45 to 60 minutes.

Theoretical Lens

The current study sought to examine the shared knowledge or understanding of Latino *intercultural competence*, or the skills that facilitate cultural interactions, via a mixed-methods approach. The qualitative portion of the project identified emergent themes, from semistructured interviews of Latino adults in the community, detailing the features of intercultural competence. Then, cultural consensus analysis (Romney, Weller, & Batchelder, 1986), an innovative methodological procedure from the field of anthropology, was used to identify the shared cultural model of Latino intercultural competence. The value of the present research is to clarify the experiences of the Latino group, which has particular significance to the current U.S. demography and sociopolitical context as well as to contribute to the general modeling of the cultural adaptation process (Torres, 2009).

Data Analysis Procedures

The research team that analyzed the qualitative data consisted of one Latino (the Principal Investigator), one Latina, and two European American women (Torres, 2009). A Latino male served as an auditor by independently reviewing the emergent themes to determine that the categories adequately represented the information generated by the interviews. The first step in the cultural consensus analysis was to test for a shared cultural model of Latino intercultural competence. This analysis was conducted using the software program ANTHROPAC, which uses the participant ratings of importance as units of analysis and the informants as variables in a factor analysis.

The second step of the cultural consensus analysis involves calculating the level of expertise for each participant. This analysis is essentially the factor loadings of each participant on the first factor indicating the magnitude of each informant's knowledge correlated with the aggregate knowledge of the group (Dressler & Bindon, 2000). These coefficients of expertise are used in the third step of the cultural consensus analysis to calculate a weighted mean of each item's importance ratings. Averaged across the sample, these calculations give higher weight to participants who have higher cultural expertise. These composite scores are considered to be the shared characteristics of Latino intercultural competence (Torres, 2009).

Rationale for Mixed Method Design

Mixed methods research has become increasingly popular and may be considered a legitimate, stand-alone research design (Creswell, 2002, 2003; Greene, Caracelli, & Graham, 1989; Tashakkori & Teddlie, 1998, 2003). It may be defined as "the collection or analysis of both quantitative and qualitative data in a single study in which the data are collected concurrently or sequentially, are given a priority, and involve the integration of the data at one or more stages in the process of research" (Creswell, Plano Clark, Gutmann, & Hanson, 2003, p. 212). When both quantitative and qualitative data are included in a study, researchers may enrich their results in ways that one form of data does not allow (Brewer & Hunter, 1989; Tashakkori & Teddlie, 1998). Using both forms of data, for example, allows researchers to simultaneously generalize results from a sample to a population and to gain a deeper understanding of the phenomenon of interest. It also allows researchers to test theoretical models and to modify them based on participant feedback.

The current study (Torres, 2009) used two separate and sequential methodologies including qualitative semistructured interviews and a systematic ethnographic technique known as *cultural consensus analysis* (Romney, Weller, & Batchelder, 1986). Cultural consensus analysis measures the degree to which participants agree on the definition of some cultural domain (Dressler, Balieiro, & dos Santos, 1998), assumes that cultural groups have a shared pool of knowledge distributed across social divisions and identifies this preferred cultural model through a form of reliability testing. Cultural consensus analysis also evaluates each participant's command of this cultural model, or expertise, compared with the aggregate. Finally, this analysis identifies the characteristics to a research question or cultural construct by estimating the distribution of the knowledge as it applies to participant expertise (Dressler et al., 2005).

References

Brewer, J., & Hunter, A. (1989). *Multimethod research: A synthesis of styles.* In Hanson, W. E., Creswell, J. W., Plano Clark, V. L., Petska, K. S., & Creswell, D. J. (2005). Mixed methods research design in counseling psychology. *Journal of Counseling Psychology, 52,* 224-235

Creswell, J. W. (2002). *Educational research: Planning, conducting, and evaluating quantitative and qualitative approaches to research.* In Hanson, W. E., Creswell, J. W., Plano Clark, V. L., Petska, K. S., & Creswell, D. J. (2005). Mixed methods research design in counseling psychology. *Journal of Counseling Psychology, 52,* 224-235.

Creswell, J. W. (2003). *Research design: Quantitative, qualitative, and mixed methods approaches* (2nd ed.). In Hanson, W. E., Creswell, J. W., Plano Clark, V. L., Petska, K. S., & Creswell, D. J. (2005). Mixed methods research design in counseling psychology. *Journal of Counseling Psychology, 52,* 224-235.

Creswell, J. W., Plano Clark, V. L., Gutmann, M. L., & Hanson, W. E. (2003). Advanced mixed methods research designs. In Hanson, W. E., Creswell, J. W., Plano Clark, V. L., Petska, K. S., & Creswell, D. J. (2005). Mixed methods research design in counseling psychology. *Journal of Counseling Psychology, 52,* 224-235.

Dressler, W. W., Borges, C. D., Balieiro, M. C., & dos Santos, J. E. (2005). Measuring cultural consonance: Examples with special reference to measurement theory in anthropology. *Field Methods, 17*, 331-355. In Torres, L. (2009). Latino definitions of success: A cultural model of intercultural competence. *Hispanic Journal of Behavioral Sciences, 31*, 576-593.

Dressler, W. W., & Bindon, J. R. (2000). The health consequences of cultural consonance: Cultural dimensions of lifestyle, social support, and arterial blood pressure in an African American community. In Torres, L. (2009). Latino definitions of success: A cultural model of intercultural competence. *Hispanic Journal of Behavioral Sciences, 31*, 576-593.

Greene, J. C., Caracelli, V. J., & Graham, W. F. (1989). Toward a conceptual framework for mixed-method evaluation designs. In Hanson, W. E., Creswell, J. W., Plano Clark, V. L., Petska, K. S., & Creswell, D. J. (2005). Mixed methods research design in counseling psychology. *Journal of Counseling Psychology, 52*, 224-235.

Hanson, W. E., Creswell, J. W., Plano Clark, V. L., Petska, K. S., & Creswell, D. J. (2005). Mixed methods research design in counseling psychology. *Journal of Counseling Psychology, 52*, 224-235.

Romney, A. K., Weller, S. C., & Batchelder, W. H. (1986). Culture as consensus: A theory of culture and informant accuracy. In Torres, L. (2009). Latino definitions of success: A cultural model of intercultural competence. *Hispanic Journal of Behavioral Sciences, 31*, 576-

Tashakkori, A., & Teddlie, C. (1998). *Mixed methodology: Combining qualitative and quantitative approaches.* In Hanson, W. E., Creswell, J. W., Plano Clark, V. L., Petska, K. S., & Creswell, D. J. (2005). Mixed methods research design in counseling psychology. *Journal of Counseling Psychology, 52,* 224-235.

Tashakkori, A., & Teddlie, C. (Eds.). (2003). *Handbook of mixed methods in social and behavioral research.* In Hanson, W. E., Creswell, J. W., Plano Clark, V. L., Petska, K. S., & Creswell, D. J. (2005). Mixed methods research design in counseling psychology. *Journal of Counseling Psychology, 52,* 224-235.

Torres, L. (2009). Latino definitions of success: A cultural model of intercultural competence. *Hispanic Journal of Behavioral Sciences, 31,* 576-593.

Conducting Qualitative Research

Tomas Ferraro

Walden University

Disadvantaged and Ethnically Diverse Populations

The first, and perhaps, most important issue as MRE (Marriage and Relationship Education) relates to disadvantaged and ethnically diverse populations is the research on the effects of MRE with couples from diverse racial/ethnic and economic backgrounds which, unfortunately, is sparse, making it impossible to draw definitive conclusions about MRE's efficacy for diverse groups. This is a crucial issue because publicly funded programs are being directed primarily at more disadvantaged groups that face greater risks for relationship problems (Ooms & Wilson, 2004).

Second, most of the relationship quality measures were self-reports whereas many of the communication skills assessments were observational. Observational measures of communication skills typically yield higher effect sizes (Blanchard, Hawkins, & Fawcett, 2007). While couples may be able to display for researchers various communication behaviors learned in MRE, couples may not yet recognize or otherwise attend to positive changes in their overall relationship. In fact, there is some evidence that increases in communication skills can have a negative effect on relationship quality, at least in the short run, presumably because more relationship problems are being attended to but perhaps not fully resolved (Dindia & Timmerman, 2003).

Increased Participation

To increase the participation of the disadvantaged and culturally diverse, I would offer initial MRE as a free seminar at a location easily accessible to their neighborhoods, offer a simple meal and speakers they could relate to.

A seminar indicates that there will be many people in attendance versus a one on one meeting with a counselor. Having the seminar in a location where drive time is reduced, will help inspire many to attend. Free food always attracts a crowd, and so would this. Finally, having speakers of various ethnic and socioeconomic backgrounds will solidify and give credence to what is being addressed and to the surveys offered.

Measures and Data Collection Methods

One of the first tools for data collection would be the participant-oriented approach. According to Sheperis, Young & Daniels (2010), the purpose of this transactive relationship is to obtain descriptive accounts of the program from all who participated in it. Because there are multiple participants, each with a personal experience, different realities are depicted.

I would also employ program evaluation measures, asking the participants about the effectiveness of the program, what information they found useful, their personal relationship to what was being said, and if they would return for another seminar.

Finally, research within the population of number of marriages, number of divoces, number of separations, number of reconciliations, and the reasons mentioned behind the divorces and separations to see if communication was key. Within the research (Hawkins, et al., 2008), more than two-thirds of the programs in these studies had a primary focus on communication skills training, and researchers typically directly measured participants' demonstration of these specific communication skills. Thus, it is not surprising that communication skills would be most affected by the interventions. Second, most of the relationship quality measures were self-reports whereas many of the communication skills assessments were observations.

References

Blanchard, V. L., Hawkins, A. J., & Fawcett, E. B. (2007, November). Does relationship education improve couples' communication? A meta-analysis. In Hawkins, A., Blanchard, V., Baldwin, S., & Fawcett, E. (2008). Does marriage and relationship education work? A meta-analytic study. *Journal of Consulting and Clinical Psychology, 76*(5), 723-734.

Dindia, K., & Timmerman, L. (2003). Accomplishing romantic relationships. In Hawkins, A., Blanchard, V., Baldwin, S., & Fawcett, E. (2008). Does marriage and relationship education work? A meta-analytic study. *Journal of Consulting and Clinical Psychology, 76*(5), 723-734.

Hawkins, A., Blanchard, V., Baldwin, S., & Fawcett, E. (2008). Does marriage and relationship education work? A meta-analytic study. *Journal of Consulting and Clinical Psychology, 76*(5), 723-734.

Ooms, T., & Wilson, P. (2004). The challenges of offering relationship and marriage education to low-income populations. In Hawkins, A., Blanchard, V., Baldwin, S., & Fawcett, E. (2008). Does marriage and relationship education work? A meta-analytic study. *Journal of Consulting and Clinical Psychology, 76*(5), 723-734.

Driving Your Clients M.A.D.:

Intervention Strategies in Music, Art & Drama

Tomas Ferraro

Walden University

Driving Your Clients M.A.D.: Intervention Strategies in Music, Art & Drama

Introduction

To ameliorate the flow of this paper, it has been divided into various research areas in which quantitative and qualitative methods play an important role in determining the importance of the arts as intervention strategies for various groups. The reference section has been divided into what research was quantitative, qualitative and mixed methods.

While quantitative research aims to measure the impact of the arts on student learning by testing the claims of its advocates through controlled, experimental methods, qualitative research methods may be applied in an effort to describe the impact of the arts in education within the heuristic world of arts education practice, a world in which arbitrary factors tend to impede the efficacy of experimental design.

Early Childhood

Quantitative research has shown that early intervention of the arts: music, visual arts, drama, and dance, can enhance brain development in infants and early childhood (Furfaro, 2007). Scientific research about the brain shows an ongoing development from just 42 days after conception. As infants grow, so does the brain as it develops and supports the new functions of the infant, from crawling, to walking.

Early childhood activities in which dance is introduced, can help a child with balance, and physical awareness. Drama can be used to increase social, intellectual and social interactions, as well as, cooperation. Drama can also be used in auditory and visual discrimination.

Visual arts, painting, sculpting, drawing and design, can help a child with visual and fine motor skills. Music can be incorporated to help with memorization, creativity, visual discrimination, self-expression, and communication skills (Malamat, 2004).

Gail Lindsey's research on children having a nurturing environment before they start school, also includes a study by Simmons and Sheehan (1997), that found a child's critical brain development and potential is determined in these early years. The researchers discovered that "the manner in which a child is raised affects how the brain chooses to wire itself" (Lindsey, 1999). If experiences and environment are important to brain development, what effect do art experiences have on that development?

In the arts area of dance an overall review of studies was presented in the fall, 2000, *Journal of Aesthetic Education.* It was a meta-analytical study where the researchers viewed 3,714 possibly relevant studies in literature, computer databases, identified journals and recommendations from primary researchers to select seven studies that were scientifically viable. These studies had quantified outcomes, used control groups and were done with non-impaired students. Four of the dance education studies dealt with the teaching of dance and corresponding reading skills. These studies were done on 527 students. The authors found only a small positive correlation between the teaching of dance and reading skill growth. This effect grew with the sample size but was still judged as weak overall (Deasy, 2001).

The three other studies dealt with the teaching of dance and changes with nonverbal reasoning abilities. These studies were done on 188 students. There was a clearer positive correlation in these studies. The studies were judged as more homogeneous and therefore more reliable and valid for their meta-analytical study (Deasy, 2001).

At Risk Students

The No Child Left Behind Act of 2001 was implemented to change the culture of America's schools and close the achievement gap by "teaching students based on what works." What works seems to be like finding a needle in a haystack. States have sought and funded strategies to improve academic outcomes, yet a cookie cutter approach to educating students often prevails: one size fits all. Students are rushed through a basic curriculum designed for students with homogenous learning styles without consideration of atypical learning styles. This leads to boredom, underachievement, and discipline problems (Respress & Lufti, 2006). To conquer this difficult problem, educators are making use of nontraditional pedagogical approaches such as brain-based learning to address the needs of these students. Many schools are at the other extreme of the dull, boring, and rigid learning environments in which students are the passive recipients of information. Fortunately, well-designed arts programs provide just the kinds of environments that students need. Research indicates that participation in the fine arts can alleviate many of the aforementioned quandaries. Social scientists have reasoned that students who participate in the fine arts tend to experience greater academic achievement and are less likely to have social, emotional, or behavioral problems. According to Franklin, Fernandez, Mosby, and Fernando (2004), participation in the arts positively influences brain performance. For instance, music, painting, dance, and drama have been cited as essential to academic and emotional development. They help to reduce stress, improve learning outcomes, enhance intrinsic motivation, regulate brain chemistry, augment body memory, and literally rewire neural pathways.

Fine arts require higher order thinking skills, individual and group efforts, and an atmosphere of controlled liberation that teaches responsibility. The concepts of fine arts programs are developed upon the findings of whole brain research. Whole brain research is central to learning theory. There have been several contributions made in the areas of music, dance, drama, and visual arts. Recent research reported by the American Psychological Association suggests that music lessons, and even simply listening to music, can enhance spatial reasoning performance. The studies of Rauscher and Shaw substantiate an unmistakable causal link between music and spatial intelligence (Dickinson, 2002). Spatial reasoning is involved in many other things, such as solving mathematical problems and creative scientific processes and the ability to orchestrate most anything (Catterall, 2002).

According to Catterall (2002), drama has also attracted wide attention among researchers. Drama shows consistent effects on narrative understanding as well as on component skills: identifying characteristics, understanding character motivations, reading and writing skills, and interpersonal skills such as dealing with conflict. Drama develops quick-witted spontaneous thinking, problem-solving ability, poise and presence, concentration, and both conceptual and analytical thinking skills (Dickinson, 2002). Research also indicates that fine arts programs reduce delinquent demeanor and ameliorate self-esteem.

The program curriculum of the HEARTS Family Life Center is designed to reflect an integrative approach to teaching and learning. Instruction and activities are planned and executed with major accentuation placed upon the facilitation of experiential learning in four fine arts areas: art, drama, music, and dance. Predicated upon their communicated interests on the Student Interest Survey, students are assigned to a music, drama, dance, or art module.

The sample population consisted of sixty-six middle school students, grades six through eight, in this project at the university school. Thirty-three of these students were placed in the participant group and thirty-three were placed in the comparison group. Both the participant and comparison groups consisted of sixteen males and seventeen females. The racial makeup of both groups was ninety-four percent African American, six percent bi-racial, and one percent other. The students were between the ages of

eleven and fourteen. They were selected based upon baseline data regarding problem behaviors, grades, attendance, socio-economic background, family problems, and problems in the community. The analysis of this program examines the extent to

which the fine arts improves academic achievement, school bonding, and reduces violence. The analysis is based upon quantitative data analysis (statistical analysis of assessments, grade point average, and disciplinary referral data). A Quasi-Experimental Design is used to determine if students who received intervention strategies scored significantly higher on outcome measures when compared with students who did not receive intervention strategies. A pre-test and post-test design is used in comparing the participant group against the comparison group. The Analysis of Variance (ANOVA) is used to determine statistical significance at the .05 probability level (Respress & Lufti, 2006).

The results presented address whether or not participation in the fine arts enhances academic achievement, self-esteem, and commitment towards school and reduces students' propensity towards violent acts. The results presented determine if African American students who received intervention strategies scored significantly

higher on outcome measures when compared with a comparison group that did not receive intervention strategies. Although these results are positive, it is recommended when working with African American middle school students. Additionally, after school programs should consider revising their program activities and curriculum to be inclusive of the fine arts. Furthermore, teachers should address the various learning styles of students in their classrooms by offering a curriculum that requires both rational and creative thinking. Finally, parents should encourage their youth to participate in the fine arts and utilize the fine arts when assisting their youth with homework assignments.

The Arts in Prison

The criminal justice agenda is a central focus of the government's drive to increase social inclusion. Arts activities are considered to have a range of benefits from increased self-confidence to transferable skills, which can help divert people away from pathways to crime or break the cycle of re-offending. While several important studies have generated evidence to support such claims for the arts, and although the body of evidence supporting the case for the arts has grown significantly over the last ten years, questions remain about the quality of research methods and findings (Hughes, Miles & McLewin, 2005).

A number of evaluations have attempted to measure the impact of taking part in arts programs on offending by young people. For example, an evaluation of *Hull Cop Shop* (2000-2002), a mobile police unit moving into areas with high rates of youth disturbance, which included the offering of arts and sports for young people, achieved a 62-78% reduction in youth causing a disturbance (Unit for the Arts and Offenders, 2003).

Similarly an evaluation of a persistent youth offenders project incorporating arts and drama workshops with a range of social provision, found a significant drop in police charges (compared to charges for six months prior to participation) amongst a group of 37 participants and that *'participation in an organized activity, good use of leisure time and motivation with education appear to have the greatest impact'* on reducing crime (University of Portsmouth, 2002:31).

An evaluation of drama-based cognitive behavioral programs for sex, violent and persistent offenders within a youth offending team (Hewish, 2001) analyzed convictions of offenders one year prior to, during and one year post participation and found that from 38 starters, convictions were reduced from 21 in the year before participation to 13 in the year following: 67% of non completers were reconvicted within the year following participation, compared to 43% of completers. The data for this study was incomplete, due to difficulties carrying out the evaluation, but, despite this, the results indicate the promise of the approach. Once more, a lack of other evidence means that a causal connection to participation in the program cannot be established. In addition, the small sample size means that it is not possible to test for statistical significance. An evaluation of a number of arts projects with young offenders ('demonstration' projects specially commissioned by a partnerships of arts and federal agencies) across the U.S. reported reduced disciplinary infractions in both alternative education and correctional facilities, improved attendance in alternative education settings and reduced recidivism among young people. Furthermore an independent longitudinal evaluation of one program claimed that involvement improved the incident rate of misbehavior by 75% (Hillman, 2000).

Music in Therapy

Assessment and clinical evaluation in music therapy are increasingly addressed as a topic of research from a theoretical and methodological perspective (Sabbatella, 2004). Although in clinical practice more and more music therapists are asked about the assessment tools they use and the reliability and validity of these instruments to document the music therapy process (data collection, measurement of data, analysis - interpretation and reports), nowadays not all assessment and clinical evaluation protocols used are based on standardized or systematic assessment models (test or evidence based assessment).

The celebration of the Assessment Institute co-sponsored by the Research Committee of the American Music Therapy Association during the IX World Congress of Music Therapy in Washington, DC (1999), could be considered a landmark in this field, as it was the first event addressing assessment at an international music therapy congress. After this event two special issues on assessment were edited by the Journal of Music Therapy (2000, vol. XXXVII, Issue 2) and the Music Therapy Perspectives (2000, vol. XVIII, Issue 1) and several papers with a focus on music therapy assessment were published.

A comprehensive literature review on assessment and clinical evaluation in music therapy revealed that research in this area started basically in the late nineties and is growing. Although a considerable number of references with the highest number of publications on the topic were found in 2000, not much literature is available on theory and method of assessment and clinical evaluation.

Arts in Education

Educators have put forward two main justifications for including the arts in formal school curricula. One argument is intrinsic to the arts. It maintains that the arts are important components of human culture in and of themselves and that, as such, they ought to be included as school subjects on an equal footing with other cultural disciplines such as literature or history. The intrinsic argument can lead to either of two pedagogical approaches (O'Farrell & Meban, 2003). On the one hand, an acknowledgement of the intrinsic value of the arts can lead to the adoption of the various disciplines such as dance, music, theatre and visual arts as academic subjects for the edification of all students as part of their preparation for future lives as culturally adept adults. On the other hand, recognition of the arts as important elements in the culture of the wider community can lead to a focus on skill development with a view to training talented youngsters to supply the world with a new generation of professional artists. Both of these approaches reflect the legitimate concerns of arts educators who may look upon a formal school program that omits a study of the arts as one that has failed to reflect the realities of society. The second general argument in favor of incorporating the arts in school programs is instrumental. It advocates using the arts as an effective means of achieving the educational goals of the curriculum as a whole.

Because qualitative research aims to provide a rich description of one, specific arts education setting or program, the choice of a subject for the research is very important. It is customary for researchers to select a setting or program that has been identified as exceptional in some way so that the results of the study will have the potential to provide insights that may be of use to

In the case of the study by McCammon and Betts, the school chosen as the site of the study was exceptional because it had been the subject of a number of teacher development projects in theatre education over the course of six years prior to the commencement of the study. McCammon and Betts set up a case study in the school intending to examine its culture to determine what aspects may have led such a large number of teachers to volunteer to participate in arts based approaches to learning. This was the primary focus of the study although, like all qualitative studies, this one was open to respond to any important issues that might emerge (O'Farrell & Meban, 2003).

To achieve a high level of credibility for their study, McCammon and Betts employed a methodology termed "focused data collection" which refers to the gathering of data though participant observation. The researchers also interviewed three groups of students and Betts conducted telephone interviews with some parents of these students. Interviews were conducted according to a set protocol in which each group of students and each adult respondent were asked the same open-ended questions. Questions focused on the respondent's feelings about being involved in theatre lessons and their perceptions on how and why the arts integration program worked and how they had been changed by the project. They also elicited the participant's view on the arts and his or her perception of the school climate. The researchers began their study with an interest in the apparently high level of support in the school for the theatre education program. What they were able to demonstrate, as a result of their analysis, was that their initial assumptions about the school culture were confirmed. In reporting their results the researchers included extensive excerpts from interviews to demonstrate how the positive school culture was manifested (O'Farrell & Meban, 2003).

Arts and the Elderly

The maturing of the baby boom generation has prompted increased research into strategies to promote healthy cognitive aging or improve cognitive decline.

A theatrically based intervention was given to 122 older adults who took acting lessons twice a week for 4 weeks. The training consisted of multi-modal activities (cognitive-affective-physiological) typically employed in college acting classes. Comparison groups consisted of no-treatment controls and participants instructed in a different performing art, singing. Assessment of effectiveness was performed using a battery of 11 cognitive/affective test measures that included word recall, prose comprehension/recall, word generation, digit-span ability, and problem solving. It was found that the acting group improved significantly from pretest to posttest over both other groups. Digit-span was the only measure that failed to improve. No aspects of the intervention supplied specific training or practice on the test measures. Previous versions of the intervention with community-dwelling adults had produced similar findings but the current participants were older, less well-educated, and lived in subsidized, primarily low-income, retirement homes (Noice & Noice, 2008).

Music Therapy in War-Torn Areas

Children suffer as a result from exposure to war violence. Separation, death in the family, witnessing killing, injury of family or strangers, arrest, torture, forced displacement or involvement in the military, rape and sexual assault, are just a few possible experiences children may have survived. Extreme poverty or deprivation, such as shortage of food, water, shelter and clothes, often play a role in the challenging circumstances of children and their families, and

Currently, there is evidence of a growing number of projects undertaken by international humanitarian aid agencies that use music and music therapy in their psychosocial aid programs. Music therapists are becoming increasingly involved in voluntary work in war-torn and developing countries (Heidenreich, 2005).

Music therapy does not require technical or talented musical ability. Music therapy generally utilizes simple improvisations with easy to use instruments. It does not have to sound harmonic nor pleasant to the ear. Musical improvisation allows emotional expression and offers the possibility to play free of judgment and norms, and does not impose performance pressure on clients. Music therapy maintains the attitude that anyone can freely make music and use it in his/her own way.

There were three sources of data for this research; media, literature and human subjects. The information was gained from Internet websites and literature reviews. Subject interviews were conducted with therapists and organizations that are involved in the use of music therapy in international humanitarian aid. A questionnaire was designed based on field observations and literature collected. In conjunction with this semi-structured questionnaire, unstructured, indirect and external observation was used. The music therapy department visited during the field research period was equipped with an observation room and an observation mirror.

The results of this study demonstrate that music, initially, is often not specifically used as therapy, nor is it identified as 'music therapy'. Yet, many projects that use music in their programs have therapeutic goals. The main goals of the programs are: the improvement of the emotional situation through the expression of feelings, individual building capacity, self-esteem and self-respect. In most cases, social learning occurs in group settings.

Music and musical improvisation can provide an alternative form of communication. The relationship in a counseling situation can be experienced as less threatening than through direct verbal interaction. Research done by Gupta (2000) about trauma treatment in Sierra Leone and Rwanda shows significant decrease in the symptoms of traumatization using music therapy. The negative feelings experienced by children changed remark- ably after a period of trauma healing with recreational and expressive activities such as music, arts, writing and story telling. Interviews and questionnaires were collected from more than 300 children aged 8-18 years of age before and after a 4-week psychosocial program. More than half of the children reported they felt a sense of relief while drawing pictures, talking or playing, and expressing their bad memories from the war (Heidenreich, 2005).

Conclusion

A review of the literature in utilizing music, art and drama as an intervention to therapy is overwhelming. Research, whether quantitative, qualitative or mixed method, vividly shows that introducing the arts into therapy has great and positive benefits for the client, no matter what age or what circumstance.

Art, in its many complexities, should be encouraged as a form of therapy in helping clients recognize their current challenges, and in helping them overcome the blockades which restrain them from achieving their therapeutic goals. In doing so, counselor training should address not only the desideratum, but successes that have been documented through the literature and research, and provide training for counselors in the arts as a therapeutic tool.

References

Quantitative

Catterall, J. (2002). Critical Links: Learning in the Arts and Student Social and Academic Development. *New Horizons for Learning.* Retrieved from www.newhorizons.org/strategies/arts/catterall.htm

Deasy, R. J. (Ed.). (2001). *Critical links: Learning in the arts and student academic and social development.* Washington, DC: Arts Education Partnership.

Dickinson, D. (2002). Learning Through the Arts. *New Horizons for Learning.* Retrieved from **www.newhorizons.org**. strategies.arts/cabc/odd lei fson.html.

Franklin, C.)., Fernandez, M.D., Mosby, A., & Fernando, V. (2004). Artful learning. *Leadership.*

Furfaro, D. A. (2007). A literature review of brain research and the influence of arts education on early childhood brain development. *Research Paper.* Bemidji State University, Minnesota.

Lindsey, G. (1999). Brain research and implications for early childhood education. *Childhood Education.* 75(2), 97-100.

Malamat, B. L. (2004). *Keynote Address.* Presented at Fields of Mind Conference at University of Saint Thomas, ST. Paul, MN.

Qualitative

Hillman, G. (2000). Arts programs for juvenile offenders in detention and corrections: A guide to promising practices. *Office of Juvenile Justice and Delinquency Prevention and the National Endowment for the Arts.*

Hughes, J. (2005). Doing the arts justice. *The Unit for the Arts and Offenders Center for Applied*

O'Farrell, L. & Meban, M. (2003). Arts education and instrumental outcomes: An introduction to research, methods and indicators. *UNESCO*. Queen's University, Kingston, Canada.

Respress, T. & Lufti, G. (2006). Whole brain learning: The fine arts with students at risk. *Reclaiming Children and Youth* 15:1, 24-31.

Sabbatella, P. E. (2004). Assessment and clinical evaluation in music therapy: An overview from literature and clinical practice. *Music Therapy Today.* Vol. V (1)

Mixed Methods

Heidenreich, V. (2005). Music therapy in war-effective areas. *Intervention.* Vol. 3, No. 2, 129-134.

Conducting Time Series Research

Tomas Ferraro

Walden University

Conducting Time Series Research

Research Problem

The initiating problem with this study is:

- It does clarify the type of school Kaya attends, e.g., public, private, charter, etc.

- It does not specify what grade level Kaya is in.

- It does not specify if Kaya has the same teacher all day, or if there is a rotation schedule.

Therefore, the following observational report is based on the only information given, not taking into account the child's age, how long the problem has persisted throughout her education, nor any information about Kaya's actions at home, or a physician's diagnosis or report.

Time Series Design

The type of behavior Kaya is exhibiting lends itself to Momentary Time Sampling. According to Sheperis, Young, and Daniels (2010), MTS is advantageous as it does not take away from observation time and that interval behavior can be recorded at anytime it occurs. MTS can be calculated as a percent of intervals.

Through observation, Kaya's behavior could be noted at various intervals throughout the time period while also observing the possibility of contributing factors such as, how other children react to her, the environment in which her acting out takes place and how the teacher deals with it.

Multiple Baseline Design

A multiple baseline design across behaviors would be appropriate in the case of a student exhibiting several disruptive behaviors. This type of design is also effective, as the treatment would involve all behaviors instead of focusing on one at a time (Sheperis, et al., 2010).

The chart below clearly identifies the levels of behavior as they relate to the days of the week. Since the activities differ, it is hard to calculate if the exact activity is a contributing factor to the behavior.

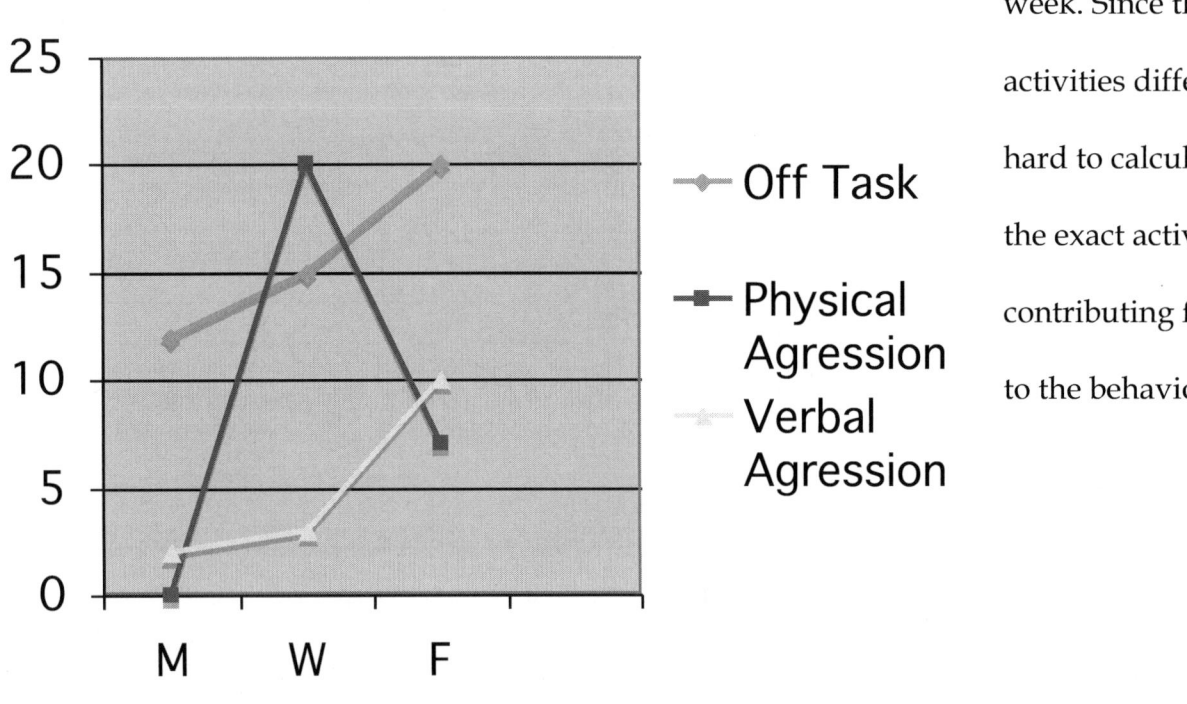

Narrative Approach for Education and Families

Having been a teacher for 30 years, and already possessing a Master's degree in Educational Counseling, one of the aspects of my practice is to work with students having problems within the school environment. School Psychologists focus on learning disabilities, while school counselors, especially those at the middle and high school levels, may focus on grades and if high school students are meeting the required classes to proceed to college, but very few counselors have the time and resources to address the needs of the "average" student, let alone the complexities of a family life that may be a contributing factor in the child's success or challenges. Therefore, the article I chose to review is "Family Factors and Student Achievements: An Avenue to Increase Students' Success."

Data Analysis Procedures

Data on family influences and academic outcomes for students were reported in 125 of the over 160 manuscripts reviewed. Findings were summarized in five family factors: parent expectations and attributions, structure for learning, affective home environment, discipline, and parent involvement. Information gathered about home influences is integral to designing home-based learning interventions for students.

The five family factors are quite consistent with the global suggestions educators often make to parents during conferences.

However, simply suggesting to parents what they can do at home is not implicated by the literature. Rather, studies report increases in academic outcomes for students when educators seek the assistance of parents and directly support and instruct parents in ways to support school learning. The findings are discussed in three sections: (a) literature reviewed, (b) integration of five factors, and (c) recommendations for professional practice.

Only a few studies were found that included more than one of the five factors. For example, Clark's (1983) results from his frequently cited observational study of family life for poor black secondary school students showed that certain patterns are present in homes of high achieving students. Family life of these students was characterized by frequent dialogues between parents and children, strong parent encouragement of academic pursuits, warm and nurturing interactions, clear and consistent limits, and consistent monitoring of how time is used. Parents of high achievers felt personally responsible to help their children gain knowledge and basic literacy skills, communicate regularly with school personnel, and be involved in school functions (Clark, 1988).

Recommendations for Practice.

School psychologists/counselors need to:
(a) be knowledgeable about family influences on student achievement
(b) assess the degree to which children's home environments are characterized by factors correlated with achievement,
(c) promote recommended practices for involving parents in education
(d) design home-school interventions that address students' learning.

It is time to educate parents about their importance for their child's learning. It is recommended that school psychologists use the five family factors as guidelines in assessment and intervention for students and their families. School psychologists need to

determine the degree to which children have had an opportunity to learn at home

and consider the home an avenue for promoting children's school success.

Within the context of my private practice, I would incorporate the student's family life into the equation of school and school life, as well as peers and other pressures the student feels to get a complete narrative of what the student's life is like. In education narrative researchers typically develop life histories to inscribe their findings (Sheperis, Young and Daniels, 2010). And in this particular case of developing an overall life experience for the client, the narrative form of qualitative research seems appropriate.

References:

Christenson, S. L., Rounds, T., Gorney, D. (1992). Family factors and student achievement: An avenue to increase students' success. *School Psychology Quarterly* Vol. 7, No. 3, 178-206.

Clark, R. M. (1988). Parents as providers of linguistic and social capital. In Christenson, S. L., Rounds, T., Gorney, D. (1992). Family factors and student achievement: An avenue to increase students' success. *School Psychology Quarterly* Vol. 7, No. 3, 178-206.

Sheperis, C. J., Young, J. S., & Daniels, M. H. (2010). *Counseling research: Quantitative, qualitative, and mixed methods*. Upper Saddle River, NJ: Pearson Education, Inc.

Psychosocial Treatments in Older Adults

I chose this literature review, "Psychosocial Treatments for Major Depression and Dysthymia in Older Adults: A Review of the Research Literature," (Zalaquett & Stens, 2006) due to the fact that I am interested in working with those who are caring for elderly parents experiencing dementia and Alzheimer's disease, which can also lead to depression. The research suggests that 1-2% of adults 65 and older, living within a community, experience depression (Johnson, Weissmann, & Klerman, 1992), while 50% living in a nursing home display depressive symptoms (Koenig & Blazer, 1996). It is further noted that depression is often undiagnosed and untreatable in older adults (Zalaquett & Stens, 2006).

Research into an overview of therapies, which included: cognitive-behavioral therapy (CBT), interpersonal therapy (IPT), brief dynamic therapy (BDT), and reminiscence therapy (RT), were noted to have mixed results. CBT, for example, needed to be adapted to meet the needs of older adults (Knight & Satre, 1999). Most of these therapies focus on one's ability to change, see things more in a positive light, and reenter the world as a viable and successful member. However, there are limitations which therapy cannot address, such as poverty, limited access to health care and other socioeconomic factors.

The review of research literature (Zalaquett & Stens, 2006), suggests that older adults who have major depression can benefit from psychosocial treatments with CBT being efficacious as a treatment for older adults who are cognitively intact and not suicidal. It is also noted that current research of psychosocial methods of treating depression in older adults falls short of meeting the country's demographic needs.

The literature also comes up short when addressing what percentages of lifestyle and socioeconomics create depression, and which can be successfully treated and which cannot.

The article does not address depression brought on by Alzheimer's disease or dementia, which should have been noted in the review. As I am an advocate of euthanasia, in the general sense, this brings about other issues of depressive disorders, how the client, and general population functions under a health system which is currently reactive versus proactive.

However, before we can continue with our own advocacy, we must defer to the article "A Critical Analysis of the Social Advocacy Movement in Counseling," (Smith, Reynolds and Rovnak, 2009), in which they propose that the advocacy movement itself be overhauled to avoid promoting various agendas of a personal or political nature.

References

Johnson, J., Weissmann, M. M., & Klerman, G. L. (1992). Service utilization and social morbidity associated with depressive symptoms in the community. In Zalaquett, C., & Stens, A. (2006). Psychosocial treatments for major depression and dysthymia in older adults: A review of the research literature. *Journal of Counseling & Development, 84*(2), 192-201.

Knight, B. G., & Satre, D. D. (1999). Cognitive behavioral psychotherapy with older adults. In Zalaquett, C., & Stens, A. (2006). Psychosocial treatments for major depression and dysthymia in older adults: A review of the research literature. *Journal of Counseling & Development, 84*(2), 192-201.

Koenig, H. G., & Blazer, D. G. (1996). Minor depression in late life. In Zalaquett, C., & Stens, A. (2006). Psychosocial treatments for major depression and dysthymia in older adults: A review of the research literature. *Journal of Counseling & Development, 84*(2), 192-201.

Smith, S., Reynolds, C., & Rovnak, A. (2009). A critical analysis of the social advocacy movement in counseling. *Journal of Counseling & Development, 87*(4), 483-491.

Zalaquett, C., & Stens, A. (2006). Psychosocial treatments for major depression and dysthymia in older adults: A review of the research literature. *Journal of Counseling & Development, 84*(2), 192-201.

Using Action Research in the Real World

Action Research is defined as "practitioner action for change with reflection on practice and careful gathering and analysis of data" (Rowell, 2006). Rowell (2006) also states that action research has evolved both as a method of inquiry and as a means to mobilize and guide communities, classrooms, and professionals in taking action to improve social conditions and conditions of practice.

One of the focuses within my private practice will be group counseling of teens in regards of peer pressure, bullying and other negative phenomena that infiltrate the adolescent world. Within group work I hope to show to the teens participating that they are not alone with their concerns and problems of growth, school and social life. Developing action research will help me define what topics are of importance to teens, how teens relate and interact within certain topics, and developing not only a therapeutic alliance and "buy in" from the teens, but the parents as well.

In public practice, I advocate for more counselors at the elementary level to accurately assess students at the primary grade levels in order to define concerns that may inhibit a child from obtaining their true potential and having them qualify for special services in a timely manner. Action research here would be gradual and diplomatic as some of the perceived problems may stem from the living environment of which a counselor may or may not be privy to. Rethinking, and possibly redeveloping counseling strategies may be the key in getting the help some of these kids need for a successful educational career.

As with group counseling of teens, a "buy in" component needs to be developed with the

Reestablishing a progressive agenda for the future of the school counseling profession means fostering a sense of critical consciousness among counselors and among those they serve Rowell, 2006). Perhaps it is in the domain of a kind of emotional literacy that counselors will be able to better help children, youth, and parents with problems of everyday living. In this sense, helping may be better understood as a learning process.

Reference

Rowell, L. (2006). Action research and school counseling: Closing the gap between research and practice. *Professional School Counseling, 9*(5, Special Issue), 376-384.

Til Death DO Us Part

Death with Dignity

Tomas Ferraro

Patricia Graham

Julie Mejia

Walden University

Death with Dignity

Legislative Action

Within the realm of Euthanasia, there are currently only three states which prescribe to physician assisted suicide (PAS). These are Oregon, Montana and Hawaii. Since the patients must be terminal, legislative action must eventually involve all 50 states and must include patients who are non-terminal, but possess extenuating circumstances in which to consider euthanasia an alternative than living on a machine or in a vegetative state the rest of their natural lives.

The Death With Dignity Society

A. Hawaii's Death With Dignity Society is a foundation dedicated to preserving a patient's right to predetermine their end of life medications as well as a choice of prescribed methods of which to end life. A brief statement of their philosophy is as follows:

"Hawaii's existing law already empowers patients to make autonomous decisions regarding their end-of-life care and treatment for pain. Further, Hawaii does not have a criminal prohibition against aid in dying. Hawaii law also contains a unique provision that gives physicians broad discretion when treating terminally ill patients. Specifically, Hawaii law provides that:

'When a duly licensed physician or osteopathic physician pronounces a person affected with any disease hopeless and beyond recovery and gives a written certificate to that effect to the person affected or the person's attendant nothing herein shall forbid any person from giving or furnishing any remedial agent or measure when so requested by or on behalf of the affected person.' — Hawaii Revised Statute § 453-1

Under the law, a physician may give or furnish any measure requested by a patient who is "hopeless or beyond recovery." With aid in dying, a physician prescribes medication that may then be ingested by a terminally ill patient to bring about a peaceful death; a physician does not administer the medication. Supported by this framework, a standard of care already exists that accepts other life-ending practices such as withdrawing life-sustaining treatment, stopping of all food and fluids, and palliative sedation. It is reasonable to assume that amidst this background Hawaii is a jurisdiction in which physicians can provide aid in dying subject to standard of care" (Tucker, 2011).

B. The Ethical Consideration in Promoting Death with Dignity as Social Change

It is important to review the ACA Code of Ethics (2005) to make sure that this type of social change is ethical. One cannot consider the broader effects of social change without taking ethics into account.

The first standard to take into consideration would be A.4.a., avoiding harm. At first glance, endorsing, or counseling a client who is struggling with the possibility of euthanasia, would seem unethical in terms of condoning such an action. However, if the client is in such unbearable pain, or if an illness is terminal, therapists may be doing greater harm to the client by taking an anti-euthanasia stance, by evoking one's own personal values, a clear violation of standard A.4.b. (ACA Code of Ethics, 2005) ensues.

The next standard to consider is A.9, End of Life Care for Terminally Ill Clients (ACA Code of Ethics, 2005). A.9.a considers the quality of care a client receives, but within that definition it can also be applied to quality of life. Should a counselor find euthanasia to be an alternative to which they cannot subscribe, and should the client be looking for counseling to help them in their perceived need to end their life, then perhaps, according to standard A.11.b. (ACA Code of Ethics, 2005), that counselor needs to withdraw from the therapeutic relationship.

Perhaps unsurprisingly, fairly uniform opinions are found about the elements comprising quality of care at the end of life, with relief from pain and other symptoms at the forefront, reflecting widespread concerns about the process of dying.

C. Gaps or Limitations: A Review of the Literature

The reviews show a preponderance of research about views on euthanasia and physician assisted suicide. These findings suggest public support for euthanasia has hovered between 60% and 80% since the mid 1970s.

Within Mak, Elwyn & Finlay (2003), most research in the euthanasia debate has been quantitative focusing on the attitudes of healthcare professionals, relatives and the public. A few recent qualitative studies have provided evidence about the perspectives of patients who desired death.

Surveys (Sulmasy, 2001) have been the primary way of conducting quantitative empirical research. Most explore opinions and attitudes, while some have attempted to answer more narrowly defined research questions about euthanasia. Surveys of health care professionals found 48% of physicians in Washington State thought that euthanasia was never justified, and 54% thought it should remain illegal.

Surprisingly, the study found that those most in favor of legalization were least likely to perform PAS (Physician Assisted Suicide), such as psychiatrist. However, in Oregon 68% of physicians thought euthanasia should be legal in some cases, while 46% said they would prescribe PAS if it were legal. 40% of Michigan physicians supported legalizing PAS.

However, in Hawaii, support for end-of-life choice is even stronger than the national average. A 2004 QMark follow-up poll reported 75% of Hawaiian voters supported this end-of-life choice. In 2002 a QMark Poll of 400 Hawaiian registered voters reported 79% supported end-of-life choices as personal and private decisions rather than the government making these decisions for individuals. A 2004 QMark Poll asking the same question reported 86% in support of individual decision-making at the end of life (Web).

Barriers to Death with Dignity

Questions have arisen about these surveys and the definitions used to either "lump" or "split" in reporting their results, yet, this is the best data available. None of the surveys answers any normative questions, but they do bring to light many of the issues (Sulmasy, 2001).

Cohen, Fihn, Boyko, Jonsen and Wood (1994) sent questionnaires to 1355 randomly selected physicians in the state of Washington, including all hematologists and oncologists and a disproportionately high number of internists, family practitioners, psychiatrists, and general surgeons. To avoid ambiguity in the survey, instead of "physician-assisted suicide," the phrase "prescription of medication [e.g., narcotics or barbiturates] or the counseling of an ill patient so he or she may use an overdose to end his or her own life." was used. Instead of "euthanasia," the phrase "deliberate administration of an overdose of medication to an ill patient at his or her request with the primary intent to end his or her life." was substituted.

Of the 1355 eligible physicians who received the questionnaire, 938 (69 percent) responded. Forty-eight percent of the respondents agreed with the statement that euthanasia is never ethically justified, and 42 percent disagreed. Fifty-four percent thought euthanasia should be legal in some situations, but only 33 percent stated that they would be willing to perform euthanasia. Thirty-nine percent of respondents agreed with the statement that physician-assisted suicide is never ethically justified, and 50 percent disagreed. Fifty-three percent thought assisted suicide should be legal in some situations, but only 40 percent stated that they would be willing to assist a patient in committing suicide. Of the groups surveyed, hematologists and oncologists were most likely to oppose euthanasia and assisted suicide, and psychiatrists were most likely to support these practices (Cohen, et al., 1994). The attitudes toward physician-assisted suicide and euthanasia of physicians in Washington State are polarized. A slight majority favors legalizing physician-assisted suicide and euthanasia in at least some situations, but most would be unwilling to participate in these practices themselves.

In jurisdictions that permit euthanasia or physician-assisted suicide, patients with cancer comprise the largest group to die by these methods. Wilson, Scott, Graham, Kozak, Chater, Viola, Faye, Weaver and Curran (2000), investigated the personal attitudes toward these practices of patients receiving palliative care for advanced cancer.

Seventy patients (32 men and 38 women; median survival, 44.5 days) took part in a survey using in-depth semistructured interviews. Most participants (73%) believed that euthanasia or physician-assisted suicide should be legalized, citing pain and the individual's right to choose as their major reasons.

Participants who were opposed to legalization cited religious and moral objections as

Forty (58%) of the 69 participants who completed the entire interview also believed that, if legal, they might personally make a future request for a hastened death, particularly if pain or physical symptoms became intolerable. Eight of these individuals (12%) would have made such a request at the time of the interview. These 8 participants differed from all others on ratings of loss of interest or pleasure in activities, hopelessness, and the desire to die. They also had a higher prevalence of depressive disorders. However, they did not differ on ratings of pain severity. Many patients with advanced cancer favor policies that would allow them access to both euthanasia and physician-assisted suicide if pain and physical symptoms became intolerable (Wilson, et al., 2000). For patients who would actually make requests for a physician-hastened death, however, psychological considerations may be at least as salient as physical symptoms.

Ideas for Death with Dignity as Social Change

Qualitative research provides at least partial explanations of the trends seen in the quantitative research. For example, older women are more likely to be concerned about burdening others during a final illness, while men express more self oriented views, including the desire to live longer. Qualitative research shows that attitudes about death develop against a backdrop of varied cultural and historical influences, are deeply affected by biographical and experiential influences, and are likely to change with time and across age groups (Seymour, French & Richardson, 2010).

Lavery, Boyle, Dickens, Maclean & Singer (2001) did a qualitative study of 32 people with HIV-1 or AIDS, who were enrolled in the HIV-1 Ontario Observational Database at Sunnybrook and Women's College Health Sciences Centre, Toronto, Ontario, Canada. Participants were chosen who had deliberation about euthanasia or assisted suicide, and the meaning of these experiences with in-depth, face-to-face interviews.

Participants' desire for euthanasia and assisted suicide were affected by two main factors: disintegration, which resulted from symptoms and loss of function; and loss of community, which is defined as progressive diminishment of opportunities to initiate and maintain close personal relationships. These factors resulted in perceived loss of self. Participants saw euthanasia and assisted suicide as means of limiting loss of self (Lavery, et al., 2001).

Goal 1: Education

The first goal in any change is to educate the populace about the problem or concern needing the change. This would require a detailed account as presented previously in this paper.

Goal 2: Change Legislation One State at a Time

Once the people are informed, they can help through Participant Action Research (PAR) to find the officials they'll need to elect into office to implement changes in legislative policy and law to allow for PAS and death with dignity.

Goal 1, Objective 1: Inform, Educate and Reach Out

Through social websites and other forms of mass communication, reach out to those who are interested and/or support this issue already. Promote, as Hawaii has done, social change and

Goal 1, Objective 2: Educate Legislators

While the citizens are forming their PAR and societies to help implement change, the legislators will be sent a power point program filled with pictures and data to help educated them abut the need in their own state and how they can meet that need.

Goal 2, Objective 1: Create Political Action Committees

Create PACs who will find, support and get candidates elected that support death with dignity.

Goal 2, Objective 2: Get Policies Passed

Once candidates are elected, support and help those newly elected officials to pass legislation to legalize PAS and death with dignity.

C. Evaluation

The success of this social change project will be evaluated in many ways:

1. Educational success based on the number of people acknowledging if the information was useful and helped them with a paradigm shift in their views toward death with dignity. There will be a scale, tracker and mini evaluation form to fill out with each social networking site.
2. The interest level in creating, and the creation of Death with Dignity Societies using Hawaii's as the template.
3. Participatory Action Research done by the local populace in an effort to change viewpoints and seek out potential candidates for office who support death with dignity.

5. Election of officials in support of the social change project.

6. Passage of laws that support the social project.

7. More states joining together to support Death with Dignity.

8. National law supporting a person's right to die with dignity.

9. Constitutional amendment implementing Death with Dignity at the highest level, a person's constitutional right to die.

Personal Reflection

1. What did you learn about the issue, others, and yourself?

2. How did this change your perspective of how to be involved in social change?

3. How will you become involved after residency?

References

Cohen, J. S., Fihn, S. D., Boyko, E. J., Jonsen, A. R., & Wood, R. W. (1994). Attitudes toward Assisted Suicide and Euthanasia among Physicians in Washington State. Retrieved from **http://www.nejm.org/doi/full/10.1056/NEJM199407143310206**

CompassionAndChoicesHI.org (2011). retrieved from
http://compassionandchoices.org/document.doc?id=941

Lavery J., Boyle J., Dickens B., Maclean H., Singer, P. (2001). Origins of the desire for euthanasia and assisted suicide in people with HIV-1 or AIDS: a qualitative study. In Mak, Y. YW, Elwyn, G., Finlay, I. G. (2003). Patients' voices are needed in debates on euthanasia. Retrieved from http://www.bmj.com/content/327/7414/556.1

Mak, Y. YW, Elwyn, G., Finlay, I. G. (2003). Patients' voices are needed in debates on euthanasia. Retrieved from **http://www.bmj.com/content/327/7414/556.1**

Seymour, J.E., French, J. & Richardson, E. (2010). Dying matters: Let's talk about it. Retrieved from http://www.bmj.com/content/341/bmj.c4860.full

Sulmasy, D. P. (2001). Research in medical ethics: Physician-assisted suicide and euthanasia. Retrieved from **http://books.google.com/books?hl=en&lr=&id=-5a0nza21ZMC&oi=fnd&pg=PA247&dq=Quantitative+research+on+euthanasia&ots =oDdxcGxdLB&sig=aSzNZrMY0fSVQ55mwvy3JAiwR_A#v=onepage&q=Quantitative%20research%20on%20euthanasia&f=false**

Tucker, K. (2011). Hawaii Death With Dignity Society. Retrieved from
http://hawaiidwdsociety.org/home/

Wilson, K. G., Scott, J. F., Graham, I. D., Kozak, J. F., Chater, S., Viola, R. A., Faye, B. J., Weaver, L. A. & Curran, D. (2000). Attitudes of terminally ill patients toward euthanasia and physician-assisted suicide. Retrieved from **http://archinte.ama-assn.org/cgi/content/abstract/160/16/2454**

Commentary on Universities and Professors

Walden University

Online universities are a great way to get an education, a degree or an advanced degree, especially if you can't take the time off from work to attend classes. However, one must ask questions to get answers that might have been provided by professors in person.

For an example, I signed up to get my Master's degree in Mental Health Counseling and started my classes without ever asking, when the time came for my internship, who was going to provide it. Other classmates were talking about how they were doing theirs at the current place they were working. I wasn't working at any mental health facility so I just assumed the university would assign me to one. This was not the case. Suddenly, after I finished my classes with a 3.8 GPA, I found myself struggling to find a place for my internship. But it wasn't as easy as I though it should be. Places already had interns or their internship program began at a different time than the time from at Walden.

I received very little help from Walden in finding a place. Hence, even though I did very well with my classes, I never got the chance for an internship or to finish my Master's degree in Mental Health Counseling.

One of the things I wanted to do with my degree and license was to help those out that lost homes and/or loved ones during natural disasters. Now, everytime a natural disaster comes about, I just sit home and watch it on the news.

Cappella University

With my educational background in counseling I was allowed to enter the doctorate program at Cappella. Once again, I did well in all my classes, save one. There is a fine line between what you want to write and what is considered plagiarism. On my final paper, in my final class, my professor got a hold of me concerned I had committed plagiarism. I ask if I could take a look at it and change things. At first he agreed. I asked him where the plagiarism had taken place. He didn't answer and decided to fail me. Not just the paper, but the class. I could not even begin my doctorate dissertation without the class. I asked the administration about it to which they replied that the teacher has the final say. A lot of time and money went into that program only to be left wondering why he agreed then taking back.

Check out online universities carefully so you're not wasting your time with classes or programs you might not need. Remember, that even though the instructors may be dedicated to giving you a quality education, the admin is there to make money. These are for profit institutions.

Other books by T H Ferraro

Here Thar Be Pirates (Poetry)

Thinking Out Loud (Political and Social Commentary)

What's This Room Used For? (An introduction to cooking)

What You See Is What I Saw (The photography of Tomas Howe)

Tell Tommy (The male perspective on the male perspective.)

Books to look for soon:

Ignorance Is No Excuse, But It's A Damn Good Reason (Reflections on the penal system)

Deranged Greeting Cards

New Education Book (Easy GED Prep)

Memoirs Of An Alien (Autobiography)

The Playground Of Learning (Education in the 21st century)

T H Ferraro

T H Ferraro began writing as soon as he could manipulate a crayon. His imagination stemmed from his family taking road trips in the summer, reading and being grounded, though being sent to his room was not a punishment as he enjoyed his alone time with his imaginary friend "corner," and the toys in his room.

Ferraro loved school especially story time and when teacher's encouraged students to write.

In 6th grade he wrote a series of short stories called, "The Adventures of Soapy Suds," about a poodle detective.

The stories were good enough that his teachers encouraged him to read them in front of the class and while the orchestra (where he played clarinet) was waiting to go onstage.

Writing short stories gave way to songs and poetry as he began to discover the opposite gender.

College provided new writing challenges but he proved to be a talented writer of essays, achieving three master's degrees in education. He taught various grade levels including 8th grade composition and High School English writing right along side of his students, which inspired many of them.

After several years and trying his hand at political satire, which was his first experience in being published by newspapers, he decided to compile all his writing commentaries together in the book, "Thinking Out Loud."

His poetry compilations became the book, "Here Thar Be Pirates," while shorter works took on a life of their own. For his poetry, Ferraro has won several awards and was named Poet Laureate for the Cyber Nation of Amandium, writing its national anthem and poem.

Made in the USA
Monee, IL
05 April 2021